Thistle Field Fence

BY
MAGGIE ROWE

Thistle Field Fence

ISBN 978-1-62806-323-3   (print | paperback)

Library of Congress Control Number 2021912874

Salt Water Media
29 Broad Street, Suite 104
Berlin, MD 21811
www.saltwatermedia.com

Cover image by the author; cover design by Salt Water Media

For Mabel, and for Granny, and for Marion Elizabeth,
who loves babies and who always read to us.

Acknowledgements

I'd like to thank my poetry mentors and friends, including W.D. Snodgrass's breakfast poets, Friday Night Writers, and Cape Henlopen Retreat poets, as well as class and staff members of the Cancer Support Community where I teach. I would especially like to thank the Delaware Division of the Arts for their supportive fellowships and sponsored writers' retreats.

Several of these poems first appeared in my 2011 chapbook *Every Mother Moves To A New Country* from Finishing Line Press. "I Choke On Mortality" and "The Book I'm Writing" were published by *The Sun* magazine; "Like a Solemn Friend Inebriate With Rain" by *RHINO Poetry*; "I Heard There Were Dolphins" and an early version of "Mirror, Shutter, Window, Shade" by *Oberon*; and "Rassouli's Madonna" by the *Sunday News Journal*. "Wexford Boy" was published in the anthology, *On The Mason-Dixon Line*. "Open Door" appeared in *No Place Like Here: An Anthology of Southern Delaware Poetry and Prose*. "Coppelia Runs" appeared in *A Collection of Dance Poems*, and "Finding Divinity" was first published in *Poems Of Shadows And Light: A Wellness Community Collection*.

"The Artist Bars the Door, Drawing His Knives" was commissioned by the Delaware Art Museum. "The Night We Took Fish" appeared in *Cape Henlopen Poets 2010*. Parts of the poem "Every Mother Moves To A New Country" (divided here into chapter divisions), "I Wonder About The Chores", "Swansea Train Station, February 1979, 3 a.m.", "Quaker Hugh, After Striking Down a Redcoat", "I Take Exception to Your Shade of Blue, Mr. Key" and "We Dip Our Toes into an Estuary the Morning After the Wedding" were first published in *Art and Poetry 2004-2006* by the Biggs Museum of American Art.

Contents

1

What to take

The day before we're to set off for America, all I can do
is sit at my mother's table copying recipes.
In the sweat of the night my arms strain with
possessions:
train leaving, airport gate almost closed;
how can a mortal person know
what will be needed in a new place?
If I left the family photographs
why are they still the heaviest things I own?

Heyday

In the mouth of a cowslip between fat petals
a bee quivers; a plump fox moseys past,
while back in the morning of the old country
daisies stir across a farm, saffron and white
like fried eggs, a thousand thousand little fried eggs
sizzling across the field on slender hoists.

The fence decays, a cart wheel leaning on it,
the one that used to go places in its day,
now it's all break down and raise up,
the history of a field laughing,
wheel eases back into soil, taking the scenic route
and fence posts compost themselves down,
the borders they held out-of-date.

The broad-tailed fox trots by full of thought,
fat with neuron and synapse,
over eggs, over grass, over the humbled posts
of the old place once constrained,
and all the nourishing fields of the past yield
to the fresh purpose of the bee and the easy-hipped fox.

Arriving, Dublin

A blunt needle piercing
thick gray felt,
our plane drops through cloud;

below, I see a whale
passing the mouth of the bay
and then what I might expect:

ships, blue and green,
heading for open water;
islands; crops;
the first houses.

Once I'm back in America
I must remember that

during my dark hours

dawn is already lighting
Dublin's harbour,

and whales swim there
like knees moving under silk.

Thistle Field Fence

I stand at a fence for a thousand years,
my hand through the wire while I look away.
The stallion which has been watching me
from trees at the far end of the field
thunders past, snorting, and stops, pretending to eat around thistles.
I don't look. He chews his way over to me
and raises his great head to smell my hand quickly,
noisily. The soft wrinkles of his nostril are so close to my skin
I'm in heaven. That muscled skull
brushes my hand so that the world sways and stops,
ignites, and thunders off.
The horse
thunders off, igniting
the world, which sways and stops and brushes my hand
with its muscled, heavenly skull,
the soft wrinkles of its noisy nostril close to my skin.
It has raised its great head to smell my hand quickly.
I wasn't looking as it chewed its way over to me.
It pretends to eat, then thunders away through the thistles, snorting,
to trees at the far end of the field,
where it watches me like a stallion.
I keep looking away, my hand through the wire.
The fence and I stand for a thousand years.

I Wonder About the Chores

"Pastoral," Unknown Artist, circa 1830,
Biggs Museum of American Art.

I am traveling between worlds,
Nellie loaned to me as far as the town,
a stage to take me from there.

All the small fretting
of the work of this house:
I have left it.

The gate that stuck against its post,
the poison ivy by the raspberries,
the crotchety old pump.

The way to hang the copper
so it would fit in the space by the door.
Where the flour bin was, and how deep the remainder.

I always loved the sweet peas,
how they bloomed and swelled quickly
before summer could burn them.

I picked huckleberries in summer on the ridge,
stripped chestnuts in fall, hung clothes in winter winds to dry
and pulled spring lambs from the muddy cut.

I found the stream for watercress
and wild roots to fill out a stew
when the cellar was empty.

I knew the kindness our young cow required
to let down her milk: the low voice,
the smoothing of her flank.

I understood how to keep brothers from fighting.
What to say to a mother so she wouldn't despair,
to a father to keep peace.

I wish I knew what skills will be needed
in the next place. *If there will be kindness.*
I wish I could prepare.

Night Birds Dip

"The doorkeeper's feet are seven armlengths long" -Sappho

Night birds dip through the crest of the evening,
the child at my breast sighs now and sleeps;

neat lawn slabs lap their dusk-shrouded houses,
the sounds of the town seep away.

I listen for the moon call, night howl, wind breath,
I listen for a death song on the stilling air;

I catch no sound. There is no song for death
in the grey of the evening when the wind goes down.

Bones unflesh quietly behind an earthen door,
proportions counted for a housewifely exchange:

infant, child, girl, maiden, woman, mother, crone,
rearranged secrets of the milky graves.

Silent as they linger, the doorkeeper's toes
are five-petalled buttercups ghosting the grass,

her portal feet are seven armlengths long,
the ages of a human on a mortal pass.

Remember the purple-scented flush of summer rain falling
thick-dropped down through the blackcurrant leaves?

Armfuls of lilac stems in Sunday morning vases,
dark-skinned plums hanging damp on the trees?

No one says that the fruit may not be taken,
sweet flesh eaten and the seed passed on;

no one sees where the raven drops the plum stone;
the baby sleeps and the evening light is gone.

Swansea Train Station, February 1979, 3 a.m.

The station café has been closed for hours.
A cold wind blows across the waiting room.
There are no other passengers.

The train conductor opens the doors
and my husband stows our two suitcases.
We are off to America, a new continent.

We will be gone two years, we think.
My mother knows better.
She hands up our new baby, sleeping.

Tender

I have so much to tell you
but can hardly speak
for the grace of it

as whatever else the world contains
it has this, the antidote,
the best truth of home.

Icicles outside may fall like arrows
and the strength of the world
break around my shoulders,

but I see you, child, and am quiet.
I brush your hair to curves,
I hold you in the crook of my arm.

I become worthy
because you are tender.
Everything that matters starts here.

Coppélia Runs

A surge, a wait; a bend;
    giving in, a pause by the door jamb for a plié,
        sweep into high kick and turn, then down to the kitchen
    floor
            next to the coal scuttle,
a whisper of toes across the room *en pointe*,
    pretend tutu crisp from the waist,
        arms like the necks of birds fishing in stage-lit water.

Christmases and birthdays I hoped for slippers
    with glistening straps. Aunt Bride took me and my sister
        to scenes from Swan Lake and Coppélia
            which I could see when the dancers moved left.
Swan Lake, right and centre,
was a long disappointment of the backs of heads,
    but, by chance, Coppélia with painted cheeks
        danced in her stiff body on the left of the stage:
she bent and froze - still, still, still -
    until she was wound up by a man and danced again.

Bare-legged, our best dresses tossed by a night wind,
    we caught a bus back to Aunt Bride's room,
        ate cream of mushroom soup in mugs and shared her bed.
In the morning we used the toilet down the hall
    and Aunt Bride told my sister she had
        too much marmalade on her toast.

Back home in the family kitchen, far from town,
    I remembered Coppélia, stuck in her stiff body
        with no one around to wind up her key.

Instead of dancing *en pointe*
    as I used to (to show my mother how I longed for lessons),
        since the dancers on stage had run in their bright tights,
           and running was also dance,
I took my orchestra outside and ran, over the clumping winter
fields,
    along hedgehog and rabbit tracks,
        ran, and leapt, and ran.

Resurrection

We approached the clean edge of the grave hole,
my sister and I.

Mary wound on the film of her new Bakelite Brownie,
lining up a sharp picture.

We shouldn't have seen how naked he was,
the rusted arrowhead between his ribs.

He hadn't just been left behind, slumped from a battle
but laid out feet to the east in a Christian burial.

An Anglo-Saxon warrior he was. We could see his teeth.
They took him up out of the ground to the Reading Museum.

He thought he was going to lie on the chalk under the earth
until Christ came.

Toffee

When Dad made toffee
and we put it to set
on the cupboard's top shelf,
we did not know it would fall
like a long tongue
down the back,
fill up Mum's Sunday shoes.

Ground 1

Spring's late this year; we're bored with snow and with filling the bird feeder. When the tepid sun finally shows up I step out to hang clothes on the line, and the ground's a dull, beaten brown. It looks as dead as *a three-hour chemistry class on a wet Welsh day, Jones Chem speaking in a drone and the five of us leaning as upright as we can on the old, brown benches with pipes sticking through them,* cold as the done-for branches in this American backyard, *while outside our classroom window the gym teacher's flap of hair flies back from his bald scalp as he bounces past, the boys we like heading doggedly behind him out to the soggy playing fields.* Now students ride past our yard closed into their coats. I wanted to write a love note to the old, moist ground, but here I am, grumbling again.

Ground 2

The ground speaks to me quite often.

"Come closer," the blacktop whispers, "and I'll tell you a secret. Come down here!"

"No," I say, "you'll take my skin. You'll break my arm."

"I won't," it says. "I'll caress you with my strength, and you will love me. You will lay your cheek down on my chest."

The Ohio State Fairground chuckles through its hot, manured straw: "Come close! I want to tell you something."

I'm young, and fall for that one, the groping of my milk-heavy breast.

The Appalachian Trail with its stone creep waits for me to move on. Says almost nothing. Everything listens, chipmunk, copperhead, bear, porcupine grinding its teeth, toad with markings like chocolate drops, hawk, its slipping shadow, the almost-turned blueberries. A Giant Millipede ripples over a rock, and a rattlesnake tastes my air. Says nothing.

"No," I say to the ground now, as upright as I can be. "I won't come down."

"I'll wait," it murmurs with its brown mouth.

Ditches

You left your fistfuls of grass along the paths of childhood
the loves sprung from flower-sweet lanes,
and wetness seeped into your collars in all the autumns:
nothing for you to leave but bits of lust gone soft in the damp
like loaves in paper biked from town,
trees draining overhead, streaming ditches
along the watery quiet of the farm road home.
What, then, America? Ohio's bitter snow lasts
through any reasonable spring, other countries' spring,
when bulbs have already come and gone
on the other side of the sea.
                              Don't thaw
if you can't handle whispers,
if you don't want to see grief running.
If bouquets hardening on the sill
won't let you pretend they'll live forever.
That you'll live forever. That life will wait
while you sort out this marriage, raise these bright children,
hold your breath this long. It doesn't.
Each day takes payment; your body pays,
racking up debts as though it can handle them.
But after all the breakfasts and the evening meals,
the children gone, the body well-used, where will you be?
Down which sweet summer road will you walk, when you are old?

States of Skin

December
Birds boil up from the pines into a red morning,
thousands of them swimming in the sky,
the pond trembling in its bowl outside my window
thinking it's blackcurrant jelly,
and I soften in my skin as though it's spring.

January
Leaves fall in to rot
and everything knows death has arrived.
Frogs have already left, dug into mud,
gone so deep their skin can still protect them.
Who would willingly stay in that place
when the bite comes?

February
I melt the rigid silence down to water
with a kettle and a large pot.
A heron stares in through my window
wanting fish. There are so few ponds.
I feel my heart thrash in its throat.

March
A warm hand on the pond's skin
brings up goldfish by the dozen
I wasn't sure were there,
strong and subtle, surfacing from decay.
Their wings flash. They can't help tossing off light.

We Dip Our Toes into an Estuary,
the Morning After the Wedding,

the young women stripped to their skivvies
leaping into the cold depths,
a seal rising to look.

There are no boys the right age,
only small brothers, cousins
and older men having a smoke.

We aunts and uncles long
to plunge ourselves into that fresh water,
but don't, with our return journeys beginning.

Or perhaps what keeps us from it is imagining
our middle-aged flesh in wet underwear,
nipples and hair showing through.

So we keep our clothes on and wade, and swing pebbles.
Remember being young, burning in dark water.
Aberystwyth Bay, March, 3 a.m.

I count thirty-four swans easing towards the horizon.

The Book I'm Writing

is a book about loss and heartbreak,
also delusion, distaste, quiet villainy, and sabotage.

There's a strong pulse of hope near the beginning,
the rhythm of which weakens as the narrative develops.

It might have some heroism.
It will have whining,

especially if there is – and there always is –
pain or vomiting involved.

It's set near the coast:
There's a running metaphor

involving rogue sea waves
and the crushing of the human spirit.

There are choices made about whom to forgive
and whom to set up in the display case near the front door,

their irritating quirks dusted off
whenever dislike wants justification.

It's a character-driven work,
the laziness of the protagonist

leading directly to the forfeiture of hope.
In spite of this, birds sing, babies are born, etc.

Rassouli's Madonna
"The Voyager"

There's something lacy going on
in the skirts,

which makes me think
the picture's all skirts,

the light of the mother
leading
and, nestled in her petticoats,
a blue child sleeping,

forming its gold
in the folds of the mother.

There's a horizon too
outside, and perhaps

whatever's beyond it
the real source of light,

but the light of the mother
is in the foreground

layered with the quiet
in which a baby grows
wrapped in lace,
in velvet folds,
the baby's eyes closed
for now

and, for now,
the mother's eyes open.

The Rain's Heavy Today

I look out at the bird feeder for a kinglet
or the shy female cardinal
from yesterday, but see crows.

I don't like dressing for funerals,
even if the friend visits me in a dream
and wakes me smiling.

We wade into the chapel through torrents,
under inadequate umbrellas,
our fancy shoes leaking.

Our friend looks lovely
in her picture, out of the weather,
surrounded by chrysanthemums.

The army trumpeter I meet
in the ladies' room toweling her hair
plays *Taps* to sheets of rain on the porch.

Even stripped of our coats
we steam up the place while the priest speaks,
while the sweet sorrowful note lingers.

We arrive sodden and squelching but,
when we leave, the wide January graveyard
is quiet again, and soft.

Alice B. Toklas's Third Rose

*"Civilization began with a rose. A rose is a rose
is a rose is a rose." -Gertrude Stein
"...when she gets to that third rose she loses me."
-Erv Harmon*

This rose I gave to Gertrude in the fall,
a yellow rose for spring and love and lust;
the third one was an eyesore, I recall.

Cezanne, Matisse, Picasso blazed our hall
and forced the careless caller to adjust;
this rose I gave to Gertrude in the fall.

The weather then broke green all over Gaul,
the roses burst, the bushes were robust:
the third one was an eyesore, I recall.

Still life brushed could not be still at all:
red roses scrambled up the wall untrussed;
this rose I gave to Gertrude in the fall.

The first rose rose rose fiercely tall,
the second rose was yellow, lovers' trust;
the third one was an eyesore, I recall.

A modern rose is summer's richest scrawl
though winter's withering leaves it undiscussed;
this rose I gave to Gertrude in the fall -
the third one was an eyesore, I recall.

2

Homesick

My body, raw as unbaked clay, sinks into its grey pose,
moisture mottling its surface.
A pain in my skull shakes its dusty feathers
and settles down, clawfoot, for eternity.
I fold myself into the chill earth like a pebble.
If I surrender grief, will angels lift it away,
that great, dark flopping thing,
and relight my heart like a Tilley lamp,
the mantle flaring up, burning the inside of my ribs,
so I feel as though I'm twenty again
and loved, and in love?

Blue Road

Ice-cream bars are twopence
and every part of the blue road back from town holds its story,
where a bull killed a man, where we come for water,
and everywhere there are buttercups in the Irish hedges
yellow as fool's gold.

After Granny cooks fish, she gives us their eyes
white, like chalk, like sticky round chalk,
and we kneel down, scraping our knuckles, to draw
on the warm, blue road.

At Uncle Jimmy's there is no toilet.
When I ask where to go, he leads me to the back door,
one arm around my shoulders, the other sweeping over Ireland
and says *Child, you can go
wherever your heart desires.*

Hired for Two Hours, Our Open Boat Left Skibbereen's Harbour

weighed down with parents, grandparents,
seven brothers and sisters and myself;
under the bench seat a bag with a towel,
ham and jam sandwiches in bread bags,
boiled eggs, fruit cake and bottles of squash.

We motored past rocky pieces of land,
the seagulls AAAK-AAAKing around us,
chill water splashing, wind spraying salt in our eyes.
We looked for jellyfish and jostled for leg room.
Grandad tried in vain to light his pipe.

We were rounding the second-to-last,
uninhabited island of the bay, the water under us
beginning to lift itself higher to meet the looming,
chasmic waves of the Atlantic, no other boats in sight,
when our engine spat twice and cut out.

Perhaps there was nervous chatter.
Mum had never liked boats
or being out on the water. Dad tried
to pull the motor into action, but it was dead,
the petrol tank under the seat empty.

I remember the silence of nothing left to say,
all the rules of family gone,
not catching each others' eye,
sitting stiffly except for the baby climbing onto laps,
his blond curls blown back by the wind.

As we drifted past the last island, we saw a house!
I don't remember how we were saved,
except for the shouting for help. Did we have oars?
I remember Dad jumped into the sea with a rope,
and the people had petrol.

Heroics and hope. Dad's muscles. Everything alright—
move on, eat sandwiches. Don't talk about
how the current will always sweep our family towards that
thunderous grey horizon, how we'll always wonder
if that's how we're going to die.

Wexford Boy

Our grandfather joined the I.R.A.
as a boy in the Wexford hills,
defying the English with prayer and guns.
At eighteen he dried gunpowder at the family fire
knowing no better, and in a moment
caught enough scars there
to prove the worth of any man.

The prison camp yard in Cork could not restrain
those Catholic and Protestant boys,
who dug themselves out with a fork,
went barefoot over the wire,
and walked home across the hungry mountains
expecting to be shot.

The soldiers lay in wait at his home farm
so his family, harassed, turned him off,
passing his inheritance to a brother.
With Independence came a job working on roads,
like the jobs for many a country's hero,
and decades of labour stretched ahead of him.

But the road-worker's house had a garden,
and there his cabbages were round and loved,
and his leeks, and his rows of berries,
and when his English grandchildren came
he sat them on his trousered knee
peeling the scars from apples for them.

Door Knob

You're racing through long grass,
through cow parsley and marguerites,

chased by mummies,
weird men from the footpath

and Baby Jane's angry eyes.
You break through the wire fence—

it hurts to breathe—sprint past the hen run,
leap onto the door stone, grab the knob.

It spins loosely through agonizing minutes
while a man from the footpath pants up behind you

and Baby Jane cackles. It spins uselessly, hopelessly,

until —*a miracle!*— it catches and turns, and
you fall into the house, sweating and alive.

There you are, your mother says.
Is it your turn to lay the table?

You can't remember, but go to the drawer
and count out knives and forks and spoons,

set them round the table and sit,
your heart finally slowing, on the long bench,

to wait for dinner.

Big Sister

After the sixth
and seventh children were born
and my hair was cut short
so no one would have to plait it
and I stopped cleaning my teeth,
I bought with my pocket money
a small tin of condensed milk
and ate it without sharing
by the weeds behind the barn
in my striped t-shirt
among purple irises
and dock leaves big as plates
while the ducks quacked,
ate the thick, sweet cream
with a small spoon
ate it all.

Small Luggage

Our dad rode his bike as though it were part of his body,
leaning it like an extra limb as he threw a leg over,
or on arrival brought it back, feet crossed over a single pedal
to coast in upright.

Weekdays he rode alone to the train station
raincoated through soaking winds
or shirt-sleeved in high summer,
but Sunday mornings,
from a child seat on his crossbar no bigger than a hand,
the small luggage of his offspring got tipped sideways
as he tossed the frame over to mount,
a cardiganed package flying unsecured over ruts and road grit
through the crazed buffeting of terrible lorries.

Once we could ride alone
we pedalled cartoonishly behind that tall man,
who wasn't made to falter by growling traffic
or the loose wake of his children–brakes failing,
chains softening, hurtling toward ditches–
that graceful man cresting the hill ahead of us singing in Latin
with a small, behatted person balanced on his bar.

Paternity

When Dad took on the job
he was good at it

working hard to make it work
everybody happy now

yes, everyone excited
watching him cook

wondering what might escape
while we helped

while we made our mistakes
dropped, tripped, argued

broke, pushed, spilt–
but he was up all through

the left-over greens and potatoes
we cooked in a goose-egg omelette,

he won us over
with homemade fudge

sweet enough to hurt our teeth,
he stayed up right through

the nine-egg cake from "Mrs. Beeton's":
an egg each to crack

and turns to stir
and browning in margarine wrappers—

a cake slow enough
to welcome Mum home

a cake good-smelling
as a new baby,

and when he could stay up
just a little longer

we would go to bed in our cold rooms
listening to him sing *Killarney*

to whichever of us
could not get to sleep.

Of All the Birds

Of all the birds that dropped down naked from the trees,
eye-bulbs bulging, mouths urgent cups of red and yellow,
scarcely birds yet,
we raised perhaps three dozen in those careful years,
in boxes lined with cotton, tucked in against the pipes.

We fished spiders from the toilet bowl,
dried them on the rim and let them go.
We caught the crazy moths that beat themselves against the light
and took them out, their dusty wings still restless in our grip,
outside to the lampless evening air.

We were powerful.
There were summers when we saved whole nests
of blind and hairless mice,
scooping them in handfuls from the cornfield
before the stubble fires were set.
We rescued cats: wild kittens abandoned in the barn,
the cat impaled on our barbed-wire fence,
a twisting ball of fur and broken bone.

Dad brought in rabbits, five in one hand,
orphaned by his gun in the vegetable patch.
We reared them with care, squirted milk into each pink mouth,
felt their fur grow, took them for exercise out to the lawn,
until one by one they escaped back into Dad's ordered rows.

You were the child who died, when eight of us survived,
the first-born son, carrying the light of your father's name;
yours was the coffin lined with silk,

a typed receipt in the bureau drawer.
Though we were alive, and spread life generously,
bestowing it on all comers, we could not bestow it on you, John.

The Picnic

We drove to the high ridge of the chalk downs
above West Hendred when I was a child,
and sat in the wind at the top of the world
with every cloud of heaven surging over us
and the wild, dry grasses curving to our waists.

We ate shelled eggs and sandwiches,
fruitcake, and greengages sweet as nectar,
the juice blowing away from our mouths in the wind.

Afterwards we ran to the White Horse,
carved into the hillside before Stonehenge was built:
senseless channels in the hill's face.
We put our hands into its grooves
and tossed the chalky pieces in the air.

We walked on top of prehistoric barrows
whose bones and pots and flints
had all been scattered to museums
and the mounds resealed with earth.
The grasses again blew over them, tall, indifferent.

Driving home in the car we fought over plums.
Across the valley behind us, a clear picture now
against the steep, green slope,
the White Horse shone in the evening sun.

Clapham Common, Dusk

After all the other children have gone home for their tea
the greenery turns wistful. Sweet wrappers catch
in dirt under the railway bridge.
The time for pleasure has passed
says the wind, tossing the empty swings.
Why are you still here in the aftertime, little girls?
A filled train screams overhead, then there is silence.
You don't belong here, says the wind, or in any of these houses of strangers.
The grass sloping away from lamplight is stained with worry
and two little girls hurry, silent, through it,
something breathing on their heels.
Their granny's gate rattles and catches.
They slip through, watching bushes,
slamming the gate shut, running for the curtained house.
Nearly safe.

Grandad Had Two Jokes

Our London Grandad grew tobacco in his garden,
drying it in the garage next to his harvest of hops
from which he cooked up stinking vats of beer.

He tamped sticky brown tobacco clumps into his pipe
which he sucked and sucked at to get a draw. The smell was rich
and made me think of Indian markets and Chinese junks.

Grandad's first joke was that he cleaned his teeth with boot polish
to get them nice and yellow. We all believed him, he was so serious,
until Granny said *Oh, Father!* and we found him out.

His second joke was telling me I'd given him his terrible cough:
for years I was ashamed when I heard that mucousy hacking.
I thought he might die, and it would have been me that killed him.

The joke we played on him was at Easter. Granny would "cook"
two hard sugar eggs that looked exactly like boiled eggs,
even to the speckling on the shells. We'd put one in his egg cup

and one on his plate, then sit down, strenuously not giggling.
We'd hear his steps crossing the tiled entrance hall,
and the rattle of the kitchen door handle. He'd come in

buttoning his shirt collar, sit, and with great ceremony
try to crack the eggs. *What's the matter with these eggs?*
he'd growl, staring around the table.

Nothing, we'd say, stifling little noises, eating our eggs.
Then he'd give us a grin, showing his yellow teeth.

Surfaces

The brick wall deeply scoured the skin from my thigh: one minute I was balanced on the wall, the next, down, shocked, burning. I boarded the school bus unable to turn home, pulling my skirt over the wound. The headmaster in his office uncovered it inch by inch, his witch-hazel swabs searing my open flesh, gathering its bright drops: he dressed it again with Germolene spread like pink butter onto bare bread, packing it with gauze.

A week later I sat in the bath at home, shivering under icy drops from the high tap, puncturing the thick-skinned grasp of the water with my torso, my thin, white knees.

The bandages had bonded to my scars like moss in brick, skin fibres weaving through the greying cloth as intricate as hairs in a robin's nest, as intimate as family telling who you were; and soaking eased away the crumbled edges of the wound, but when I pulled the deep-set centre pain came, and blood, and amber beads.

Fending off my mother's hands I was prepared to wait the night out, but she broke in again and in a rush I did it, tore the whole bloody mess away—old Germolene, grey bandage, scar, rose from the grip of the water naked, letting the fear out.

John Stibbs

I hated him when I was six, new in the school
and sneaking sweets from my coat pocket,
sucking familiar comfort in the folds
of the strange, dark clothes: he told Miss Hunt,
Miss Hunt who handed me a mantilla
to cover my sinful head, gripping the boys
with warty fingers while they sang *Virgin most pure,*
Star of the Sea, pray for the wanderer, pray for me.

I hated him for five years in the private parts of my soul
as we moved from the bare front row in church
to the fifth row back, where there was a flaking pillar
to pick at during Stations of the Cross.
I scorned and avoided him until we were eleven,
when I learned to draw planes watching his careful formula,
and found then that I'd always liked his quietness,
his reddish hair, his freckles.

John Stibbs wasn't a bad boy
but one day Mr. Bell, white with anger,
called him to the front and went to fetch his stick.
Each crack of that sharp edge into John Stibbs' hand
shocked me, each time that boy's hand fell
and Mr. Bell tapped it up,
leaned back and whipped his stick down.

I stared at John Stibbs' ribbed socks, his shaking knees
until my eyes blurred, and sickened I couldn't bear it,
and if I could go back to that place,
be a different, braver girl, I'd blaze up from my desk,

take away that stick, and make Mr. Bell be perfect.
At the end of the term, of the year, of the school,
I watched John Stibbs walk away, too shy to catch his glance
or choose one word for him from the mass I had inside,
and lonely caught the hot bus home.

I Take Exception to Your Shade of Blue, Mr. Key

which makes me think of evening
in a strange playground –
all the other children,
who know where they live, gone

and (in my case) I see my sister,
think I may follow her home
except she says *no, you may not—*
ask Mum, she says—*she'll tell you you can't—*

and it's night so
I start running,
not knowing the way.

Mr. Key,
there can be no quarrel with your greens:
even the dark ones have a chance of change
if they tilt a little—
they are moving as I watch,

and petals!
exquisite oiled creams blushing,
buds holding themselves on the cusp—
now *they* have a world of beginnings in them;

audacious pinks like sweet tents, saucy and fine;
yes, I would believe everything

if it weren't for that blue at the bottom
like a boiling storm

rising behind the flowers.

Orphan boy, how your grandfather
helped you blossom!

But somewhere inside
you are running a strange road, lost.
I know it by your blue.

(After "Hollyhocks" ca. 1881 by John Ross Key, grandson of Francis Scott Key)

Hands

I'm eleven, absorbed in my work, valuable.
I'm helping out at the dig of an Iron Age fort,
writing numbers on bones in permanent black ink.
My blackened fingers steady the bone pieces,
and strands of hair catch in my mouth
from the dusty wind of the summer downs.

I'm twelve. After we're told to stop writing in pencil
the fresh pink eraser on my desk is no longer exciting:
it can't help me be perfect. Clumps of blue ballpoint ink
smear onto my white, lined page because I'm left-handed.
I believe it's because I'm clumsy.
I'm growing breasts. I believe my father dislikes me.

I'm thirteen, in the bathroom, washing and washing my hands,
the skin of my fingertips chewed off. When I dry my hands I
accidentally touch my thumb with my finger:
to erase the error I must use my thumb to touch
each fingertip in order, counting. The number of rounds
is non-negotiable; it will increase over the year.
I use the edges of my palms to open my bedroom door.

Fog

When I think of you, it's a night with fog so thick we can scarcely see three feet in front of us, your sister and I edging our steep way home.

We hear a noise, and fall silent, like two bodies plummeting from a cliff: someone is walking towards us on that lonely, Hound-of-the-Baskervilles track.

We slip sideways into the lumpy field, hoping whatever experience is approaching–and we fear the worst–will pass us by,

but we've been heard, and the footsteps come up to us, and stop. Someone is listening. We can't disappear; we're shaking.

A menacing shape, a hand reaching for Jenny–I grab her other arm ready to run for it, but she doesn't come with me because it's you, *her brother*, sent for us.

Five years later I move away. We hear you died, of loneliness. No-one saved you from your fog. If your sister and I could have, you know we would. But all I can do is write.

this move from London has cut you

adrift: you are a kite unstrung above

the empty field, a kite leaving, a speck

far up in the blue-white socket of the sky

The Valley of the Sow

Of the Tuatha De Dannan, the holy tribe of Danu, Goddess of Light, to Wales came Gwydion, teller of tales and master illusionist, druid of the gods, teacher and friend. Gwydion fought the powers of Arawn, King of the Underworld, and won good gifts for humankind, bringing back by his wits the deer, the dog and the lapwing. Then Gwydion heard of a new beast, the pig: small, with flesh better-tasting than that of the ox, sent as gift by Arawn to Pryderi, Dark Prince of Dyfed. Gwydion, the illusionist, made from fungus horses, hounds and shields to trick Pryderi in barter for the swine. Gwydion and his people hurried their new beasts away from Pryderi's castle, knowing the illusion would not last. The places where they rested on their flight are known as Mochdrev (Swine's Town), Castell-y-Moch (Swine's Castle), Mochnant (Swine's Brook). Pryderi gave chase and battled with Gwydion, darkness against the light, until the light won.

At Pant-yr-Rhwch, Sow's Bottom, farm at the bottom of the Valley of the Sow, in the county of Dyfed, under the moist flanks of the hills near Llywyn-y-groes, Dad lies in the soft Welsh mud silently cursing machines.

Three young heifers jostle him, blowing grass breath in his face, dripping their saliva. He hammers the stuck bolt above him.

Clang! Clang! Clang! Clang!

When he stops hammering, the hills of the Celtic gods close in again around him and the low sky rests on him. He sits up to push the calves away, wiping his face with his coat.

Clang! Clang! Clang! Clang!

The bolt shudders and shifts. With numb fingers, he loosens the rust. The soft sound of a voice floats towards him faintly, faintly: "di – in – ner!" and it's the call of Brigid, Goddess of the Fire and the Hearth and the Poet's Flame, the call to rejuvenation sounding faintly down through the centuries and the Celtic mists.

Dad stands and stretches painfully. He collects his tools together and sets out over the fields. In the woods he pauses to find acorns, filling a pocket with the bitter nuts.

Across the stream, the home field rises towards the house. He passes bee hives and vegetables, stopping at the sheds below the farm yard. The two young pigs look at him, suddenly still, their flat noses twitching. He tosses the acorns in and they shriek with joy, rooting busily in the straw.

The pink stone house squats silently at the top of the yard, grey-tiled and full of promise. Dogs lift themselves up in the porch, glad to see him. He opens the door to the kitchen, the inner sanctum, the warmth. He rubs his hands. An aroma comes to him of crisp pork chops, and Welsh cakes browning on the stove. He closes the door.

Smoke from the farmhouse chimney drifts up through the Valley of the Sow and disappears in the afternoon sky.

Teen Ghost

November in Wales is a clammy beast dripping chill rain: at night, disconsolate, it rattles the house, screaming; our grey farm road in the early hours is a stripe on its back oozing cold sweat, hedgerows of stinging nettles and brambles are its bony stickles. Its drool runs down my neck as I stand waiting for the school bus.

I kissed an American boy in England in summer before my family moved to this new country, and he writes still, though we won't meet again. I'm stuck here with this other, terrible kind of contact: you by the window in your white dress, dissolving, sobbing as though your heart would break. Why do you cry? It won't solve anything.

I study physics at my desk by the window, write letters to friends dropping back, listen to the rain beat on the cowsheds. I try to sleep sitting upright with the light on. I hate being able to hear you! You're dead! All your sobbing won't stop you fading away.

Of Course I Loved You.

I don't know how you felt.
I used to ache.

Red flakes of paint drop from the old tractor
and crumble into the ground.

Water drips slowly into the trough by the door,
and the shadows of roses dance over it.

The yard is empty now,
the milking sheds are empty at this time of the day.

The trees drop their water to the grass,
the windblown hedge sprays its own moisture.

When it rains, the tyre tracks fill with water,
fill with bright tear water, and all the sky is in it.

The Night We Took Fish from Our River and the Police Came

What a black night, thick rain,
branches knocking windows,
water tearing through gutter pipes.
We heard a car's engine roar up the hill,
saw blue lights flashing in the farmyard.
I grabbed both beautiful sewin
from the weighing scales
and ran upstairs
to hide them under my sleeping sister's bed,
then back down to the kitchen,
which was full of teenagers in raincoats.
I watched the porch door open
and saw a fishing gaff propped
against the inner door—
someone stepping quickly over,
as if in greeting,
to hide the gaff with his body from view.

The policeman entered,
looked around,
wished us *noswaith dda*, good evening,
asked about our neighbour at the next farm—
what we knew about him,
whether we'd seen him.
Surprised,
my father said he came for milk
twice a week, carrying his can.

It was hard looking innocent
when so many of us were
dripping on the floor and fresh blood
was pooled on the kitchen table.

The policeman didn't mention poaching—
had bigger fish to fry. He told us
our neighbour had been on the run
for years, was wanted for murder,
wore a wig, carried a loaded gun.

Cardiff Night

The clocks go back, and in the space—
there is a space—a night hour rushes in
to blaze the dusk and tinsel-wink
the deepened afternoon.

My god, we civil servants, hard-shelled
insect-soft inside, pulsate with stifled beat, yes,
barely breathe throughout the day and, numbed,
stir homeward through the raucous streets.

On such a rainbowed, fairground night
tearing and bursting our way—
amber, green, red, yellow, white—
through the writhing lights,
when numb, packed, scarved and jacketed
we stood and swayed together past the shops and stops,
our slavish shells began to peel and crack,
and we leapt out and off,
under the city sky,
under the bright Welsh winter moon,
into the evening's cool, to catch our breath.

The Thin Path

I smell the green of it, and the brown. The track is marked mud, narrow, used only for biking and walking. It stretches behind me across a meadow, puddled in spots, and in spots too muddy to take a clean step. The emotion of it is hard to place–a very deep memory. Perhaps I was carried by my father along such a track. I stare down, mesmerised as it passes under my feet. Then I'm walking in a wool skirt, my hair ribbon loose, following our mother's shoes, our father's bike: he helps a younger sister balance on the seat.

Later I'm carrying a picnic bag, holding a small brother's hand. We're always going to places out in the country, or along by the river in Oxford. The day's a little cool, with a chill wind blowing and the ground clammy to sit on, or the day's a little too hot, with the cooked grasses smelling sweet, or it's late afternoon and we have to walk a long way back, with the little ones complaining that they're too tired.

For many miles and years I walk that track, behind a bike wheel or someone's legs. When I leave Britain I don't realise I might never see such a track again, or miss it, yet thirty years later here it is. It's curving with its muddy bike tracks through White Clay Creek State Park, and I walk it every week, crossing American meadows with my daughter.

3

My midwife forbids the fan

Slick with sweat,
a hooked fish thrashing on the bed,
I reach down to cradle his head as it turns;
one shoulder, then another; my insides tear and burn.
Half-born, he looks at me, his eyes
obsidian, shining like ink.
I put my hands around the ribs of his body
to help him out of mine
while he waits quietly for what may happen next.

The Flower of Her Throat
For our great-grandmother, Mabel, 1874-1928

From secrets her mystery rose on a thin stem—
no pictures; no mention to us of her name.
The light of her face had faded long ago
but the flower of her throat did not curl down;

though mosses in the winter wall shrank back
and her babies one by one turned blue and left,
though coals in the stove lay thick with ash
and fog closed in over the sigh of the sea,

though all the patted cakes, knit coats, hopes, loves
all the fires a mother built, had gone,
though she folded her little ones in lavender,
though spring would not come.

She threw out the last crumbs, smoothed the cloth,
left her winter place in a fresh dress, tidily,
her pearls boxed away. They found her like chamomile
tied to a kitchen beam to dry, protected from grief,

and the light of her face had faded,
yet the flower of her throat did not curl down.

I Choke on Mortality and Wish for Something Less Orange

A week before reading of the sad incident in the paper
I have a dream in which, wearing an orange skirt,
I pick daylily petals from the floor,
    try to eat them, and gag. According to my friend Clare
I'm already dead, unable to swallow the fact
of the brevity of life: yes.

Two weeks later, in the park, my dog and I examine a butterfly
as blue as human milk, rows of jet points pricking
out the edges of its wings. My dog jerks forward
and swallows it. A red-eyed cicada crashes into my ear
and blunders off; for seventeen years it plotted
its splendor of green and ruby stripes.
The caterpillar on our path, immaculate
in orange lines tricked out with black jewels, rests.
My dog eats a cigarette.

On the way home I tell my neighbor Kay the title of my poem;
she thinks it will be about the child in the News-Journal
who choked on a piece of orange and died.
I didn't know it, but it is, it is.

Someone Else's Children

'I want to be able to say that history called us to action, and we left the world more peaceful for our children.'–President George W. Bush on 'Operation Iraqi Freedom,' Oct. 3, 2003.

'Fifty-two killed and sixty-three injured by landmines and unexploded ordinance ... in just one week ... most of the deaths and injuries are caused to children.'–Mines Advisory Group, Kirkuk, Iraq, April 21, 2003.

On our way home from school we found a bomb
in the grass next to the wheat, and bore it back proudly.
Our brother Mike thumped it down on the kitchen table.

When Mum came in from feeding the hens
she let out a shriek,
grabbed it up and threw it into the duck pond.

We got the bomb squad out
and they took it away and exploded it.

I wrote about the event for 'Sparky' magazine.
They changed it so it said
Mum had picked the bomb up gently
and put it carefully into a bucket of water.

They sent me five pounds and a transistor radio
for it being the Star Letter,
and children read it all across England.
But it still wasn't true, what they changed it to.
Even though people read it, it still wasn't true.

Break Clay, Kitchen Table

This metal will be a cup
          in fifty years, this clay
a piece of bread:

during another era
          kids lost their soft back
watching monsters

in the tablecloth,
          eating dry
mouthfuls.

The clock
          has no way to know what
burrowing occurs

between laid plates, between
          the slices of
a knife.

The neighbour whipped
          his son's bare rump
against their table

in front of us–
          no remedy for that,
no unmemento.

Who knows what happens
        in the sheets
of a home?

Cut bread
        into every choice.
There are plates enough

in all the houses
        and children,
crops to lay on them.

One day, cup will be
        metal
and bread, clay.

I Take Off My Breasts So I Can Go Running

I unscrew my breasts
and lay each carefully in the kitchen sink.
The chest marks left are surprisingly small,
like petals.
Relieved, as if having set down groceries,
I run away lightly across the stubble fields.

I was full in love with my children,
and if I added up our stories
it was a lifetime of sweet exchange,

but once, on a wet Welsh day, lusting to run,
I burst away from them at the village races,
left them calling for me, did not look back.

They came along then at their own small pace,
accepted my prize coins; silent, saw my shame.

My breasts in the sink are forlorn, alien;
I've forgotten which way up they go.
Pressing them, grey, against my heated skin
I'm afraid it's too late.
The chest-mark petals, though, tingle
with recognizing blood.

Full Moon Over Yi Palace

Only a bright fat arc
hovered above Rite Aid,

the laundromat,
and the Yi Palace Chinese restaurant,

yet a sparkling edge
outlined the whole deal

and the rest of the disc,
which should have been dark,

had a glow, because
the shadow on the moon

was shimmering all over
with small lights.

This is what I think of
when I see the thinness of a person,

that beyond the visible curve
shifts a full bed of embers.

Gardening Without Gloves

Rising through the dawn
birds' noise clatters through the tent;
we cocoon ourselves against the mausoleum air:
we're awake, we've been awake
from time to time throughout this fine, strange night
and the humming world was with us.

In the kitchen I make pancakes thick as buckwheat bricks,
eat them with strawberries;
the children have Aunt Jemimas with syrup and cream—
they go happy to school, to any day
which follows this best night.

You sleep indoors: no room for four in a two-man tent.
The radio clatters you awake, music and news,
you make sandwiches as you always make them,
eat raisin bran as always for breakfast.

You're an arrow shedding its airstream as it flies
aimed I don't know where, holding your momentum to you,
reluctant to stop in case you lose the power to fly,
as if the air would never hold you up again and let you pierce it,
as if the world would fall away to dust if you saw it in a single
frame,
as if the past would take you back to it, and you lost, and gone.

I can only plant things using the skin of my hands,
getting dirt in my nails, pressing my knees in it;
it's the only way I know to bless it and feel when it's ripe for seed.
Under the bindweed mats the earth teems

with may beetles, globular black ants
and the blind grubs that I'll see in my dreams tonight:
blessings of the dark goddess, picking the bones clean.

You have gone to the airport and I missed saying goodbye,
here with dirt on my knees.
You take without complaint whatever I can give you
not knowing what it is you want, not able to dream.
And I can't dream for you, can't even lay claim to my own dreams.
No wonder our children have always stuck to Aunt Jemima
and the safe American Way.

Lindisfarne, This Old Death

The sea crashes and sighs.
Our wooden boat churns past the monks' island;
gorse drops off the last ledge.
Far beyond it, puffins dip to their bare outcrops
sparked white in the distant grey,
and wind sprays salt over the sea's swell.

The rock where monks were slain a thousand years ago
is inaccessible except at low tide.
I visit it with your mother and the children,
walk over the exposed sand,
                                        wishing I could cry out
from the pain of having lost you,
or, if not you, yet, the joy I used to have,
once believed I'd have again,
would earn and deserve soon
if I kept my head down.

The monastery was built here for safety
off the far edge of the world,
but Vikings found it,
ships snaking in from the north,
and they sacked the high church
and massacred monks at their prayer.

Now the years slip by and I grow old,
walking with bare feet on that beach
with seagulls, those old monks, screaming in my chest.

Going Underground

If I could fold it
right
the flower
would open

the cut flower
dies in the vase
and the brown shrub
may not grow
back

the cut flower
dies in the vase
and the brown shrub
may not grow
back

the brown flower
dies on its stem
and the squirrel
raps on the window
for food

you say *I can feel it
snowing.* You say
*it's snowing
big flakes*
and lying I tell you
you lie.

Thirty-Nine

I sprint
to the sea through splats
of October rain.

The bay grins baptismally
and ducks me, I come up choked
and laughing,

hop shivering
back through the salt marsh
a seedcase spine
embedded in my sole.

My English mother
walks towards me
wearing her rain jacket.

The water's lovely
I yell, *try it.*
I knew you would say that,
she tells me,
giving me a towel.
You're just like your father.

There Are Red Leaves

"Misty Mountain," 1860, William Louis Sontag.

If you walk the path you've always walked
and plan for things you hoped would come to pass,
what do you do if the ground falls away
and all you see ahead is grey air full of sorrow?
If you used to know where you were going,
but now your path has fallen off
and the landscape no longer sustains you?
Perhaps, even though you're used to walking straight
on visible roads, the path onward isn't.
Perhaps what you trust is unreliable, what you see, unhelpful,
and the path is down and in and through dark.
Perhaps turning your belly to the grass will make you safe.
After all, here, like a route marker,
there are red leaves growing at the entrance to a cave,
a cave you'd never find if things were easier,
if the road were clear, or you could fly.
Who knows what will come next?
Who knows what will happen after the softening, the falling in?

Isis Dreams Back Her Lost Self

Awakened in the night, I stir with dreams of you.
My husband sleeps on, breathing in the dark;
our children doze, the couched dogs too
drift and start, and gradually my flushed heart
calms; I remember what I dreamed, and why
my skittish mind forgot: you touched my hair.
Dear one, *you touched my hair*, and how can I
stand that now, awake, and you not there?

I searched the years, the lonely nights across
to find your scattered parts: limbs,
torso, head—your banishment my loss.
I dreamt you in fragments sought, simply
drawn by longing, and you came to me somehow.
Will you return? And teach me wholeness now?

Rutted Run

You cannot go backward, says the dream.
You cannot fix the rutted way of your old marriage
with all your backhoes, diggers;
with all the road dug up.

How narrow was the house you lived in?
As wide as a double bed
with a staircase on each side.

My ex has slipped away into the party crowd.
Are you looking for him? asked my sister.
He was here. He was just here.

I give out popsicles, enough for everyone.

Fire on the Road

Can you die from the not-
writing of your stories?
Beyond the floating door cloth
seethes a forest blackened by night.

Today there was a fox
like fire on the road,
its body stiff as wood,
the edges of its fur
still breathing like flame.

Dry

The lightness of water
     is conveyed on canvas
by an absence of paint;
the lightness
     of the movement of water
running in its currents
     through winter grasses:
wet and dry, there's the balance,
summer's grasses spent on the shores,
     rocks holding everything down,
water
     an absence of paint on the canvas
bringing clarity,
the way the center of a sundial
brings clarity with its shadow.

Mars once had surface water
and an atmosphere that held it in,
     but solar winds blew that away
and Mars dried out.

On earth a river runs;
the artist paints those parts of it
     that are not water
to remind us.

Mirror, Shutter, Window, Shade

The mirror of my apartment

I rub my skin hard with the squeezed cloth
to scour pain from my stretched lips.
The face of my girl is sorely missed;
I glimpse it now and then
slipping past this closed mirror, a ghost.

The shutter of her room

I wish I knew how to be a parent,
keep all these battered organs in one body,
not lose any to the night, to the cold moon,
to the house where my first child sleeps.

Through the window of my passing car

I see summer has gilded her hair.
I see her legs have found the shape of the road
and are lit by the paths she has taken.
She's all grown now: bright as the flicker
we saw in the grass last night and as quickly gone.
If I stopped the car she'd be changed, trapped,
and I myself chaff-blown to the flat land near this town.
I suffer a temporary loss of balance.
Daughters fly past my window.

Shade

Years later I enter an antique shop
to find earrings for someone else,
but a round brooch gives me the eye,
a brooch made of butterflies, old silver
and buffed enamel the shade of love renewed,
and it smiles and mentions her name.
That night in my dream butterflies in their hundreds,
as brilliant as sun in ice, fly up.

Wealth

We were poor and made everything: gourmet
cake, wine; without your boss's roses
there wouldn't have been a bouquet

and afterward half the guests got sick,
my brother Mike in the hospital,
you alone with the vomit bowl,

while Dad and I went out to save the hay,
closer than we'd ever been,
tossing bales, growing ill, rain coming in.

You and I were poor, ready for everything:
my unexpected pregnancy and your PhD,
America with a suitcase and a new baby,

too poor for a car or a telephone, cold Ohio,
me not allowed to earn a wage, touch-and-go
on your starvation stipend,

the baby light enough for us to get free food, we
somehow went to Florida, swam in the ocean,
picked oranges right off the tree.

We were poor and did everything,
twirled haggis in a cloth, played softball,
made Christmas crackers in the fall,

drove to Colorado in a borrowed Jeep,
went to court, illegal aliens they said,
had another baby in our own bed.

We moved east, citizens: a dozen years,
me more-and-more yin, of course
to your more-and-more yang; we divorced.

I always was a low-achieving writer
and you so brilliant and focused, never
had to miss a day of work either.

You now: wealthy, with a wealthy wife.
My spouse and I: new son, what a life!
Our two in their twenties. Poor, doing everything.

Rest Stop Restaurant, 5 a.m.

The night workers are counting down
the last two hours of their shift.

After a fight I come here,
drink coffee as though I have choices.

I am not without plans;
have my toothbrush,

but once my eyes are dry
I know I will return, fulfill

all the obligations of the day.
I dreamed you cut off my skin

with a knife, and I let you,
out of politeness.

What kind of sleep is that,
which tells me such things?

I Heard There Were Dolphins

Crossing the early breakers
in my nursing-mother suit
I'm suddenly alone in a trough
where grey waves rise like walls

like walls crash in, and fear-struck
glimpse you on the beach shrinking;
scream *I can't get back* and back
your reply comes faintly: *you must.*

You won't come for me, then.
Think we might both drown.
You would let me go, then.

Many walls rise before I
tear my eyes from them,
flail, praying, towards shore,
deliver myself, choking, to the sand.

Still salt-sick when we leave the beach
I see the lifeguards arrive
like Dobermans, sprightly,
sniffing the morning sea.

I heard there were dolphins here last summer,
and they swam with the swimmers
out beyond these breakers.
This summer I only met walls
the colour of a shark's eye.

Shoes in the River

The day after the fright we go out by canoe
peering at dozens of shoes on the riverbed,
none of them his.

In my dreams pieces fall away under water;
his features sliding off his face,
potent dreams after years of fear that one of my children
would be lost under the surface
and I would hunt for that child every night of my life.

Yet at the moment in question
when I saw his face go down,
dropped pebbles from my shirt,
pressed my body through the thickening water,
I knew there was no possibility I could fail,
miss my grasp, lose him to that dark draft.

What a beautiful river! Sparkling,
with dead trees in it, and spent shad.
We see five-foot muskees, bass, bald eagles,
kingfishers, otters and merganser ducks
negotiating through will and luck and need
with the Delaware, but we got a bargain:
a boy back, for the price of a shoe.

Easter Monday

Amish families walk home from town,
women in white weekday bonnets,
men in straw hats carrying babies,
boys in breeches, girls in fresh dresses.
They have taken a day trip
on the Strasburg Scenic Railway
and are heading back to evening chores
chatting and smiling.

The farmyards hold lines of wash
hung out at daybreak, now crisp and dry.
Mules in a home field frolic
rolling stiff-legged and nuzzling each other,
the furrows they've already plowed
stretching into the distance.

Driving my car, I pass a black buggy,
its horse running at a good clip;
from its rear shadow arms and legs wave
and children's faces pop, grinning.
I wave back. We're on a road
between bright farm fields
and all have a holiday, even the mules.

Unmoored

"You can't untie a boat unmoored."
       —Osip Mandelstam, 'The Necklace'

Like a wild pinto
with a bristled mane
and muddied haunch
nosing ranch ponies
over their corral fence

the rowboat visits
moored yachts,
boats so valuable
they're held in place
with chains and locks.
They rise and fall a little,
dream of open water.

The rowboat,
which has been upriver
sniffing muddy wallows,
noses their clean
fibreglass hulls.

Children try to catch it
with a rope,
but it shimmies
and slips away
to sunrise-pink rushes
and tree fires at sunset.

It passes like a brief shadow
over manatees
as well as stones
and great fish.

Nighttime,
it pulls into hidden banks
and winks at stars.

Releasing, Tomorrow

At 4 a.m. I check on my youngest still working in his room—
calculus, lab report, essay.
The last thing he wants is for me to hear his chair creak
or see me at his door
or hear me say *skip school* at his 6 a.m. call.

Worry is a mother's default setting,
even though I know by now
a mother's worry only tells him that he needs one,
tells him he must prove himself
though he is tired, and he must carry both of us.

Driving back from school
I pull off the road to watch the creek.
A cardinal watches too, vivid in his bare shrub,
a male that shed the scent of his mother's shell
long ago, though perhaps in his voice she lingers.

The creek is frozen grey and white,
scattered birds chipping from the bank,
tree branches twisted like old arguments
against the white-faced sky, thaw held off,
releasing tomorrow, they say, with storms.

Varnish, Ornamental Trim, Legs

The basis of my poem is sliced
swiftly and accurately
by a gentleman with a bad shoulder at Lowe's.

Back home I lay my poem out flat,
tap on ornamental trim, and sand it to a silky finish,
an orange extension cord looped through a window.

Varnishing's difficult, trying for perfection
while wind tosses down debris from the maple
and suicidal gnats drift in for a permanent landing.

Fibres rise up again all over
and I grind them down in a dedicated fashion,
hammering down obtrusive edges of trim.

Another layer for clarity, more drying,
then I flip the poem over to give it legs.
Four leg plates, five screws for each plate:

I try to work quietly as everyone's asleep.
Next morning my poem stands in the corner like an interloper,
matching nothing in the room.

Morning Pond

Monday. Five small fish skitter under the lily. A cardinal, which must be playing poker up in the trees, cries *Cheater! Cheater! Cheater!* Its fellow players fall silent. The largest frog observes my weeding, calm as a buddha.

Tuesday. A mosquito floats to my neck, singing. Instead of eating mosquito larvae, the exuberant posse of fish plays tag among the irises. A dog in the distance barks like a rusty gate catching.

Wednesday. The air's like broth thickened with cornstarch. Even the birds sound grumpy. Excitement: a short Green Heron silhouetted in the shrubbery! Then mixed feelings. Fewer frogs today.

Thursday. Rain dots excitement across the surface, like a chef sprinkling drops on a hotplate. Four large frogs the same colour as the edge stones wait for me to go away; on the opposite side another lopes along, thinking of what to say. A cardinal eyes the bird feeder from a safe distance until I leave, then sails in quickly before the irritation of blackbirds returns.

Friday. The day lilies are letting their last few glories draw in and drop, but the mint has started to offer its soft, bristly spikes of blue flowers to the sky. The largest frog leaps heavily into the dark water like a wayward heart.

Saturday. A petal like a drip from a raspberry swirl cone briefly decorates a frog. The fish posse glimmers down among the reflected trees. Frilly peach lilies congregate along the far edge, whispering about butterflies like July bridesmaids.

4

"View on the Allegheny River"

This pastoral of flatboats tells my story,
its sky's inscrutable belly purpling
against the green thighs of its holy mountains,
the Allegheny silvering itself at sunset
through banks of sycamore and maple.
Every day there is a hauling to be done,
a leaning on rudder oars, laundry drying, dinner cooking.
When this boat reaches St. Louis
it will be broken up for lumber,
but now, under saffron clouds,
horses' quiet feet are shaping the evening shallows,
moving me on, and the water flows,
and the deck stove breathes smoke,
and red coals give the belly its sweet hot eye.

Finding Divinity

In the dream my dog says a man's waiting to shoot me
on the third floor of my house. In the silence I can't hear the killer;

my heart beats thump *thump* thump *thump*
which sounds to me now like the *mea culpa, mea culpa.*

"Here's something to do," said my therapist in preparation for
surgery, "knock your breast bone, say *I am worthy, I am worthy,*"

but I see now what's required. I must turn and face the assassin.
I must hope for a clean kill.

I relinquish my legs, pieces to be cut from my cervix, my hidden
mouth, my silence.

In prayer the nymph Syrinx begged Gaia to save her from Pan
and in that moment became a place of reeds

where gods rested and wind sang,
and, in love with her melody, the earth god cut his flutes.

I stop running. When I ask for aid, I'm made a reed
and, in my singing, a harvest.

How else could I encounter the lips of a god?

An Aging Politician and the Hearts of Finches

You're very like a finch in winter,
red and full of zest.
A weathered coat
protects you from the blight of cold,
this scouring wind
that empties valleys with its breath
and tosses even titan pines
most swaggeringly adorned
with their weight of snow,
while silent birds sit
puffed and patient under them.
And still,
beneath the brutal rind of ice,
sap holds sweet
in the packets and parcels of its cells.
So now I see how your hopes stay liquid,
how hearts of finches hold their blood
even when the air is chilled
and the woods seem so very bleak.

Corkscrew Swamp, Florida

We looked so far down into the sky
that clouds, fish and floating leaves
passing over each other in a rich, busy fashion
went on forever.
We fell through tall trees towards the water
as though we were falling up,
like my concussion
which left my thoughts spiralling tracks,
like insects across the surface of red waters
while beasts moved silently below,
each thought trying to fix onto another and failing,
the lost trails sparking out of sight
in a great damp mix.

After months, an osteopath touched my skull
like a small heron wading,
and it all made sense. I cried
because the thought that I had died
had been stuck in my bones
until he let it out:
an alligator rising from swamp
to glisten on the bank. A jawed beast, with teeth.

Blistered with Pockets

I got disembowelled last week,
if a sigmoid colon counts.
It wasn't as bad as I thought it would be
the week beforehand,
when fear sat hot on my chest in the night,
aged my skin to a thin glue
and showed me my bones.

Is it too late to run away to Canada?
I asked as they strapped me down.
A handsome fellow from Georgia did the deed.

They let me out
once I kept down some cream of wheat,
and, released, I sat, slowed enough to do it,
on our front step in the darkening evening
watching birds shuffle through leaves
and Howard, the neighbors' cat, slip home.

Now my stomach's swollen;
it looks as though it's been in a Rocky movie
then blasted with buckshot.
I've had afterdreams of being held down in linens
on the bed of an oxcart and suffocated;
of having my face probed
by a bird with a giant, pointed beak.

But two days before the surgery
in my favorite dream, of redemption,
I saw a train enter a station. Its doors slid open

and a short, thin, ugly child covered with blisters
stepped down from the train to the platform,
holding the edge of the door.
A tall figure in white approached,
took the child by the hand and, with kindness,
led the little one away.

Like a Solemn Friend Inebriate with Rain,

the day leans on my shoulder.
I am thick with sympathy,
        cannot set him by.

We stagger together to the bathroom
        to piss and take aspirin;
the coffee lurks in our favorite mug
making stains,

and next to it the toast softens on its plate
        weighty with indiscretion.
Dear friend! Stop drinking so much!

I know how thirsty you were,
        that dry spell parching May
                while the ponds dropped and dropped.

When June crashed in under cover of darkness
        and all the old soldiers poured over you
                you couldn't fight them,

all the old griefs and needs.
You drank and drank
        until you ran with moisture,
                glistened with excess.
Friend, rest.

Step

For a moment I think it's your white foot
stepping
from behind a tree at the end of the yard
but it's only a squirrel, light in the sun

and you're dead, little dog

though life goes on out there
and, in here, there's no need to walk carefully
or save a gravy pan;
no need to think of you at all

though eyes do still play their salty tricks.

Funeral Cake

During my friend's service
finches started to collect in a thorn bush
outside the church window—

hymns for us, while beyond the glass
they chittered and bustled about
in the brittle November air.

I was all right until the violin, when Massenet's Thaïs
drew such answering notes from my sinews
it made tears drip from my chin;

then I glanced up through the window
as the finches gathered their energy,
launched, surged west and, shrinking,

looked to me suddenly
like fistfuls of chocolate jimmies
thrown onto a iced blue cake.

Homemaker

I don't know what your view of heaven is,
but sometimes I want mine to be domestic,
with time held in fine-thread handkerchiefs
wearing eyelet lacunae outlined in satin stitch,
and we can see through the threads of the body
and into the bodies of our children,
and it all makes sense on that other plane,
if not this one.

Here there's a mother who breathes
to make the threads move,
who turns away the sharp teeth
of those mechanisms time brought with it,
who wraps you like a child in a fine, white cloth,
who feeds you small cakes, shaped like flowers.

Singing

The road sings through the pine barrens in the early morning,
plumes of mist rising over the waters.

The driver of the truck in front of me, its small flatbed
filled with old tires, sings a slow morning song of love.

A hawk, a tumble of dusty feathers barred brown and white
at the road's edge, sings its last song of beauty in this world.

The yellow school bus sings its song of welcome,
flashing its lights for fresh-washed teens.

My husband, whom I left in Cape May,
sings his song of the whole bed, turning and snoring as he wishes.

In Delaware my dentist sings his song of care
injecting my gum: I am new-crowned.

My car sings its familiar song on the way to work, to the old farmhouse
whose flowers shout their notes clear up to the midday sun.

My poets sing their own songs of joy, beauty, death and life.
How can we keep from singing?

Unexpected Harvest

What a shock, after the parsley would not come up
though we watered it daily and pinched its weeds,
after we'd given up hope yet stubbornly watered on,
then had finally seen the row of reddish nubs, like sleepy monks
rising from the earth, their tight green curls askew,
and we had rejoiced, and tended, and watched the serrated row fill
out;
what a shock to step into the garden and see them gone,
eaten back to bareness, and fat striped caterpillars belching,
as we imagined, in their place.
What were these pillagers? We knew what they ate.
Against all reason we bought more parsley from the store
and fed them in a screened bucket until they cocooned.
Then, what a shock, one morning,
to see the bucket full of swallowtails!
Great blue and gold wings quivering, gorgeous!
We let them climb our hands, dry off in the sun, and go.
I don't know. You plant parsley seeds,
you get nothing but trouble and glory.

Coriander is the Colour of My True Love's Eyes

I'm building a writing hut
with six by six posts,
        struts two by four,
                two by six joists, and also beams:
it sounds so squared and straight,
but wood's sold by thin measure,
the post blocks I cut
        slant a bit,
and the five-foot joists
        splaying spoke-like from their center post
           are a little off.
Living branches rustle around my frame;
a heron clomps along my roof beam.
Waits for something to happen.

The local museum has a walnut and oak spice box,
its pieces rabbetted, dovetailed,
        lapped, tenoned,
           stiled,
its drawer fronts tapered in,
        drawers to nest saffron threads, nutmegs,
           orchid pods packed with seed,
jewels, pocket watches.
The way a husband says his wife's name
        when he loves her.

Your great-great-grandfather made a poplar bed
and carved pegs to join it,
        each peg a different shape,
            its number pencilled on.
The bed's a spice box.
        I will write of it in my hut.
Your eyes are the colour of coriander;
by candlelight your summer legs are cinnamon.

Fox

Something in the froth of a girl's hair
like a spring tree reminds me,
whispers relief into my ear,
that I've had enough of beauty
in my own day–two husbands,
three children–and now something
wild in this season
leads me into other kinds of riches.

Lilies spread their hands
across the pond, fingering the fish
and the mild-eyed, courting mallards:
everything is tender as it should be.
The girl with frothy hair needs youth
to play it right; she has her hopes –
I can see her gleam with them
in the ripeness of the old way.

But my body starts blazing:
cracking out of its tight tunnels.
I dig a fresh den, drop into it,
rest until evening. Cover my breasts–
which made their milk in other springs–
with sleek swaths of fur, until I'm animal.
Dusk comes; I find my way.

I Think of You

The first rays of the early morning sun
fire through my solitary forest walk,
setting ablaze in narrow conflagration
each slender leaf, each bright, selected stalk;
beneath their burning ministrations, which hold
every chosen web and branch within their spell,
turning to bathe my face in particles of gold
I think of you, my dear, and wish you well.

The Lacewing's Eggs

Cardiff Museum, domed and monumental calm.
Here is the treading of a quiet floor, the whispering
of the silence of the dead, of mute art (of bones).

Human bones. Humans aren't so various and maintainable
as to be like these dead: *Orthoptera, Coleoptera, Psocoptera*
trays of crickets, beetles, lice, thistle-light and perfect
trapped in death, that knew no shell-less life—
they're now just shells.

Tidier, perhaps, to have the soft inside
and let the changing of it hide behind its form:
easier on the eye to live with forms.

Yet there's a hymn of magic in the lacewing's eggs,
the still white grains floating up,
gathering eternity on filigree stalks of silk.

A Room of Her Own

"Women, then, have not had a dog's chance of writing poetry.
That is why I have laid so much stress on money and a room
of one's own."–Virginia Woolf

The room, you understand, is not just physical,
a door to lock, a desk, a chair;
you can tell by the way thoughts are piled up
and the structure not as solid as the plan of a room would be
with a blueprint, a key, measurements, this next to that,
and space for vents.

I won't ask you if this is how you want me to sit, to turn my head,
to hold my hands. I won't ask if you'll be pleased by my sitting for you,
my reward to be rendered in oils: tentative, waiting, shadowed,
you deciding where to add my points of light.

I might upset you if I say that the room is spiritual,
a corn nib packed with all a new thing needs,
DNA, etc. Call it biological then, if you must.
That can stand in for what it is.

You, all action, and I, stilled. You filling in my canvas,
so that my own pen's marks will be the crazed spiderings of a gnat
kept in line by your broad strokes.

The other part of what the room is is absence,
the solitude of thought I'd give my right arm for,
since my mind is packed like a stuffed craw with other people's lives.
The room is the absence of belonging to anyone for a while.
Do you see how there are breathing spaces between the pieces?

Perspective

The prize photograph you took
of lady companions at the shore—

one in pant suit, one in patterned frock—
showed how Aberystwyth life endured.

The ladies, made famous by your eye
for texture, life story, composition, form,

saw themselves in print, and came
to your reception smiling, arm in arm.

As a girl you were so lost in thought
that, sister, we didn't see your spark,

but how you shine out now
in your careful light and dark.

Always in Season

Transfigured by a dark, mysterious glass
This well-known room cascades with glistening lights,
This room which, other years, seemed merely bright,
Sufficient in its pretty way to pass.
Yet now I find this living space suffused
With vibrant colours in a glorious haze:
The orange note of sunsets over winter days;
And silver peaches; golden, mythic blues;
Dark fire reds; everlasting greens. And it is not
This festive time of year, this winter season
Setting the room aglow with special thought,
Nor dreamed illusions, ripe with rosy pleasing;
But love, for love is the transforming glass
That reaches hearts, and changes lives at last.

5

This rock is a battered heart

and in its caves are secrets,
monoliths and catacombs, cathedral tombs
so quiet they have birdsong in them,
the Irish graves of our grandmothers, and the Welsh
sweet with grass and roses.
I asked my husband, when I die,
to throw my ashes from a Cornish cliff,
but now I wonder, why make him go so far?
The rock of the earth is my heart
and our names are spoken everywhere
in its caves' silence.

The Artist Bars the Door, Drawing His Knives

Leonard Baskin, Angel of Death, 1959, woodcut on paper

The artist cuts the feathers
of the shoulders of the Angel of Death,
and the mouth, that's a closed cave,
and the nostrils:
oubliettes stuffed with black air that has our scent.

He gives the Angel of Death a white throat,
netted balls, the shadow
of the herald of an unlit dawn,
and its feathers take the veins of our lungs—
fill themselves with our breath.

The artist fights with blades and ink,
pins the harbinger to the threshold;
fights to mortalise it, detain it in the breach;
fights until the eyes of the angel flicker and roll back;
fights so the paper it's on cannot be turned to ash—
whatever worlds end, whatever fires burn.

This Candle

Not much church-pure
about this candle.
Not much of the preformed white columns
we lit as children
to ask for mercy, melting silently.

This one's green, rippled,
with a wax pool hot in its womb;
dried orange peel like skin shrinking back
from brown clove bones,
which cry out and break in the flame,
the tough fruit pieces
blackening and bending to the wick.

This candle asks for nothing.
It reeks of Yule, cave fires.

Death Waits with Half-Moon Eyebrows

My eyeballs are on fire.
I'm afraid to fall asleep. Sitting up, I fall asleep.
My throat swells shut.

Light pools behind my closed lids, a film-noir
of city lampposts, rain seeding the silent river
where Death waits, a stiletto in her purse.

I wake fighting for air, my heart in a panicked beat.
I get juice down but can't manage aspirin,
read another hour, close my eyes.

Death leans against a post,
rain dripping from the brim of her fedora.
The only lifelike thing in this place of concrete and shadows
she is no beauty, or it's hard to tell, her makeup is so thick.
I wake again, gasping. This isn't it! This isn't it!
I close my eyes.

She is all red and black.
Studies her nails. Flashes a glance.

Whetstone Park

That spring, the strong water of the Olentangy
carried the thaw through there with fish lively in it

and tree branches marking its surface,
black blue black white black blue,

piecing out the sky as if there were enough,
as if there were more than enough of it

to fill out the skin of the lively day,
until the daylight froze into particles

and the soft sounds of the water stopped
and the blood of the fish leapt into an ecstasy of fixed dream,

dream fixed in that stunned night of trees,
and when the sky came back unruffled

the water and the thrashing dreams of the fish
sank down to the leaf mat ground.

The cold roots of maples and oaks,
black in their porridge of wet leaves,

had netted a strange catch of glistening fish,
fish scattered over the earth-packed paths of the woods,

fish dead in the dredge of wet leaves.
The Olentangy had gathered itself back

into its righteous channels. It would no longer carry
its gifts to the woods, or mirror their sky.

It left behind its rich vocabulary
of love spoken in the wrong place,

and the black-limbed trees open their roots
to feast on the meat of the fish.

A Barn, and the State of the World

The walls are old,
anchored in rock.
At dusk under the eaves
swallows feed their young an airy diet,
while inside
messy young barn owls stir in the rafters,
awaiting the smooth white hearts
of their parents' faces
glowing in the gloom,
mice gripped in their beaks.
Far below them, wild kittens sleep between hay bales,
their mother out stalking.

Ask me the state of the world
and I go to my usual references,
the news weighted heavily
to the dark side.

I'd like to parcel it out
so that we each lift one piece
(one country, one hurt child,
one aspect of the state of war,
one innocent man imprisoned,
one chained dog,
one question of power, of industry,
of the need to earn a living,
one lost woman on an icy road
with insufficient clothing,
one camp of refugees looking
for firewood).

I hear with this way of lifting we can build a barn,
a bright structure full of sustenance.

Building a Structure for the Beloved

You come in for dinner, your brow leaking sweat.
Day after day you've been forming my hut in the backyard
which, left for me to complete,
I'm sure would have rubbled down by now
into curses, deferred dreams, wasted wood.

Perhaps this is how we love: apply our best talents
to the holding and shaping
of whatever sacred place is needed by the other,
building up the structures formed
by the held hopes of the beloved.

Just so I protect your wish for a boat
through your years, your decades
of searching eBay, of sketching, of reading.
I don't know what it's about, the long wait,
but you won't buy one until you're ready.
Skipjacks, doreys, catboats;
drop keels, centerboards, mast positions;
outboard and inbuilt motors.

I stretch my arms around the beauty
of your lines, of your sails, of your hope of the open sea.

Gravida

The body is a courtyard
surrounded by windows,

and the moist pump at its centre
rising from a carved stone urn.

The body is the pump's water
swelling, in its clear tegument,
bigger than the cup of its vessel.

Above it the body's blind birds
soar against the waxing of the moon,

and below it the sweet cress of the body
soaks up spray from the pump's splash.

Generous pump.
The ripe body feeds more than itself.

The Cottage in the Woods

A month after the death it's time for me to come here;
I leave my companions.

The little house, next to others, looks abandoned.
I know it, though, and enter.

Down the white corridor I find a room
with a kitchen sink and a couch, and dust.

After I'm well inside I hear a low growl,
a snarl, then I'm menaced

by a black beast trying to attack me, a kind of dog,
and I'm afraid.

I duck away but can't reach the door—
I run behind the couch—

the animal comes at me from the side,
then from the front—

I grab something for a weapon
and see it's a pitchfork,

and just in time
stab it down through the heart.

Then I watch it form again out of mist
and get to its feet,

and I know I can't kill it, or run from it.
I start to talk, say *I'm sorry,*

and drop to my knee. The animal leaps at me again
but dodges away

so that we make contact for a moment,
because my hand is outstretched.

Now I can leave. Now I've understood.
The beast comes with me, back down the corridor

and out to the front porch.
I close the door behind us,

then realize that the dog needs to stay,
so I open the door again

and it slips inside, back to its bed.
I wonder: *who will take care of it?*

And I see an old woman, herself made of mist,
approaching from the woods,

the owner of the house.
It will be alright.

Slight Comfort

Slight comfort, day to day and night to night,
linked train carriages: minutes rattling by,
rails unseen and the station out of sight.

It all sweeps on, through dark, and dawn, and light,
the printed news enough to horrify:
I read it day to day and night to night;

trouble, someone's rage, a prisoner's plight,
the loss of hope: I can't figure out why
rails pass unseen, the station's out of sight.

There seems no sense to it. Nothing that might
show love, no big enough plan to justify
a child's pain, day to day or night to night.

So why does kindness bathe my skin tonight,
soothing my anguish beneath the moon's eye,
rails unseen and the station out of sight?

I find that beauty or joy quite
lucid in the quiet earth and subtle sky
can comfort, day to day and night to night,
though rails are unseen, the station out of sight.

Like a Skein of Geese

Like a skein of geese singing directions
across our lifeless eastern winter skies,
or irises, lost under a late snow,
uncovered, blue and gold and shining still;
like mulberries, where the tree was only brown,
swelling rosy black and fat with juice
all over branches where a busy song sparrow
nourishes her hatch of young; like heavy rain
thrown on the summer ground, coaxing dust
and cracked clay back to earth, for late
shoots to creep out, delicate and green,
or the smooth-skinned melon found in the fall
under leaves, unexpected, luminous, whole:
serendipitous friend, you feed my soul.

Quaker Hugh, After Striking Down A Redcoat

"And then there was Instant Silence,"
Howard Pyle, Biggs Museum of American Art

The painter paints me hero: so I stand
rigid, fists fixed, taller than the rest;
my deed attests I am no longer pacifist,
but sanctified in umber oils I stand
framed by the threshold of America.
I astound this smoky gathering of men
who peer thick-lidded at their stricken friend,
weak-faced and softened all by liquor;
their dealt hands seed the floor. All is red,
blood red, scarlet red: this welter of fine-thread
coats, these slouching, bewigged clowns. I wear
Philadelphia brown. My sober mother stares,
but painter blesses me—so by his hand
my foe falls into shadows, and I stand.

Street Musicians

In a dark mood, cropped
you miss the scent of angels

forgetting they are street musicians
drawing cries from what's to hand

forgetting they wrestle in caves to win.

Wallet

Since you asked me for your wallet
I removed your credit cards and driver's license
from its soft, worn flaps
and replaced the two twenties with singles,
so you could have it in your hands
and feel like yourself again.

It still had your parks pass
from our trip to Yellowstone,
where I bought it from a case of leather goods
 for your 62nd birthday. A small deception:
I colored its brightly embroidered pony with ink
to be subtle, more your style.
All your jeans pockets had its shape.

By the time I brought it to your hospice room
you didn't need it; you were already travelling.
A month later I was still carrying it myself,
but now I've set it down on your workbench
with the hawk feather that landed on the grass
the day I brought your ashes home,
the grass next to the washing line
where I stood for a long time, waiting.

Condor (When Sorrow Comes)

When sorrow comes and stays,
lurking in the back rooms and rearranging the toothbrushes,
I'll tell it *dear heart, you need an adventure.*
Let's away and find one!
I'll wear the red cape and the seven-league boots.

I know you like your skeleton costume with its white bones,
but at least put on your Day-of-the-Dead finery;
you always forget you have it. I'll help you with the earrings.
Ah--now you're dashing!
Away! Let's away to the jewelled sands and the blue hills of the
condor!

Doris, Mother of the Nereids

I press glistening crystals of sand
onto my arms, my legs, my breasts, my back.
I take up pieces of rosy coral to string for my neck
and green salt seaweed
to set on my head for hair.
There.
Now I am human.

The sea rushes in and out.
Gulls fly over: I have an ache from their cry.
Small crabs tickle my feet.

I turn about, watching my arms sparkle.
It's heavy though, being human.
Everywhere I look, life is breaking and mending,
breaking and mending.
When I walk, I leave marks behind
from the heaviness of it.

I take off my hair, my coral necklace.
I try to brush off the sand, but it sticks
and the crystals bite.
I brush and brush the beautiful heavy pieces,
which fall and fall.

I rise up.
The necklace and seaweed rest where I stood.
I fly home swiftly over the waves to my daughters.

Beautiful Rose

"Like rose petals covering a dung heap"
was how a monk in the Middle Ages
described a woman, womankind,
in order to warn his brethren
against the temptations of the flesh.

Bell, bella, bellissimo, bellissima, the beautiful, the most beautiful.
Bellum, bellum, belli, bellorum, bellis, bellis, war, my war, your
war,
our war, their war.
Belladonna, the beautiful lady, the most poisonous beautiful lady,
the sins of the flesh all rolled up in one,
the tempting fragrance of the devil—and, lucky for him, female—
that greatly-sinning sex that consorted with the serpent
and damned men to knowledge and life.

"Rose – where did you get your skin?" asks Rumi.
"From dung," she replies. "It's a wonderful fertilizer."

Addendum

Death of Aethelflaed, Lady of the Mercians
Britain, 12th of June, 918 A.D.

At Tamworth, sickness drew me to my bed:
my dreams were foul and filled with bloody men.
Judith laid cool linens on my aching head
and held my bowl. I could not whisper then
of serpents writhing all about the floor
too numerous to set my foot between,
of clinging branches scraping through my hair
the air so thick I could not draw it in.
A roar like battle rose and dammed my ears,
mud settled in my throat. And what a groan
I uttered! Warfare's common rattling prayer
which frees the ghost and leaves the flesh to worms.
Silence. O, sweet note of lark, you call me home
in summer wind across the chalky loam.

Ballad of Aethelflaed, Lady of the Mercians

Flaed, with her hair bound behind her
And jewelled veils on her head,
Went north from her family's fireside,
Took old Ethelred to her bed:

'Flaed, you are young and lovely,
Your body is supple and strong,
But we need you to marry a sickly man
And to Mercian people belong."

'As I am King Alfred's daughter,
Father, then you know
That if it will help our nation
To this old man I will go."

> *White three-petal grows in the reeds of the marsh*
> *Where her army fought and won,*
> *And no one remembers my lady's name*
> *When they speak of what men have done.*

What was on her mind
When, full of life, she lay
With her husband, wrinkled and weary
Every hair on his body gone grey?

'Come to me, dream of glory,
Let me feel the weight of your thighs;
I will press your conquests to me,
I will catch your hot blood on the rise,

I will cast my ripples inside you,
Take your warm touch to my breast
So all my hungry longings
In you may find their rest."

White three-petal grows in the reeds of the marsh
Where her army fought and won,
And no one remembers my lady's name
When they speak of what men have done.

Aethelflaed gathered their army
As her husband sickened and died;
She remembered all of the lessons
She had learnt at her father's side.

The birds in the brush were silent,
The buffeting winds were still:
With muffled, horse-held purpose
Flaed descended the hill.

And with her were all her forces,
Wintry spears in their arms,
Who by nightfall had drawn fierce Viking blood
And repossessed their farms.

White three-petal grows in the reeds of the marsh
Where her army fought and won,
And no one remembers my lady's name
When they speak of what men have done.

Alfred's son, Edward, succeeded him,
Joined with his sister's plans:

Together they pressed back the Vikings
To limit the Danelaw lands.

And Flaed was loved for her wisdom,
Her strength grew in message and verse;
The Danes at York gave her that city
And back to their hillsides dispersed.

At Derby and Leicester she prospered,
Though many a good man was lost:
Flaed mourned two of her faithful thanes
And everyone counted the cost.

> *White three-petal grows in the reeds of the marsh*
> *Where her army fought and won,*
> *And no one remembers my lady's name*
> *When they speak of what men have done.*

"When I was young, and grieving
I was full and hot with tears,
But, now that my battles are over
With the passion of so many years,

Now, when grief comes to me
It dries, like a linen swath
Pressed tight against my open wound,
A cold, coarse-woven cloth,

And, even though we have succeeded,
No one is left unscarred:
Each nation pays with its heart's blood
For the land it has to guard."

White three-petal grows in the reeds of the marsh
Where her army fought and won,
And no one remembers my lady's name
When they speak of what men have done.

'Brother, why hide my name now?
Why carry my daughter away?
The people will always remember me
Though I know I die this day."

White three-petal grows in the reeds of the marsh
Where her army fought and won,
And no one remembers my lady's name
When they speak of what men have done.

Witness

That winter when / we sisters smeared
the cherished children / thick with fat,
their gowns greased / for hale hearts
through deadly dark, / when finches froze
and thrushes fell / through scrubby briars
limp and light / we ate our fill of fowls.
Ever-watched waters! / The slick sea-craft
stayed from our sight. / Our winter warriors
struck steely blades / from ore and fire,
priest-pardoned, / keen to kill.

In spring the stinking / cloths were cut.
Wielding wood, / the youngest of yellers
pricked and parried, / hiding in hedgerows,
where birds sweet with song / whistled no warning.
The sun rose seaward, / but red-tongued roiled
cold salt crests, / those hungry hounds
forming a foaming / path of pain
to our dark day. /
               War-ships washed in,
blighting our beaches / with menacing men.
O! Ferocious, our fathers, / clashing in combat!
Brave fought our brothers / friend and dear friend,
side-by-side runners / sworn to the sword.
O! Evil invaders / who struck without ceasing,
renewed beyond number / black hulls on the brine.
Embattled and bleeding / our strongest were silenced,
they fell to the foes / outnumbered, outwon.

With terrible tread / from the blood of the beaches
the monsters of morning / came to our keep.
Kicked and killed after / our fierce little fighters,
struck down our sages / and wobbling babes,
then ravished our virgins / and milk-breasted mothers
they dragged from the ditches / crying for Crist.
With blessing of blackness / while those fiends were afeast
on our best beasts, / our sows to the spit,
I abandoned my branch / in the pine's high peak,
my perilous perch, / shaken and shocked.
This woeful day's witness, / I kept my own counsel.
As I was, a maid alone, / I tell this truth.

Postscript

Glory
February 5th, 1979

Hurtling silently through the late afternoon,
heading west and further west,
immigrants to America;
our plane broke through a bed of clouds
that were every shade of pink
and hovered over them
like a hummingbird in full thrill
over a spread of flowers,
the garden of Eden stretching to every horizon.
We were shocked speechless by the beauty,
the two of us with our newborn daughter,
our plane holding us
in the grandeur of the setting sun
as we moved west with it
only a little outpaced,
so that after an hour the pinks dimmed
and Ohio's hills, visible here and there,
darkened and twinkled with lights.
We could make out a fine bright movement:
the highway, sprinkled with grains of light
drifting in and out of towns.
This was America! Glory, glory.

CPSIA information can be obtained
at www.ICGtesting.com
Printed in the USA
LVHW020335030821
694218LV00012B/828

TABLE OF CONTENTS

S. Utah Wilderness Alliance
1471 S. 1100 East Salt Lake City
84105

MAP SYMBOLS

Town or City	□□	Viewpoint	▲
Buildings or Homes	□■	Stream or Running Water	~
Campgrounds		Intermittent Stream	~
Backcountry Campsite	▲	Potholes	P.H.
Camp Sites		Escarpment~Canyon Rim, the Reef	
Picnic Site		Peak, or Standing Rock	
Cemetery		Lake	
Hotel, Motel or Lodge		Mine or Quarry	
Ranger Station or Visitor Center		Waterfalls, or Dry Falls	
Guard Station		Spring or Seep	Ⓢ O
Airport or Landing Strip		Grass or Sagebrush	
Radio Tower		Forest (Pines)	
Old Railway Grade		Forest (Pinyon-Juniper)	
Interstate Highway	70	Forest (Deciduous)	
U.S. Highway	24	Pass	
State Highway	9	Natural Arch	Ⓐ
Road, Maintained		Pictograph	PIC
Road, Not Maintained		Petroglyph	PET
Mile Posts	3 4	Indian Ruins	Ⓡ •
Trails		Narrows	Ⓝ
Routes (No Trail)	••••	Geology Cross Section	
Car-Park, Trailhead	Ⓟ		

ABBREVIATIONS

Canyon	C.or Can.	Reservoir	Res. or R.
Lake	L.	Ranger Station	R.S.
River	R.	Guard Station	G.S.
Potholes	P.H.	4 Wheel Drive Road or Vehicle	4WD
Creek	Ck.	High Clearance Vehicle	HCV
Campground	CG.	Wilderness Study Area	WSA
Picnic Grounds	PG.	Kilometers	Km(s)

Acknowledgments

It's impossible to recall all the many people who helped me with information for this book. There are many, but special thanks should go to the following people: Jim Kenna, Terry Humprey, Blaine Miller, David Orr, Trish Lindeman and Becky Gravenmier, all BLM personnel at the Price office; and Clyde Kofford, Owen Price, Leah Defriez Seeley, Eldon Doorman, Kirk Johansen, Owen McClenahan(and his book, Utah's Scenic San Rafael), a Mrs. Hatt, Blain Luke, and Wayne and Betty Smith. All the above people live in Green River, Price or Castle Valley. And of course Dee Anne Finken who wrote the BLM publication called--A History of the San Rafael Swell. Her short history is included in this book.

Many thanks go to my mother, Venetta Kelsey who watches over my small publishing business when I'm gone, and who helped proof-read this manuscript.

The Author

The author experienced his earliest years of life in eastern Utah's Uinta Basin, namely around the town of Roosevelt. Then the family moved to Provo where he attended Provo High School and later Brigham Young University, where he earned a B.S. degree in Sociology. Shortly thereafter he discovered that was the wrong subject, so he attended the University of Utah, where he received his Masters of Science degree in Geography, finishing that in June, 1970.

It was then real life began, for on June 9, 1970, he put a pack on his back and started traveling for the first time. Since then he has seen 146 countries and island groups. All this wandering has resulted in a number of books having been written and published by himself: Climbers and Hikers Guide to the World's Mountains(3rd Ed. due in 1990); Utah Mountaineering Guide, and the Best Canyon Hikes(2nd Ed.); China on Your Own and the Hiking Guide to China's Nine Sacred Mountains(3rd Ed.); Canyon Hiking Guide to the Colorado Plateau(2nd printing); Hiking Utah's San Rafael Swell(2nd Ed.); Hiking and Exploring Utah's Henry Mountains and Robbers Roost; Hiking and Exploring the Paria River; Hiking and Climbing in the Great Basin National Park(Wheeler Peak, Nevada); Boater's Guide to Lake Powell--Featuring Hiking, Camping, Geology, History and Archaeology; and Climbing and Exploring Utah's Mt. Timpanogas.

Elevations of Important Locations Around the San Rafael Swell
(in Feet and Meters)

Price	1628(5341 ft)	Mexican Mtn.	
Woodside	1400(4593 ft)	Airstrip	1375(4511 ft)
Smith Cabin	1375(4511 ft)	Mexican Mtn.	1949(6394 ft)
Green River	1244(4081 ft)	Temple Mtn.	2064(6772 ft)
Hatts Ranch	1280(4200 ft)	Temple Mtn.	
Goblin Valley	1525(5003 ft)	GhostTown	1658(5440 ft)
Hanksville	1300(4265 ft)	Delta Mine Ruins	1463(4800 ft)
Emery	1900(6233 ft)	Tomsich Mine Ruins	1463(4800 ft)
Moore	1920(6299 ft)	Tomsich Butte	1768(5800 ft)
Huntington	1760(5774 ft)	North Butte	1943(6389 ft)
Cleveland	1750(5741 ft)	Square Top	2258(7408 ft)
Elmo	1740(5709 ft)	Lucky Strike Mine	1768(5800 ft)
Cleveland-Lloyd		Family Butte	2253(7392 ft)
Dinosaur Quarry	1750(5741 ft)	San Rafael Knob	2414(7920 ft)
Cedar Mtn.	2336(7663 ft)	Swazy Cabin	2195(7201 ft)
Buckhorn Well	1700(5577 ft)	Copper Globe Mine	2170(7120 ft)
San Rafael Campground	1557(5108 ft)	Ghost Rock	2219(7280 ft)
Window Blind Peak	2175(7136 ft)	The Wickiup	2128(6982 ft)
Assembly Hall Peak	1925(6316 ft)	Dilli Butte	2137(7011 ft)

Metric Conversion Table

1 Centimeter = 0.39 Inch
1 Inch = 2.54 Centimeters
1 Meter = 39.37 Inches
1 Foot = 0.3048 Meter
1 Kilometer = 0.621 Mile

1 Mile = 1.609 Kilometers
100 Miles = 161 Kilometers
100 Kilometers = 62.1 Miles
1 Liter = 1.056 Quarts(US)
1 Kilogram = 2.205 Pounds

1 Pound = 453 Grams
1 Quart(US) = 0.946 Liter
1 Gallon(US) = 3.785 Liters
1 Acre = 0.405 Hectare
1 Hectare = 2.471 Acres

METERS TO FEET (Meters x 3.2808 = Feet)

100 m = 328 ft.	2500 m = 8202 ft.	5000 m = 16404 ft.	7500 m = 24606 ft.
500 m = 1640 ft.	3000 m = 9842 ft.	5500 m = 18044 ft.	8000 m = 26246 ft.
1000 m = 3281 ft.	3500 m = 11483 ft.	6000 m = 19686 ft.	8500 m = 27887 ft.
1500 m = 4921 ft.	4000 m = 13124 ft.	6500 m = 21325 ft.	9000 m = 29527 ft.
2000 m = 6562 ft.	4500 m = 14764 ft.	7000 m = 22966 ft.	

FEET TO METERS (Feet ÷ 3.2808 = Meters)

1000 ft. = 305 m	9000 ft. = 2743 m	16000 ft. = 4877 m	23000 ft. = 7010 m
2000 ft. = 610 m	10000 ft. = 3048 m	17000 ft. = 5182 m	24000 ft. = 7315 m
3000 ft. = 914 m	11000 ft. = 3353 m	18000 ft. = 5486 m	25000 ft. = 7620 m
4000 ft. = 1219 m	12000 ft. = 3658 m	19000 ft. = 5791 m	26000 ft. = 7925 m
5000 ft. = 1524 m	13000 ft. = 3962 m	20000 ft. = 6096 m	27000 ft. = 8230 m
6000 ft. = 1829 m	14000 ft. = 4268 m	21000 ft. = 6401 m	28000 ft. = 8535 m
7000 ft. = 2134 m	15000 ft. = 4572 m	22000 ft. = 6706 m	29000 ft. = 8839 m
8000 ft. = 2438 m			30000 ft. = 9144 m

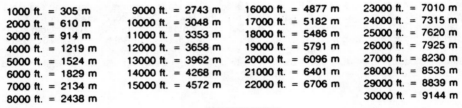

CENTIMETERS / INCHES

METERS / FEET

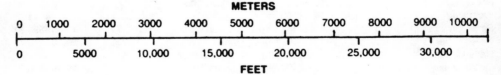

KILOMETERS / MILES

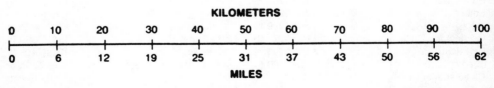

FAHRENHEIT / CENTIGRADE

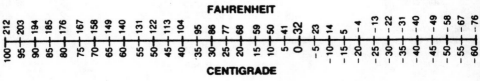

A History of the San Rafael Swell

by

Dee Anne Finken

Sponsored by the Bureau of Land Management
Moab District Office
San Rafael Resource Area
Price, Utah

Project Committee Supervisor:
Samuel Rowley

Project Committee Members:
Robert Barry
Scott Packer
Bruce Louthan

September, 1977

The following chapter is a public document about the history of the San Rafael Swell. This is now out of print, and can only be found in a few select libraries in the state of Utah. By adding it to this book it's hoped this research project by Dee Anne Finken can be kept in print and available to the general public. Special thanks goes out to Dee Anne Finken.

The author has added paragraphs here and there, all of which are in brackets, but it's basically the same as the original text. The numbers noting footnotes have been eliminated, but some of the actual footnotes have been placed in the text and placed in parenthesizes.

INTRODUCTION
Situated in southeastern Utah, in the Canyonlands area of the Colorado Plateau, the San Rafael Swell is a kidney-shaped area of geologic uplift approximately 80 kms long and 50 kms wide. Bordered on the west by the Castle Valley and the Muddy Creek drainage, on the north by Cedar Mountain and on the east and southeast by the Green River and San Rafael Deserts, the Swell is appropriately named. It is not a mountain, a plateau or a tableland; instead, it is a huge dome resembling an inverted bowl. On the east this dome rises abruptly out of the desert with the flatirons of the San Rafael Reef jutting 650 meters into the sky. On other sides the Swell climbs less dramatically to its highest point, the 2414 meter

San Rafael Knob, near the center of the Swell.

Just east of the San Rafael Knob is a relatively flat area of grassy pastures known as Sinbad Country. This central core of the Swell stretches about 25 kms by 15 kms and from it, water drains off in all directions. "Drains" however is an understatement, for over eons of time water has cut spectacular canyons through the Swell's huge dome. Reds Canyon, Devils Canyon, Eagle Canyon, Coal Wash, Saddle Horse Canyon, Black Dragon Canyon, the Black Box and the Little Grand Canyon of the San Rafael River would each classify as a "natural wonder" in any landscape other than the Canyonlands of southeastern Utah.

In some parts of the world these impressive canyons would suggest plentiful water, but again this canyon country differs. In the San Rafael Swell water comes in sudden and intense thunderstorms. Then, for a few hours, red-brown torrents of water flashflood the canyons. A day or two later the only water remaining is in small and frequently salty springs or in small pools found in pockets or "potholes" in the sandstone.

Like its intriguing geography, and substantially as a result of it, the San Rafael Swell has had a curious human history. Mexican slave and horse traders, military explorers, Mormon missionaries, railroad builders, outlaws, cattlemen, sheepherders, wild horse runners, prospectors, miners and others have left their mark on the San Rafael Swell. But for the most part, their history has not been recorded or it has been recorded in documents that focus elsewhere and mention the San Rafael Swell only in passing.

This report takes the form of the narrative on four themes—the Old Spanish Trail and other travel routes through the region, the livestock industry, minerals and energy exploration and development, and folklore of the Swell. As a narrative on these themes, the report emerges not as a complete history, but as an overview of the primary activities that have taken place in this region in the last 200 years.

The data collection procedures used in compiling the information in this report have varied. Much of the region's earliest history—including accounts of the traffic on the Old Spanish Trail—has been found in history books, library archives and diaries. Written accounts of the more recent history, especially of the livestock industry, have not been so well documented. Instead of being in historical texts, this information is found deep in the memories of those who have spent their lives in the region. To obtain this information, interviews were conducted by the author with ten local residents. Their information was included in the narrative and in a library of oral histories which has been deposited with the Charles Redd Center for Western Studies at Brigham Young University in Provo, Utah.

Morgan's Cabin, located at the beginning of Chute Canyon and at the end of the Chute Canyon Road.

THE OLD SPANISH TRAIL AND OTHER TRAVEL ROUTES

By tracing the roads and trails that have been worn in the sand and rocks, and scoured through the hills of the San Rafael region, one can get an insight into the area's history. Along these passageways, Mormon settlers have carried their faith, outlaws have absconded with livestock and mine payrolls, traders have bartered trinkets and blankets for furs and Indian children, and livestockmen have herded their stock to better grazing.

If history has recorded an accurate account of his journey, the first European travel into the present state of Utah was by Spanish conquistador Lopez de Cardenas. In 1540, under the command of Coronado, Cardenas reportedly reached the Colorado River, a short distance northeast of where the river crosses into Arizona from southern Utah.

More than 200 years later, in 1776, Spanish exploration in what is now Utah was reopened by Franciscan padres Atanasio Dominguez and Silvestre Velez de Escalante. The priests set out to discover a route that would connect the Spanish settlements in New Mexico with Monterey, California. The route of the traveling fathers did not cross the San Rafael Swell; instead, the trail they took west cut across from present day Rangely, Colorado, through northern Utah near Vernal and Duchesne to the Great Basin at Utah Lake. With a change in plans, the padres returned home by traveling south from the Great Basin and "when the mountains on their left lowered, they turned east and headed across the Arizona Strip. . . . At length they reached the Colorado River. . .." Though they failed to reach their final destination, they opened new territory for later exploration and travel by others.

The Old Spanish Trail emerged as a major route of westward travel after Dominguez and Escalante's efforts. This trail ran northwest from the Spanish settlements around Santa Fe, crossed the Colorado River near the present town of Moab and the Green River near the town of Green River, continued west to the Sevier Valley, and from there extended to the Spanish settlements in California.

There were several variations of this route in southeastern Utah. The primary route ran west from the Green River to cross the San Rafael Swell on the north by way of Cottonwood Creek at Wilsonville, and Ferron Creek at Paradise Ranch and then progressed to the Sevier River by way of the Salina Canyon.

A variation of the trail turned northwest from the Green River crossing and followed the open country at the base of the Book Cliffs to the base of the Wasatch Plateau; it crossed the Plateau by way of the Price River-Spanish Fork Canyons to arrive at Utah Lake [the present route of Highway 6, via Soldier Summit].

A second variation of the trail reached across the center of the San Rafael from Temple Mountain to Castle Valley.

These variations according to author Herbert S. Auerbach are a result of cut-offs and alternate routes that were taken to cross mountain passes, to shorten the travel distance and simply because different parties varied their course in response to their own needs.

Traffic along this trail differed greatly in spirit from the motivations of the Dominguez and Escalante expedition. In fact, Indian slave trade probably caused the route to be established and was its prime use for many years.

The practice of obtaining Indian women and children in southern Utah and selling them as servants in Spanish New Mexico and California apparently began shortly after 1776 and continued into the early 1850's. The nature of this trade-generally conducted by private individuals under government Indian trading restrictions that often made it advantageous not to keep records-makes it difficult to trace this activity. Apparently, however, the general pattern involved trading or bartering a variety of trade goods for Indian children, with young girls being the most sought after because of their value as domestic servants in the Spanish settlements. Most of the slaves were either obtained directly from Paiute, Goshute and other bands or they were obtained from the Utes after having been captured in raids.

The trading trip of Spaniards Mauricio Arze and Lagos Garcia (known because the two were prosecuted for violation of Spanish slave trade laws) presents a picture of the trade as it existed in the early 1800's. The two left New Mexico in the spring of 1813 leading a company of seven traders. They traveled to the Utah Lake area, by an unspecified route, where they experienced difficulties with the Ute Indians. They turned south toward the Sevier and Sanpete Valleys hoping for a more friendly reception, but did not find it and turned east for home. Their trail led from the "Sevier eastward over the Wasatch Plateau, then northeast along the base of the range and across the various creeks heading the Fremont and San Rafael Rivers; and then eastward to the Green River. At the Green they met Chief Wasatch's Ute band and conducted some trading, obtaining a scant twelve slaves and 109 pelts with which they returned to New Mexico."

Evidence of Arze's travel in the region has been found by a Ferron resident, Lee Swasey, who discovered the Spaniard's name and the date 1812 etched in a wall along the Moore Road in Dry Wash (Monte Swasey, long time San Rafael region resident, speculated the Old Spanish Trail traveler followed the San Rafael Reef, crossed the mouth of Dry Wash, and "probably dropped into the wash to get out of the wind and rain.." In addition, Swasey discovered the names of Fremont and Gunnison (who conducted railroad surveys in the region) along with the date 1846 nearby the Arze notation).

By the middle of the century the trade system had become more elaborate. D. W. Jones described the system he observed in 1851. The New Mexican traders, he says, would set out with a few goods which they soon traded to Navajos or Utes for horses.

> These used-up horses were brought through and traded to the poorer Indians for children. The horses were often used for food. This trading was continued into Lower California, where the children bought on the down trip would be traded to the Mexican-Californians for other horses, goods or cash. Many times a small outfit on the start would return with large herds of California stock.
>
> All children bought on the return trip would be taken back to New Mexico and then sold, boys fetching on an average $100, girls from $150 to $200. The girls were in demand to bring up for house servants, having the reputation of making better servants than any others.

Jorgensen concludes the story of the slave trade by noting that an underlying cause of the Walker War, between the Utes and Mormons in 1853, was Chief Walker's dissatisfaction with the Mormon policy of interrupting and hindering his participation in the continuing slave trade.

Up until 1830 traffic over the Old Spanish Trail did not extend as far as California but went only as far west as the Sevier Valley and the Great Basin.

(According to J. Cecil Alter, James Workman and William Spencer were the first American citizens to travel the Old Spanish Trail and commerce over the trail between New Mexico and California had become well established before 1809. Workman and Spencer, the two "Lost Trappers" escaped an encounter with Comanche Indians at the headwaters of the Arkansas River and mistakenly followed the Gunnison and Grand (Colorado) Rivers to the future site of Moab, Utah. They followed the Grand thinking it was the Rio Del Norte (Rio Grande). Reaching Moab in the summer of 1809, they followed a well worn trail that crossed the river and headed southeast. Two days later Workman and Spencer met a Spanish caravan of 40 to 50 men traveling the opposite direction to Puebla de los Angelos (Los Angeles). Trappers Workman and Spencer decided to join the caravan.

> The company continued on its way crossing the Colorado and then for several more days traveling northwest after which they turned southwest until they reached their objective on the Pacific coast. After turning southwest on the right of their route there was a range of very high mountains (likely the Wasatch Mountains). . . . the peaks having snow on them.

Jorgensen writes, "From this narrative, there can be little doubt that Workman and Spencer went through Castle Valley with the Spanish caravan to California."

There is a conflict in the report offered by Alter as extensive research of Spanish records, specifically by Hafen and Hafen, indicate travel over the Trail to California did not occur prior to 1829).

Travel and trade between New Mexico and California was begun by Antonio Armijo in 1829-30. Armijo did not pass through the San Rafael region; he followed a route running close to the present Utah-Arizona border which approximated the eastward trek of Dominguez and Escalante [on their return to Santa Fe].

The first party to journey the entire distance over substantially the route of the Old Spanish Trail was led by Americans William Wolfskill and George C. Yount in the winter of 1830-31. These two men led a party of trappers from Taos over the trail intending to trap in California. They apparently used the variation of the trail which passes through the north end of the San Rafael Swell. These pioneering efforts led to the establishment of regular commerce between New Mexico and California. In 1831 Antonio Santi-Estevan inaugurated what became an annual pack train commerce that for two decades became the distinctive feature of the Old Spanish Trail. The New Mexicans traded their handsome woolen goods for the excellent California horses and mules and for silk and other Chinese goods.

The California livestock was so prized by the New Mexicans that beginning in 1832 the theft of horses and mules suddenly blossomed in California with the arrival of the trading parties. American mountain men and Ute Indians quickly took up the horse stealing game so that well into the 1850's this activity was a major problem for the Californians. Legally obtained or not, thousands of horses and mules were trailed east almost every year and reached destinations which suggest that many of them were herded over the San Rafael section of the Old Spanish Trail.

The picture of the traffic using the San Rafael Swell portion of the Old Spanish Trail during the 1830's-40's emerges as a mixture of slaves, horses for the slave trade, stolen horses and mules, legally purchased livestock and New Mexican woolen goods.

Kit Carson, one of the West's most famous scouts, also traveled the Old Spanish Trail. According to Lieutenant George D. Brewerton who rode with Carson in 1848, the scouts followed a trail through the Wasatch Mountains at Salina Creek. It seems logical to conclude that Carson followed the trail through

THE SPANISH TRAIL AND THE OLD RAILWAY GRADE

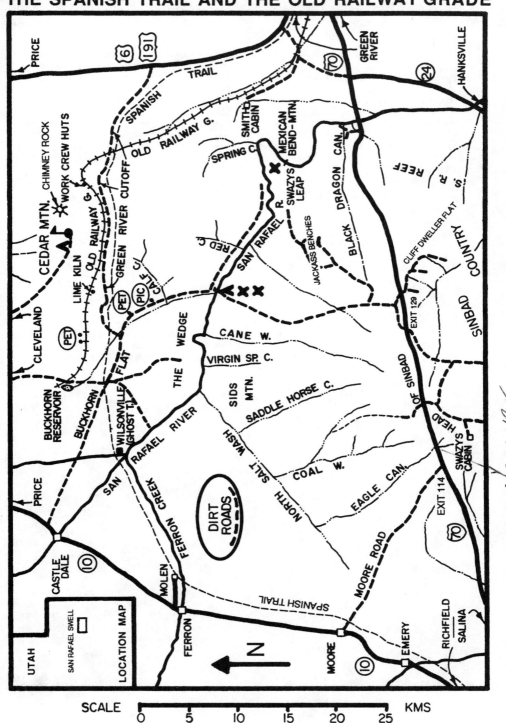

the San Rafael Swell. Carson is known to have carried mail and military dispatches on both these trips, and it is possible that on the 1848 trip he carried the first news of the discovery of gold in California. It is known that he carried a copy of a California newspaper containing the discovery news. Either that copy or another one carried over the Humboldt route was quoted when news of the discovery was first published in the East.

The San Rafael region did not feel the footsteps of westward travelers lured by the discovery of gold in California. Those rushing west, instead of crossing the rough terrain, took the Overland Trail passing through northern Utah. However, California superintendent of Indian Affairs, E. F. Beale, hoping to popularize a more southern route, did travel the San Rafael Region. But the iron horse, and preparation for it, brought the next travelers to the region. In 1853 Congress authorized expeditions to survey the best possible route for the first transcontinental railroad.

Captain John W. Gunnison led one of the authorized survey parties though the San Rafael Swell region in October 1853. Gunnison chose the Old Spanish Trail route specifically because its potential as a railroad route had not been examined. However, he did not take his wagon-encumbered party over the Swell. Instead they detoured north almost to present day Price, Utah, and then went south through Castle Valley.

Traveling with the Gunnison expedition was Dr. James Schiel who described the San Rafael region:

> From the top of some of the higher hills, which are situated some miles [kms] east of Green River, one can overlook the wild and unproductive country for long distances. As far as to the Wasatch Mountains (sic) one views a chain of open canyons and fantastically-formed sandstone hills on which not a trace of vegetation can be seen. A thin cover of gypsum gives the soil around them a look of snow fields, and neither the bare hulks of the northern Roan Mountains nor the snow-covered Salt Mountains in the east nor the rugged and towering ranges in the south are able or likely to diminish the gloom of this view.

Gunnison encountered Indians along the journey and Schiel wondered how anyone living in the region could find food,

> . . . in an absolutely sterile country. . . . There could be no thought of any subsistance by the hunt, for one can travel for weeks without finding any game besides a pair of lonely jackdaws, or a few contented lizards, which seem to represent the animal life here. It is a country where, according to the statement of a famous mountaineer, Kit Carson, "not even a wolf could make a living."

One of several uranium mines dating from the 1970's located in Buckmaster Draw north of I-70. The eastern San Rafael Reef is in the background.

On October 26, shortly after it departed the San Rafael region, Gunnison's party was attacked in the Sevier River Valley by Paiute Indians. Gunnison and seven other members of his party were killed.

A few months later John C. Fremont led another party into the region. Like Gunnison, Fremont was looking for a feasible railroad route, but his trip was not a government endeavor. Fremont's party was suffering from lack of food and the effects of severe winter weather when they reached the Green River. As the party continued west through the San Rafael Swell their situation became desperate. Finally, they cached all their equipment somewhere in the Swell or in Castle Valley and rode their pack animals, reaching the community of Parawon after considerable suffering.

The late 1840's had seen the beginning of the era of Mormon settlement in Utah, and church explorers probably entered the Castle Valley-San Rafael Swell region in the early 1850's. In 1855 Mormon missionaries crossed the region enroute to establish a mission among the Ute Indians living in the Elk Mountain area (the LaSal Mountains and Moab Valley). Forty-one missionaries under the direction of Elder Alfred N. Billings left Manti (in Sanpete County) in May of 1855 with 15 wagons, 65 oxen, 16 cows, 13 horses, two bulls, one calf, two pigs, four dogs and 12 chickens. The Mormon expedition followed Salina Canyon, moved east along the Old Spanish Trail through Castle Valley, and crossed to the Green River by way of Buckhorn Flat and Cottonwood Wash in 12 days. In so doing, they were the first to take wagons over the San Rafael Swell section of the Old Spanish Trail.

Excerpts from missionary Oliver B. Huntington's journal of the trip follow:

> May 30—The company moved on over a barren, hilly road 10 miles [16 kms] to Sweet Cottonwood Creek, then traveled 3 miles [5 kms] to Huntington Creek. On this creek we found Indians who suggested a nearer route to Green River and we concluded to try it.
>
> May 31—Took the right Spanish Trail and traveled over a good country for a road without water until 2:00 p.m., when we came to a large gulch in rocks with nearly perpendicular banks a hundred feet [30 meters] high. We camped at the head of his gulch, where we found a little water standing in the rocks. By further search Levi Greg Metcalf found two other pools down about a mile [km] from which we drew water to give all the stock a few quarts each. We got down about sunset, and at half past nine we started again and traveled over good ground until daybreak, when we came to other pools of standing water more convenient. Here we again watered all our stock, giving them all they wanted, and we thanked God with all our hearts. Traveled during the day 15 miles [25 kms] and during the night 15 miles [25 kms].
>
> June 1—Left our morning camp about 1:00. Had a crooked and sandy road some of the day. Traveled 10 miles [16 kms] and camped near the head of a small cottonwood creek on Gunnison's trail.
>
> June 2—traveled 10 to 12 miles [16 to 20 kms]—then traveled on good roads, 7 or 8 miles [11 or 12 kms] and came to Green River.

The "large gulch" with "nearly perpendicular banks" mentioned in the account was most likely Buckhorn Draw or Calf Canyon.

In 1858, a rather different wagon train worked its way eastward through the San Rafael region. An army expedition of 300 men in 50 wagons under the direction of Colonel William Wing Loring left Camp Floyd, Utah, on July 19 enroute for Fort Union, New Mexico.

Loring's expedition journeyed through the San Rafael region by way of the head of Salt Creek, Slover (or possibly Clover Creek), Media Creek, and St. Raphael, San Mateo or Sivareeche Creek and on to the Green River.

In 1870, a mail route was established along part of the Old Spanish Trail. Running a "murderous 400 kms" between Ouray, Colorado, and Salina, Utah, the mail route crossed territory that included "deep canyons, sun-parched deserts and numerous water courses including the Green and Colorado Rivers." Six Wilson brothers—Sylvester, George, Nick, Chris, Davis and Silas—settled along the route and at Cottonwood Creek, just up from the confluence of the San Rafael River, founded the town of Wilsonville. As the only mail stop, Wilsonville became one of the most important towns in Castle Valley, even though it was home for only eight or ten families. Mail transportation continued along this route until 1883 when the Denver and Rio Grande Railroad was built.

The roar of the Rio Grande Railroad through southeastern Utah was preceded by considerable confusion over surveys and studies that were undertaken to select a route that would connect existing railroad lines and complete a second transcontinental rail route.

In 1882 the Rio Grande Railroad had reached the Utah State line from Colorado, and the Denver and Rio Grande Western had absorbed the Utah and Pleasant Valley Railroad which ran south from Utah Lake up Spanish Fork Canyon to Scofield. The railroad companies set out to work on one connection linking Denver with Salt Lake City and another linking the Salt Lake-Denver line with the Southwest, and Los Angeles in particular.

Several potential routes were considered for these two purposes. One proposal was a route from

Where the Green River Cutoff intersects the old railway bed.

Southeast of Chimney Rock, the old railway bed cuts are still very visible.

Green River, through Cottonwood Wash, to Buckhorn Flat, to Castle Valley, southwest through Castle Valley to Ivie Creek and Salina Canyon, and down Salina Canyon to Salina. This route, known as the Buckhorn Flat route, would join a railway running north and south through the Sevier Valley from Salt Lake to Salina to Los Angeles. A second suggested route would leave Green River, head to Woodside, continue to the Grassy Trail Creek vicinity, and follow the Price River to meet up with the Pleasant Valley route near Colton. This route would make connection with the Salt Lake to Los Angeles line at Provo [in other words, it would run from Price to Provo via Spanish Fork Canyon and Soldier Summit]. A third alternative involved building the main line from Colorado, through the San Rafael Swell to Salina, and from there to Los Angeles. The connection with Salt Lake would be via the Pleasant Valley line from a wye located at Castle Valley. Denver and Rio Grande management decided that an immediate connection with Salt Lake was more attractive than a route to the unpopulated area near Salina, but railroad personnel on the ground in southeastern Utah were strongly in favor of giving priority to Salina route and its eventual connection with Los Angeles. Finally, Denver and Rio Grande Western Railroad Construction Manager R. F. Weitbrec informed M. T. Burgess, a proponent of the route through Salina Canyon, that Burgess was

> ...in error in the supposition that Salina Canyon is to be considered as the main connection; on the contrary, we both (Weitbrec and railroad president Palmer) look upon the line to Salt Lake as the principal stem at present....

However, Weitbrec authorized Burgess to continue work on the Buckhorn route with the cut northward at Castle Valley to connect with the Pleasant Valley line.

> .You will, however, go ahead upon the basis of your letter and construct by the southern route for three reasons:
>
> 1. There may be some reason not fully apparent to us.
> 2. Considerable expenditure must have been made already.
> 3. We fear any attempt to make changes would involve more damage through unavoidable delay, than to allow things to go on as they are.
>
> Press the line from the connection with the Pleasant Valley road eastward to the Colorado line, and do only as much on Salina route as will not interfere with the main object; to wit, Colorado connection.

So grading commenced in 1881 on a line from Green River through Cottonwood Wash to Buckhorn Flat. From there it turned north toward the town of Cleveland. Eighty kms of grading and $213,470 were invested in the Buckhorn route, but track was never laid. The Denver and Rio Grande management settled on the alternative of making the connection with the Los Angeles line south of Provo and discarded the idea of building a connection between Castle Valley and Salina. They also concluded that operating costs on the Salt Lake route would be much higher on the Buckhorn Flat route than they would be on a line running to Woodside and along the Price River. The Buckhorn Flat Grade was abandoned for the Price River route over which the Denver and Rio Grande connection between Denver and Salt Lake was made on March 30, 1883.

Work on the railroad grade employed people already settled in the region and lured other prospective settlers to the area. **The Deseret News** on January 4, 1883, excitedly claimed:

> The D&RG Railway Company has done considerable in the County (Emery) the last six months (sic);... This road has been a blessing to this county, as no man could say he could not find work, as there has been plenty of grading, both dirt and rock work, tie chopping and hauling, also several lumber mills kept very busy furnishing bridge timbers and other building material.

On the Buckhorn route, before it was abandoned, local men with teams of "Spannie" mules were hired for $3 a day to haul water to railroad working stock.

Chris Halverson, who later homesteaded (before 1900) on what is now the Rey Lloyd Hatt ranch near Green River [the Hatt Ranch is between mile posts 158 and 157 just off Highway 24 and on the San Rafael River] came to the region with plans of working on the narrow gage bridge being built at Green River. Halverson never worked on the railroad; instead, he spent the winter trapping beaver on the San Rafael River. He returned to Telluride, Colorado, but came back in 1888 or 1889 to the San Rafael region and homesteaded 65 hectares near the Green River.

Many Chinese came to work on the railroad. They earned $1.10 a day while Caucasians earned $2.00 for their efforts. Remains of the shelters the Asians built to live in can still be found in the San Rafael Swell.

> They (the shelters) are mostly fallen in, with no roofs on them. They're tiny little things; I couldn't lie down in one. Some of the doorways are still standing and they're about 2 feet

Work crew rock shelters in a shallow drainage, dating from the early 1880's.

Another work crew shelter with only the chimney standing.

Petroglyphs of railway workers, just south of Cedar Mtn.

Near the railway work crew ruins is this old watering trough.

[½ meter] wide.

Apparently the roofs were made from timber, as there are no rocks that seem to have fallen down. They were built into the side of a hill; three-sided and sort of round.

Apparently the Chinese were the unfortunate recipients of Green River youths' pranks. "The favorite pastime of the town kids was to stuff rags or paper down the stove pipes then hide until the Chinamen got smoked out..."

[One good set of ruins the author has found is very near Chimney Rock, which is located on the east side of Cedar Mountain. To get there, drive along the Green River Cutoff, the good and well maintained gravel road running between Buckhorn Flat and Highway 191-6. At the sign and turnoff to Chimney Rock (located directed south of Chimney Rock) drive northeast on a rough road, which is actually the old railway bed, about 2 kms. At a point where the road crosses over the railway bed and heads north, stop and park, then walk in a northeasterly direction along the old grade. There are places where it cuts deep into solid limestone with very little sign of erosion. About 200-300 meters from your car, and where the grade runs over a deep gully, you can see several rock huts, one with a fire place. These are located directly underneath where a tressel would have been built. Nearby is a water trough, which was apparently fed by a spring, which now is dried up.]

Use of the path of the Old Spanish Trail did not end with abandonment of the railroad grade. The wagon trail through Buckhorn Flat and Cottonwood Wash continued in use as the main route of travel between Castle Valley and Green River or the northern end of the San Rafael Desert up to recent times. Even today a high standard graveled road from Castle Dale to US 6-50 (now 191-6) at Woodside closely follows parts of the old trail [It's generally referred to now as the Green River Cutoff].

[If you're out exploring the old railway grade, there are other features and sights to see. Directly north of the junction of the Green River Cutoff and the Buckhorn Wash Road, and just below the cliffs of Cedar Mountain, is where the old grade runs. If you go north at that point (and maps don't show roads, but there are some around), you can arrive at the grade. And just at the base of the cliffs are some large boulders with petroglyphs. About 5 kms north and east of the previously mentioned road junction, and as the Green River Cutoff Road makes a sharp turn to the south and into Furniture Draw, you can find an old rough track heading to the north east. Drive this track about 2 kms to the base of the cliffs and to the old grade, then look for an old lime kiln just below a small stock pond dam formed by the grade bed itself.]

Other less famous routes also served the few travelers that ventured into the San Rafael Swell. The primary access into the center of the Swell from the north was by way of Buckhorn Draw. Outlaws may well have been the first to use this route extensively. It is known that Butch Cassidy and Elza Lay used

A so called "lime kiln", located to the northeast of Buckhorn Flat.

the Draw as part of their escape route following the Castle Gate Payroll robbery in April, 1897.

[Here's more information on the Castle Gate Holdup. The following story is from the Eastern Utah Advocate (Price City newspaper), for April 22, 1897.

Bold, bad highwaymen, created consternation and excitement Wednesday noon at Castle Gate, by holding up E. L. Carpenter, the Pleasant Valley Coal company's paymaster and making off with $7000 in gold.

The horse thieves, bandits and murderers infesting what is commonly known as Robber's Roost 60 miles [100 kms] southeast of Price on the San Rafael River in Emery County, have in the past few years committed many an atrocious deed of daring, but none so bold and audacious as this last unprecedented and nervy holdup. This tough clique is rapidly gaining a reputation not to be envied by any except such men as composed the celebrated "James gang" and they are invariably successful in their undertakings and in evading the minions of the law.

This last daring act of theirs is supposed to have been committed by Tom Gissell [actually Elza Lay] and "Butch Cassidy," and it is reasonably certain at this writing that the identity of at least Cassidy, who figured about a year ago in the Montpelier, Idaho, bank robbery, can be established.

The particulars of the hold-up, robbery and flight of the desperadoes is as follows: The pay rolls, money and checks for paying the coal diggers and company's employees at Castle Gate, was sent down Wednesday from Salt Lake City on the Rio Grande Western passenger train No. 2, which reaches Castle Gate at about 12 o'clock noon. There were two sacks of silver, one of $1000, one of $860, one sack of gold containing $7000, and a satchel holding the rolls and checks for another thousand dollars, in all $9860. These were all transferred to the hands of E. L. Carpenter and a deputy clerk who were at the depot awaiting the arrival.

When No. 2 pulled out for Helper the paymaster and deputy crossed over the tracks to the Wasatch Company's store, a two story rock building about fifty yards [meters] distant from the depot, and were just about to carry the treasure up the stairs on the east side of the building, which led up to the P. V. Coal Company's offices, when a rough looking individual, evidently "Butch" Cassidy, stepped in front of Mr. Carpenter and exclaimed "drop them sacks and hold up your hands."

The request was backed up by a six-shooter being pushed into the astonished paymaster's face, and he naturally complied. T. W. Lewis, the clerk, noted the situation at once and made a run into the store with the thousand dollar sack of silver. The bold highwayman then cooly stooped and picking up the other two sacks and satchel handed them to his confederate who was on horse-back near at hand. Cassidy's pal rode swiftly down the road, but the former was out of luck for a few moments as his horse got loose and started away. He, however, ran rapidly and caught the animal a few feet (meters) away, instantly mounted and sped after the man ahead.

While Mr. Carpenter was being relieved of the money, the mounted bandit flourished a six-shooter and fired several shots promiscuously, and the only thing done toward preventing their escape until it was too late, was the firing of three shots from the offices of the company as they flew down the road. The robbery was accomplished with so much bravado and daring that the suddenness of the act completely paralyzed the number of men who were lounging about near the scene, and there were nearly a hundred of them around and in the store who witnessed the whole affair.

Passing safely through the lower part of town the robbers stopped a short distance north of the half-way house and cut the telegraph wires. They also examined the satchel and finding nothing of use to them in it, left it on the road. The sack containing $860 in silver had been dropped near the power house in town, no doubt on account of its being too heavy to carry, so their load now consisted only of the $7000 in gold. Reaching John U. Bryner's ranch at the mouth of Spring Creek canyon and just north of Helper, they crossed his land and went about 2 miles [3 kms] up the canyon, where they turned south over the ridge and continued on a trail which makes a perfect circuit of Helper, Spring Glen and Price, and being only distant from them about three miles [5 kms].

It was 2:30 p.m. when they reached the main traveled Emery county road between Cleveland and Price, and here they cut the telephone wire, but they were too late in doing so, as messages had already gone over the line to Huntington, Castle Dale and Cleveland where posses were being organized to intercept the men.

At 4:00 p.m. the mail carrier met them this side of Cleveland and they were then but four or five miles [seven or eight kms] ahead of Sheriff Donant's posse which left Price at 2:00 p.m. The men were described as being one about 25 years of age and the other as middle age. The younger man wore a black hat, blue coat and goggles, while the man who held Mr. Carpenter up had on a light slouch hat, denham overalls and brown coat. Both men were sun-browned and appeared more like cowboys or common hoboes than desperate highwaymen. One of the men rode a grey horse with only bridle and no saddle and the other was on a bay horse loitering around Caffey's saloon during Tuesday. They had evidently laid their plans well and were there on time to prepare for the capture of the money.

Mr. Carpenter and others followed the highwaymen down the canyon on an engine, but did not see them and came on to Price where the news spread like wild-fire.

[As it had turned out it was Joe Walker who had cut the telegraph wires in or near Price, then he headed south. Late in the afternoon Butch and Elza met Joe Walker just south of Desert Lake, which is east of Cleveland. They all headed down Buckhorn Wash, and along the San Rafael River to Mexican Bend, arriving there at dusk. In the mean time two posses had set out after them, one from Huntington, the other from Castle Dale. In Buckhorn Wash the two posses met, and because of darkness, each group suspected the other of being the outlaws and opened fire on the other. No one was hurt, but one horse was shot. According to Owen Price of Orangeville, it was Henning Olsen's horse that was shot. This momentary gun battle took place at what locals called the "Merry-go-round". It's located in the middle part of Buckhorn Wash at a big rincon or abandoned meander, where is found a large alcove cave on the south side.

At Mexican Bend, the outlaws had left several other horses with a young boy. At that point they all split up. Cassidy and Lay rode on down to the Robbers Roost southeast of Hanksville, Joe Walker headed on over to Woodside, down the Price River then up to Florence Creek ranch. The boy headed to Castle Valley. The best source of information on this holdup is in Pearl Bakers book, "The Wild Bunch at Robbers Roost".

Butch Cassidy watchers might be interested in still another version as to the escape route taken by Cassidy and Lay. Owen McClenahan, long time resident of Castle Dale, says the outlaws never did go down the Buckhorn Draw, but instead headed for the eastern side of Cedar Mountain, then got down into Mexican Bend via Spring (or Nates) Canyon. This author however was never able to locate a horse trail of any kind down either of those canyons in his two trips there. However, McClenahan further states it is commonly assumed that the trail was originally built by Joe Walker, who must have used a shovel to create a better slope or a landing place for horses to jump down to. It was apparently never used by horses going up the canyon.

McClenahan and Clyde Kofford both have stated that old-timers such as Orange Seeley and others used to take sheep up what became known as the Walker Trail. From Mexican Mountain a man on foot would herd the sheep up Spring Canyon and along the trail to the rim, but the horses and camp outfits would have to be taken up Buckhorn Wash and around that way and meet the shepherd on top. Throughout the years, the Walker Trail which was never used much anyway, was slowly abandoned and storms have since washed away all traces of it. To locate this historic trail, look at Map 11, Spring and Nates Canyons in the hiking section of this book.]

Over the years the route down Buckhorn Draw and the bridge crossing the San Rafael River at the mouth of the Draw have been improved and rebuilt many times. Almost annually flash floods wash out part of the road in the Draw and floods have destroyed or damaged bridges over the river on several

The mouth of Buckhorn Wash, as seen from the San Rafael River Bridge.

occasions. One bridge was built in 1936 by the Emergency Conservation Work section (ECW) of the Intermountain Division of Grazing. **The Desert News** on May 16 of that year headlined a report of the upcoming construction "Mystic Area to Be Made Accessible By Suspension Bridge Over Treacherous Stream." The **News** said the 168 foot [51 meter] long suspension bridge, about 30 miles [**50** kms] south of Castle Dale, though not unique in the state, is unusual. "Plans," the account reports, "are for the bridge to be 12 feet [4 meters] wide, permitting two automobiles to pass. Oil prospectors are excited to see the bridge, as it makes it possible to bring equipment by automobile into the region, which before the span, was limited to transportation by wagon and on mule back.

Another route into the Swell came up Coal Wash from the Horn Silver Gulch vicinity, climbed out of the North Fork of Coal Wash, and crossed over the Devils Racetrack to the Head of Sinbad. This route was used by livestockmen taking stock into the Swell or the San Rafael Desert. It was also used by freighters, carrying supplies to sheepherders on the San Rafael Desert, who followed Road Draw and Iron Wash out of the Head of Sinbad. Although this route continues to receive some livestock use, it has never been improved, and it is still possible to see where just enough rock was cut away at the Devils Racetrack to allow the passage of wagons. [See the location of the Devils Racetrack on the Coal Wash hiking map.]

Livestockmen in the Swell frequently used yet another trail into the Swell from the west. This route came up Kimball Draw and Cat Canyon from the Muddy River and led into the Sagebrush Bench-Copper Globe area.

In 1902, a 65 km road along the ridge between North and South Salt Washes from the Copper Globe Mine to the town of Moore was built. Miner Edward Pike paid $3,000 for the road that was built by local residents who used work horses and scrapers.

The most recent element playing a role in the travel history of the San Rafael Swell is the east-west running Interstate 70 that cuts through the Swell and crosses the Sinbad region. The first two lanes of the highway were opened in November, 1970, and in 1972, 1,030 vehicles were using it daily. Construction of I-70 thus has altered fundamentally the travel situation in the Swell. During the 200 years before the interstate the Swell was a barrier to travel across southern Utah, and travel into the Swell was by rough gravel roads or four-wheel drive trucks. Now one of the major travel arteries in the Western United States cuts directly through the Swell. [As this second edition goes to press, more construction is taking place along I-70 in the middle of the San Rafael Swell. A second lane is under construction which will finally make this Interstate a 4-lane highway from coast to coast. As of the fall of 1989, a second bridge over Eagle Canyon was nearing completion. This entire section should be completed by the end of 1990.]

Cattle milling around a "stock pond", a typical scene in the San Rafael.

Assembly Hall Peak, left; Window Blind Peak, center; and the San Rafael River Bridge. Sometime in the early 1990's this bridge will be replaced with a better one.

From Chimney Flat looking north at Chimney Rock (east of Cedar Mtn.).

Looking west towards the San Rafael Reef, with Spotted Wolf Canyon and I-70.

Interstate 70 crossing Eagle Canyon, one of the highest bridges in the country.

THE LIVESTOCK INDUSTRY

Livestock—cattle, sheep, horses and burros—have grazed the San Rafael Swell at least since the days of the California horse trade on the Old Spanish Trail. Over the years the livestock business has provided the foundation for much of the history and for the way of life of the communities surrounding the San Rafael Swell. Grazing brought the first permanent settlers to Castle Valley, and ever since, it and mining have formed the economic backbone of the region. In many cases livestock grazing in the San Rafael Swell was an integral part of livestock operations based outside the Swell. Thus the history of livestock in the Swell is often interwoven with the story of these operations.

Cattle and Sheep

In the 1870's livestock operations west of the Wasatch Plateau in the Sevier and Sanpete Valleys expanded to the point that cowmen and sheepherders began to trek eastward over the Wasatch in search of fresh winter grazing. In the Spring of 1875, livestockmen Leander Lemon, James McHadden, Bill Gentry and Alfred Starr came over the mountains and began the permanent settlement of Huntington. In October of that year, Orange Seely, a Mt. Pleasant Mormon bishop, moved stock–1500 head of sheep and about 1400 cattle, over the Wasatch to winter them in the Cottonwood Canyon [Creek?] of Castle Valley. According to a University of Utah thesis, other cattle herds, owned by Charles Swasey and Jonas Erickson, were brought into the valley the same year by Henry Erickson and Lon Cahone. Two years later, Mike Molen brought cattle and horses into the Castle Valley and settled on Ferron Creek. Also, Hyrum Nelson, the Bennion brothers and John Loverage joined the early settlement move eastward.

From Castle Valley livestockmen soon moved their herds east onto the San Rafael Swell. It is not certain exactly when this move was first made, but it came no later than the early 1880's. In an interview, Royal Swasey, son of early stockman Joe Swasey, said, "Joseph Swasey was one of the first men to run stock in the area known as Castle Valley.... In the period of 1880—1885, he and his brothers moved stock into the Sinbad area (in the San Rafael Swell). At that time there were some sheepmen using the area in the winters."

Early Castle Valley resident, Dr. McLloyd Killpack, now a retired veterinarian, said a number of sheepmen—including the Petersons, Allreds and Sunwalls—came over from Sanpete.

> They used the desert and of course, the west desert (San Rafael) for their winter range.... They would take the sheep out in the winter on those big mesas that run out to the Green River, and out to the Colorado and all they'd have to do is turn them loose on the mesas, and pitch...camp and watch....

Grazing east of the Wasatch Plateau was good according to Killpack. "They would stay there all winter and get really fat.... They would come back in the spring (from the desert) fatter than they came off the mountains."

A family who has operated in the San Rafael Swell since before the turn of the century and contributed to carving the region's livestock history is the Petersons. Chris N. Peterson came over the Wasatch prior to 1900, "which was about the time he went into the San Rafael Swell," according to his son Seeley J. Peterson. The Petersons homesteaded a ranch of 350-400 hectares just east of Ferron, and from there took stock, 300 head at one time (mostly herefords and some shorthorns), to the San Rafael Swell in the winter. In the summer, the cows were herded to the Head of Sinbad, MacKay Flat, Reds Canyon, and down to the Muddy River. In the fall, the cattle were returned to the Molen ranch. Peterson also wintered his cattle on top of Sids Mountain "where it's high and there's lots of brush." During the drought of 1933-34, Peterson remembered no hay was raised, and food on the range was scarce. They herded the cattle up Sids Mountain, and though it was difficult moving the cattle up the steep trails and many of them fell off, they found good grazing and snow to provide water.

Sids Mountain, according to Lee Swasey, descendant of early stockman Joe Swasey, was discovered by Sid Swasey who one day had nothing to do and trailed a big horn sheep up one of the two or three rimrock routes onto the mountain. After his discovery of the mountain, Sid Swasey wintered stock there, and when the snow was gone, would move them to other parts of the country.

Though the steep trail up Sids Mountain was difficult to climb, cowman Rex Koffard built a cabin on the mountain; the exact construction date is not known but Seeley J. Peterson said, "It was built some time in the (1940's), but I'm not sure exactly when." The cabin later became Loren Beach's and he and his associates, Monte Swasey and Clyde Baillings, packed a small wood-burning stove up to it.

[There are actually two cabins on Sids Mountain. One is of normal size but has no roof. The other is smaller and stands on stilts which have up-side-down pans on top of the poles to keep rats or mice from getting inside. The cabin without a roof was apparently started by a man named Theo Ungerman who made an early attempt to homestead the top of the mountain. After he gave up the idea, Rex G. Kofford went out and built the cabin on stilts sometime in the late 1930's. He filed for a

Ruins of an old line cabin in the Upper San Rafael River Gorge.

The Kofford Cabins located on top of Sids Mountain. They both date from the mid to late 1930's.

grazing homestead which was 640 acres(one section or 260 hectares) rather than the 160 acre(quarter section--65 hectares) farming homestead. In the end he met the requirements of the homestead act and obtained a patent(legal ownership) on 440 acres(178 hectares) in December, 1942, for the land surrounding the cabins.

Later in time others bought and sold the property. The next-to-last owner was Energy Fuels Ltd. This mining company purchased the land in cooperation with the BLM, so they could do a land swap or trade for other more valuable mineral property elsewhere. The deal between Energy Fuels and the BLM finalized on April 19, 1985. Since that date all the land on top of Sids Mountain has belonged to the BLM and is now part of the Sids Mountain Wilderness Study Area. If you're interested in seeing the Kofford Cabin, see Map 5 on Sids Mtn. in the hiking section of this book for directions. Inside the cabin today is an old stove, a bed, table, cupboards and even some canned food, some of which has been there a long time and is surely unfit to eat.]

The Lemon family was also among the first to bring big nerds of cattle into the region, and specifically to run them on the Head of Sinbad. According to Gary George, great grandson of early settler Samuel Singleton (who crossed the Wasatch as a youngster to run cattle for Mike Molen and eventually homesteaded on Ferron Creek), Lemon was accompanied by John Duncan who brought a large herd of cattle from the Sevier Valley through Salina Canyon to run in the Muddy River Country. From his ranch Singleton along with Ernest Wilde wintered stock in the Swell and summered them on Ferron Mountain.

Just east of the San Rafael Reef along the San Rafael River, Tom Tidwell and his sons, Frank, Keep and Roland ran their stock during the early days in what is now called Tidwell Bottom. This land now belongs to the Smith family of Green River. The Smiths, father Thomas William and son Wayne, ran stock on the Tracyhte Ranch in the Henry Mountains before they came to the San Rafael region in the early 1920's. After marrying Betty Reynolds, Wayne Smith made home a cabin in the north end of Tidwell Draw at a spring in the base of the San Rafael Reef. From there he ran cattle in the Draw, in the San Rafael Box and along the San Rafael River. In the summer, Smith's stock was herded to the foot of Cedar Mountain, to Chimney Rock Flat and Joe's Hole Wash.

Life at the cabin was good remembered Betty Smith. "We lived there the first six years of our marriage in a two-room cabin. We built another room on when we had the first baby, and that was in 1936." Home was built from railroad ties, and newspapers and tar paper were tacked on the walls inside.

"We were there two years, and then we decided it was time for the washer and 'fridge' and more comforts of home, so we went to Price Trading store....and bought an electric plant (generator) so we could have lights in the cabin....otherwise we used candles or

A modern day "cowpoke camp", along the San Rafael River (Assembly Hall Peak, background).

From a hill above, one can see the old homestead at what is called the Smith Cabin.

The Smith Cabin, made of railway ties, with tar paper on the outside.

Coleman laterns.... we bought a windmill that would charge the big storage batteries.... and when the wind didn't blow enough to charge the batteries, then we had the little motor that we would run."

At the Smith Cabin was a spring that at one time was being considered for development for supplying water to the town of Green River. The plans were rejected though, when it was decided the spring would not furnish enough water for the town. It did furnish water for a garden at the cabin that included numerous fruit trees. "We had enough pie cherries to supply all of the Green River.... people would come out with their buckets and pick the cherries," remembered Betty Smith. But a geological exploration team pulled the plug on the water source. "A seismograph crew came by (about a km from the cabin) and drilled some holes and blasted and (that) dried up almost all the water (at the cabin)," said Betty Smith.

[To get to Smith Cabin and corrals, drive along Highway 191-6, about half way between Green River and Woodside. At an electric sub-station, located between mile posts 295 and 296, turn west and follow the road to the big power lines then turn north at the sign. Follow this good road north to the cabin in Tidwell Draw, a distance of about 11 kms from the highway. See Map 12 of Cottonwood Draw in the hiking section for a better look at the route].

A big corral still stands at the Smith Place. According to Betty Smith water from the spring was run through it, and feed could be left in the manger permitting the Smiths to leave the stock unattended and well supplied with food.

[At present there are a couple of corrals, a storage shed in good condition, and the ruins of the cabin. According to the Smiths, someone tore up the floor of the cabin and pushed the walls in, apparently looking for buried treasure. There are also several struggling fruit trees and the remains of a cellar and chicken coop at the site].

South through the draw from the Smith's Ranch was the Gillies Ranch. Cattle from the two ranches would drift together, and when this happened a round-up was called.

"All the cowboys would come and we would gather all the cattle from miles [kms] around and then they would all be separated. Sometimes we would have a rodeo early in the morning because the horses were fresh and they would buck the cowboys off."

Apparently the San Rafael saw very little of the conflicts between cowmen and sheepmen that occurred in other parts of the west. "They probably swore at one another when their backs were turned, but there was never any real trouble," said rancher Seeley J. Peterson. Perhaps, however, there was

Rusting wagons from yesterday, as seen at the Smith Cabin.

some minor trouble. A history compiled by the Emery County Daughters of the Utah Pioneers indicated that competition for choice grazing areas led to at least one sheep camp being burned with considerable damage done. There is also a stone monument on Copper Globe Flat which reads:

> Henry H. Jensen of Mayfield, Utah was found (here) dead Dec. 16 1890. Blood and trails in the snow showed he had walked and crawled a mile [1½ kms] after he was shot. He still held to his rifle, herding sheep for the Witbecks. It is said the Robbers Roost gang warned all sheep to "Stay out of this herding mesa." He was carried out on a pack mule to the brink of Eagle Canyon to a buckboard 7 miles [11 kms]. He was found by Will and Otto Witbeck.

Historical records are strangely silent regarding this incident, but it would appear to be quite reasonable to assume that Henry Jensen died in a dispute over grazing rights.

[This monument and location is known as Shepherds End. To get there exit I-70 at the Copper Globe Road, which is between mile posts 114 and 115. Drive along the road as if going to the Copper Globe Mine. Higher clearence cars can make it. About 10 kms south of I-70 and where the Copper Globe Mine Road veers to the right or west, is a sign pointing to Shepherds End. About 30 meters off the road is the monument].

Running livestock in the San Rafael Swell has always been a "tough proposition," and one of the major factors contributing to the difficulty was the lack of good water. Many areas of the Swell historically have been grazed only during the winter with snow on the ground providing the water source. What water was available often left much to be desired. Pearl Baker tells of at least two occasions where the water in Straight Wash poisoned horses that were watered there. One horse died and left its rider afoot in the San Rafael Desert. McLloyd Killpack remembered the Swell's salt washes that are "just the same as Epsom salts," and local residents refer to the water in the Muddy River as "gyp" water for its high content of gypsum that acts (on humans) as a laxative.

In addition to the poor water supply, livestockmen have had to be wary of some of the vegetation in the Swell. McLloyd Killpack remembered steering stock away from poisonous wiregrass and Saleratus patches. "We'd keep our cows away because one mouthful of that (Saleratus) and in a few minutes they'd just walk over and die. But we learned those things the hard way." (The scientific names of the vegetation Killpack discussed are not known. Two poisonous plants common in the San Rafael Swell and that are of concern to livestockmen are Locoweed and Halogeton).

During the depression of 1929, however, livestockmen and Castle Valley ranchers did not feel the strangling effects experienced by the rest of the country. "Life was tough, like it was everyplace," said

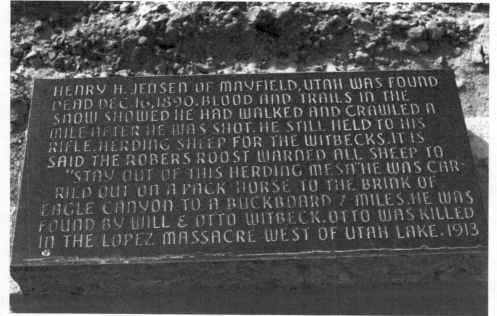

The monument to Henry H. Jensen, at a place known as Shepherds Ends.

Seeley J. Peterson, "but as ranchers and being self-sufficient, they had enough to eat. Milk, dairy products and meat were plentiful," he said. Though at one time during the depression there was no feed for the stock and so cattlemen were paid a subsidy by the government to kill, rather than market their animals. Peterson remembered that $4 was paid for a 200 kg calf.

Wild Horses & Burros, and Deer, Antelope and Big Horn Sheep

Wild horses in the San Rafael Swell also were an important aspect of livestock history in the region. It is almost certain that these animals were descendants of horses left by early travelers along the Old Spanish Trail. In addition to historical texts testifying to this, observations of the present-day horses running wild in the Swell support this origin. The horses hearded eastward over the Trail were excellent California stock, and today, similar statured horses, "thoroughbred looking horses....big horses" still run wild in the Swell. Hanksville resident Barbara Ekker described some of these present wild horses: "They call them broomtails because their tails....and manes drag the ground; they've just fabulous tails and manes." She noted that these horses have a great deal of endurance, and were once in demand by mail route riders.

[In talking to other old timers in Castle Valley, the author found that few of them really believe the horses originated from the old Spanish herds and more or less refuted what has been stated in the paragraph above. The stockmen this author spoke to on the subject, Owen Price and Clyde Kofford, stated the majority of the wild horses in the Swell over the years had originally belonged to local ranchers. They would turn the horses loose in the Swell usually during the winter months, then some would become wild before they could be rounded up again in the spring.

In the early days, Thadius Hambrick once had a large herd of horses grazing in the Swell and Kofford believes many of the horses rounded up in the 1930's could have been descendents of his original stock. In the late 1930's, not long after the Taylor Grazing Act was passed(1934), the newly formed BLM and ranchers had several wild horse roundups. Ross Petty and Charley Gunderson were in charge of the operation.

The author has been to the Copper Globe Mine and Flat(where stands the monument at Shepherds End) on several occasions and has seen wild horses each time. In the summer of 1989, the BLM took a survey of the wild horses in the Swell. They found about 55 head in the area of the Copper Globe Mine and Flat, and Link Flats just to the south. They also sighted about 35 head in the center of the Swell in the area of Reds Canyon and MacKay Flat. The BLM is now considering what to do with them as they're taking over parts of the range normally grazed by cattle. It appears that

A corral for rounding up wild horses. This one is just west of the Wickiup Mines.

30

sometime in the early 1990's they will put out bids to contractors who will go into the area with a helicopter and round up at least 25 head. If and when this happens, the horses will be sold to the public for $125 each under the "Adopt-a-Horse Program"].

For many years wild horses provided enterprising individuals with a source of income. The Swasey family traded and sold wild horses in the Sanpete Valley that they had rounded up in the Sinbad region of the San Rafael Swell. Monte Swasey, grandson of horseman Joe Swasey, remembers the family's business:

> When I was just a young feller, I can remember them bringing horses from Sinbad. They'd bring 150 at a time—and they had a big round corral down at Molen that they'd put 'em in and they'd run 'em through a chute and halter 'em. They'd usually break em' to lead in that corral.

He continued:

> They'd start out with that bunch of horses and they'd go for a fish hatchery.... Along the way, of course, they'd trade these horses they had gathered for old fish bait horses and get some boot (pay). By the time they'd get to the fish hatchery (Sigurd fish hatchery in Sevier County), all they'd have left would be a bunch of fish bait and what boot they'd gotten from trading horses.

Rounding up the broomtails was assisted by the construction of horse traps. Made of cedar posts butted tightly against each other, and with cables wound between them, the traps stood in a canyon which operated like a funnel forcing the horses toward the corral in front of pursuing riders. In front of the corral gate, a pit was dug, covered with branches, and staffed with a young Swasey whose job was to hop out and close the gate behind the entering animals.

The Swaseys built at least a dozen of these horse traps, and Seely J. Peterson said his family constructed some, too. Three known locations of traps are near the Wickiup [still standing just west of the Wickiup Mines], in Bullock Canyon and near Tan Seeps. Peterson recalled another trap in Eagle Canyon. On one occassion rounding up wild horses proved to be fatal for a San Rafael area cowman. In 1934, Vern Koffard was killed east of Moore on Sand Bench while trying to herd wild horses into a corral. The horse he was riding stepped in a hole and Koffard was thrown and broke his neck.

In addition to trading and selling wild horses, livestockman Joe Swasey tried to breed broomtails with domesticated horses. Great grandson Lee Swasey claimed considerable domestication took place by the "Swaseys (who) brought over stallions to upgrade the wild horses." Seeley J. Peterson remembered a good amount of breeding that was successful, too. However, early Castle Valley resident McLloyd Killpack remembered. "Joe Swasey brought two Norman percheron stallions to breed with the Cayuses (wild horses), but the wild horses killed one horse and just about killed the other."

The Swaseys and other Castle Valley residents sold and traded quality steeds and working horses, too. Seeley J. Peterson remembered that his family sold a carload of horses at Green River for $25 a head. Peterson said, "The thing with horses is that they're nearly all clear profit.... They run on the open range all year round.... and all we had to do was take out the colts we wanted.

The Swasey's horse business, according to Monte Swasey, was quite large when the demand for horses was high prior to the automobile and when the cavalry was still in operation. Monte said the family had 900 head of horses at one time. Apparently their horses were some of the best available in the region. Pearl Baker reports that Butch Cassidy had another man buy a Swasey horse, Gray Eagle, for use as a get-away horse in the Castle Gate payroll robbery.

With the advent of the automobile and the end of the mounted cavalry, the demand for horses decreased rapidly. As a result, wild horses increased tremendously in number during the 1930's on the San Rafael. Horace Ekker of Hanksville remembered attempting to earn some money by selling horses during this time. He rounded up sixty head, fed and cared for them, and netted a total of six dollars for his trouble.

In an effort to reduce the number of free-roaming horses, in 1939 a wild horse round-up was staged in cooperation with the Emery County Commisioner's office. At that time, according to an interview with Royal Swasey, "There were between 200 and 500 head of unclaimed and unbranded animals running wild in the vicinity of the San Rafael Desert and the San Rafael Swell." These animals were declared a nuisance to the public ranges.

North of the San Rafael Swell in the Nine Mile area, but indicative of the activities that occurred in the Swell, the Preston Nutter (cattle) Corporation was told by the Grazing Service that it must dispose of the horses. "The Grazing Service agreed to furnish the ammunition which required a release from the War Department since this was during World War II. We asked for two shells per animal, but we allowed only one which did not make for humane killing. The tally was kept in ears. Nothing was done to salvage hides or meat.... The final tally was 1140 horses killed."

In addition to wild horses, McLloyd Killpack remembered, "Of course, we had little burros, hundreds of them on the desert. We could go pick up a hundred of them in a day. . . .just ride out and round 'em up." Most likely these free-roaming animals came to the San Rafael Swell from California with the traffic on the Old Spansih Trail. Wild horses and burros can still be spotted in the San Rafael Swell, but they are few in number and are protected under Wild Free-Roaming Horse and Burro Management Act of 1971.

[The author hasn't actually seen wild burros in the Swell, but has seen many tracks of these animals as he was hiking in the upper end of Eardley Canyon (Straight Wash), in the area of Red and Hyde Draws, and the landing strip on Cliff Dweller Flat.

In July of 1989, the BLM had the first ever wild burro roundup not only in the San Rafael Swell but in the state of Utah. This roundup took place in the area of Cliff Dweller Flat just east of the head of Eardley Canyon and near Hyde and Red Draws. They contracted a helicopter and had wranglers on the ground on horseback. They kept in touch by radio. The helicopter drove the burros toward the cowboys who roped the little critters and placed them in small portable holding pens. In all they gathered up 26 head. All the burros taken in this one-day roundup were shipped to the corrals(adoption center) at Delta, Utah. All 26 were adopted for $75 each. It was noted by those involved with the operation that these animals became rather docile soon after being rounded up.

David Orr, who works for the BLM out of the Price office, states that all wild burros are found in the eastern part of the San Rafael Swell and divided by Interstate Highway 70. South of the highway they range in the Cliff Dweller Flat area. These animals are black in color and rather small. A second herd is located further north, in the head of Black Dragon Canyon and around the Jackass Benches. These animals are said to be a little larger and of a lighter color than those to the south. In all the BLM believes there are about 50-60 head still roaming free in the Swell.

Clyde Kofford of Castle Dale believes it's possible some of these wild burros could be left-overs from the Old Spanish Trail days or from old miners, but that the majority are probably descendents of a herd brought into the country by a man named Jack Murring of Huntington. This goes back to around the turn of the century. By the 1930's they had increased to the point they were considered a menace to the range and were shot for several years. The shooting stopped in the early 1940's.

There are big game animals in the Swell as well. Scattered throughout the San Rafael are small numbers of deer, which inhabit the region on a year-round basis. You can see these deer in almost every canyon except for those in the slickrock country.

There have always been antelope in and around the Swell, but the Utah Division of Wildlife Resources transplanted 300 head of these animals from other areas into the San Rafael in 1984 and 1985. They were placed in the San Rafael Desert just to the east of the eastern Reef. The author has

One of the little burros taken during the BLM burro roundup in July of 1989.

seen a large herd of antelope just east of the Reef, and near the mouth of Three Fingers Canyon. On another occasion he saw a lone animal on the eastern side of Buckhorn Flat just south of Cedar Mountain. In the summer of 1989, BLM employees reported a herd of 17 antelope grazing at MacKay Flat in the center of the Swell.

Desert big horn sheep have always been in the Swell. Most pictograph and petroglyph panels in the area depict these magnificent animals on the canyon walls. But in this century, the numbers dwindled, and it was decided by Wildlife Resources that new blood needed to be introduced. So in 1979, 12 head were introduced from other parts of Utah. Also, in 1982, '83, '84, and again in 1986, big horns of 11, 12, 16 and 18 animals were relocated into the San Rafael. They were originally placed in the Iron Wash area and near Muddy Creek and the Delta Mine, but they have scattered and can now be found in virtually every corner of the Swell, particularly around and near the Reef. The author saw a large herd of 25-30 animals, presumably desert big horns, high on the cliffs at Straight Wash as it cuts through the Reef.]

ENERGY AND MINERALS

"Without the prospector, the world's money would be wampum."

Piled rock uranium claim markers, rough roads carved by oil drillers, old mine tunnels and scattered remnants of wooden mine buildings reflect another aspect of the San Rafael region's history—the story of its mining activity. This activity has included exploration for oil and gas along with prospecting and mining for uranium, copper, gold and silver ores. Even sulphur and gypsum have been considered for possible development.

Oil and Gas

For many years numberous oil seeps and outcrops of bituminous sandstone throughout Southeastern Utah have resulted in the region being considered a favorable territory for prospecting for oil and gas.

Throughout the state in the 1890's, oil prospecting flourished, though few wells were actually drilled. Late in the decade, in 1899, the San Rafael region first became involved in this limited activity when the California-Utah Oil Company drilled east of the San Rafael Swell in Section 5, Township 22 South, Range 15 East of the Salt Lake Meridian (Sec. 5, T. 22 S., R. 15 E.). That same year, another drilling operation took place northeast of the San Rafael Swell in Township 20 South, Range 14 East of the Salt Lake Meridian (T. 20 S., R. 14 E.).

Thirteen years later, in 1912, the Des Moines Oil Company drilled the Jeffrey well 885 meters, 5 kms west of the Big Flattop Butte in the San Rafael Desert. Also that year, a group of Pittsburgh people claimed oil-placer deposits at what is now Garvin Ranch in the San Rafael Desert. Water for drilling the deposit was hauled from Lost or Buckskin Spring. Later, A. J. Denny used the camp as his cow camp headquarters; the camp is now owned by Green River Mayor Rey Lloyd Hatt. Denny reportedly worked with the Ohio Oil Company in 1921 drilling the Huntington well that turned out dry.

In 1921, at the head of Iron Wash near the crest of the San Rafael Swell, the Carter Oil Company drilled 425 meters for oil with unsuccessful results. Cattleman Seeley J. Peterson remembered the Carter Company, one of the biggest operators in the Unita Basin, also drilling by Twin Knolls. The company must not have been successful, Peterson recalled, as it never returned.

A few years later, in the north part of the San Rafael Swell, in Sec. 12, T. 19 S., R.. 13 E., the Utah Oil Refining Company drilled for oil. Instead of striking the black gold, the company located gas, including notable quantities of helium. The federal government withdrew the find and named it a helium reserve in 1924, preventing commericialization of the deposit. In 1964, however, the United States Department of the Interior issued an order to relax the government's hold on the deposit.

In the summer of 1927, near the crest of the Sweetwater Dome, about three kms east of Big Flattop Butte in the San Rafael Desert, the Texas Production Company drilled. It too did not strike oil and abandoned the well a year later at a depth of 876 meters.

Despite the dismal results, continued drilling efforts were urged. James Gilluly, in the United Sates Geological Survey Bulletin, supported drilling tests and suggested areas he thought had potential:

> First, the anticlinal crests about 1 km east of Tan Seeps; second, the flat area about 1 km south of the junction of the road from the Carter Oil camp to the San Rafael River and that from Joe Swasey's cabin, in Road Hollow; third, about 6 kms south and three kms east from....the Wickiup....

During the years 1920-1932, the state saw an increase in oil drilling with 250 wells being sunk. Drilling continued in the San Rafael region, but the activity was concentrated near the Green River considerably east of the Swell.

From 1931 to 1936, the Ramsey Petroleum Company was busy drilling on the Last Chance or Starvation Creek Anticline at the south end of the San Rafael Swell. Near the crest of the Swell, in Sec. 21, T. 23 S., R. 11 E., and in Sec. 27, T. 23 S., R. 11 E., the Standard Oil Company of California sunk wells. The company's second well, which was started in April, 1937, was abandoned in July of that year, after striking granite.

Besides plunging wells deep into the San Rafael Swell and Desert, oil companies built roads to link isolated drilling operations with populated areas. In 1920, oil workers built a road from Emery to Caineville. A year later, companies operating in the Sinbad region built a road from Buckhorn Flat down Buckhorn Wash to the San Rafael River, where a bridge was erected. This route provided the best access into the San Rafael Swell until I-70 was opened in 1970. Around 1918—1922, a road through Black Dragon Canyon into the Swell was built, but it was never more than a rough trail.

In 1949, a United States Geological Survey Bulletin reported, "Wells drilled up to the present time have failed to disclose large accumulations of oil but," the publication continued.

> . . . as a few wells have yielded small quantities of oil and some gas and many other wells have obtained showings of oil at one or more horizons, the idea has persisted that somewhere in that part of the state (Emery, Wayne and Garfield Counties), important production of oil would be obtained.

Twenty years later, **Utah's Mining Industry** reported considerable exploration was still being done and, in 1964 and 1965, nineteen wells were drilled, of which five oil wells and one gas well were producers. In 1965, Emery County reported a petroleum production worth $66,000.

A Bureau of Land Management Environmental Analysis Report on the Sinbad area of the San Rafael region summed up the oil and gas production situation in 1976, saying "potential is there, but possibilities (for realizing the resource) are complicated by economics."

Likewise, the report indicted that in the Muddy area of the San Rafael region, which contains the Ferron gas field,

> Nine wells have been drilled, but present production is very limited. Stratigraphic changes and the possibility of favorable structures at shallow depths have enticed a number of wildcats in the recent past. Resurgence in drilling in the district will no doubt find more producers in this unit.

[If you're in the upper Cane Wash, which is not far north of the Head of Sinbad, you can find an oil seep right in the bottom of the dry creek bed. See the hiking map of Saddle Horse Canyon for the exact location.]

Sulphur

Investigating the San Rafael region in 1911, United States Geological Survey Bulletin writer Frank L. Hess indicated sulphur potential very similar to that of oil and gas. Hess located a deposit 30 kms west of Green River, in the San Rafael River Canyon in July, 1911. The sulphur was found on the south side of the river, about 8 kms from the mouth of the canyon in limestone debris. There was no question that sulphur could be extracted, Hess wrote, but the scarcity of fuel, considerable distance to transportation (at Green River) and a restricted market would hamper profitable production.

Fifty-five years later, in 1967, **Utah's Mining Industry** reported there still had been no commercial production of sulphur, though it noted locations at Mexican Bend, and at the mouth of Black Dragon Canyon.

[The sulphur springs mentioned above are located along the San Rafael River at the very bottom end of the Lower Black Box. As you approach the area, you'll get a whiff of the odor, which resembles that of rotten eggs. There are also sulphur springs in Coal Wash and one of its upper tributaries, Bullock Draw. When the water first comes out of the ground, it's undrinkable, but the smell fades and the taste improves the further you get from the spring itself. There's another spring in the upper part of Eagle Canyon which is sulphur, but this one has been used to water cattle and has a watering trough. In Coal Wash and Eagle Canyon these springs come out of the Chinle Formation.]

Gypsum

Like sulphur, gypsum has been located in the San Rafael Swell with apparently little work having been done to extract the deposits. It has been found at the east end of Fuller Bottom, on the north side of the San Rafael River; in Coal Wash, 30 kms east of Emery; on the west side of Salt Wash, north of Muddy Creek, 25 kms southeast of Emery; and south of Cedar Mountain or Reds Plateau, near an unused road bed of the Denver and Rio Grande Railroad in the NW1/4SW1/4 of Sec. 6, T. 19S., R. 11 E.

In 1911 United States Geological Survey Bulletin in which Hess discussed sulphur production, Charles T. Lupton wrote that the San Rafael Swell contained an enormous supply of gypsum, but no great quantity would be mined until better transportation systems were available. Lupton suggested a railroad spur could be projected very easily through the center of the Swell's gypsum belt.

"The raw product then could be mined and transported cheaply. Such a railroad would probably induce coal mining in the beds east and south of Emery along Muddy Creek and its tributaries."

Fifty-five years later, in 1967, **Utah's Mining Industry**, like the 1911 report, was still suggesting future production:

"West of the railroad between Wellington and Green River are deposits of gypsum that show promise for future development."

Gold, Silver, Copper, Lead, and Zinc

Information relating to gold, silver, lead and zinc mining in the San Rafael is limited. **Utah's Mining Industry** notes that in 1883, the Emery District, 15 kms west of Woodside, was organized and produced small amounts of these ores. Apparently the nearby Cedar Mountain district, too, produced the metals in small quantities. In 1967, **Utah's Mining Industry** reported that the extent and quality of gold, silver, copper, lead and zinc reserves in Emery County is largely unknown. The ores in the Emery and Cedar Mountain districts, it said, are in "small deposits and give little promise of further development under present conditions. The only shipment in recent years was a small amount of silver-copper ore, with a value of only $64."

A copper operation, the Copper Globe Mine, was "one of the biggest ventures anybody ever got into out there (in the San Rafael region)," according to Ferron resident Monte Swasey. Discovered prior to 1900, the mine eventually became property of a U.S. Commissioner Edward Pike, who along with two associates, worked the mine. During World War I, three shipments of ore were pulled from the mine; more was hauled out of the mine, which was renamed the Copper Dome Mine in 1941, during World War II.

On the south side of the drifts, other miners also dug a 200 meter shaft by hand with a whim (a horse powered gear operation). Efforts there were unsuccessful and were abandoned.

[There are many things to see at the old abandoned Copper Globe Mine. To get there, exit I-70 between mile posts 114 and 115, and drive south across Justensen Flats, down into the head of Devils Canyon, and then south to Copper Globe Flat. At the signpost and the junction known as Shepherds End, turn west for about half a km. At the site are found several cabins and mine shafts, and a huge pile of stacked wood. According to Owen McClenahan, the wood was to be used as fuel for a smelter. The ore was not of good enough grade to haul out by wagon, so it was decided to smelt it on the site. They apparently built a cupola made of bricks which were made in a local town. On the first try at smelting, they got the fire going, then added the copper ore. As things heated up, the bricks ended up melting faster than the ore. The result was the collapse of the cupola, which apparently ended the operation.

The road leading into the Copper Globe is pretty good, but with one rough spot as you are going down into Devils Canyon. If you'll take a shovel, you can likely get most high clearance cars to the mine. At the mine site, remember to walk about the area, as there are several scattered sites.]

In 1902, to make transportation of the ore easier, Pike paid $3,000 for the construction of a 65 km road along the ridge between North and South Salt Washes to the town of Moore. Work by horse and scraper was performed by local residents, many of whom were farmers who juggled the construction between farming responsibilities.

[This road is known locally as "the Moore Road." It runs from the small ranching community of Moore to I-70 (between mile posts 114 and 115). This location is just across the highway from the Copper Globe Road.]

Uranium

Uranium has been heavily prospected and extensively mined throughout the San Rafael region for some time. Around the turn of the twentieth century, sheepherders and ranchers who were searching for what were considered more important minerals first discovered uranium ore in the Colorado Plateau.

In the San Rafael Swell, uranium claims were staked at Temple Mountain as early as 1898. Twenty-five kms southwest of the Rio Grande Railroad station in Green River, sheepherders discovered ores that were mined on a small scale in 1904. A Price judge, J. W. Warf, reportedly worked ores from there that were later sent to Germany. Thirty kms west of Green River, the Radium Company of America joined the uranium and vanadium ore mining activity. Mining was also done on Little Wild Horse Mesa, about 15 kms north of Hanksville in 1904. [These deposits are found in what must be the Morrison Formation, because they're on the outside of the Swell. The Morrison F. is the same group of rocks in which are found the dinosaur bones in the Cleveland-Lloyd Quarry. Most uranium ores are found on the inside of the Swell, or rather the inside of the Reef, and in the Moss Back Member of the Chinle Formation. An example of uranium mining in the Morrison Formation can be seen 6 to 8 kms due north of the Hanksville Exit on Interstate 70(where Highway 24 heads south). At that exit, instead of turning south toward Hanksville, turn north and drive a very good road into Buckmaster Draw. Several mines can be seen in the area. Mining there took place in the 1970's, as evidenced by the modern steel frame buildings. In the Buckmaster Draw area are claims with names like Billie, Hill Top, Blue Goose and Johnny Boy. They evidently closed down in about 1980 when the price fell in the uranium market].

A claim of the richest uranium ore in the area being mined in 1909 on the San Rafael River by the McArthur Chemical Company of Scotland was reported in a Daughters of Utah Pioneers history of Emery County. According to the history one 200 kg shipment was the highest grade uranium ever mined.

Other early uranium activity was at the Wardvern claim in the San Rafael Canyon; the Little Bessie and Little Vernon mines, which a 1911 United States Geological Survey Bulletin stated produced about two tons of ore; and the Little Hulda claim, which was inspected by Frank L. Hess. Hess wrote in 1911 no work had been done on the mine, but he believed a carload of ore was shipped from it a number of years earlier. He speculated that the ore was removed from shallow trenches and was shipped to Europe, though no returns were made for it.

Apparently, however, the most extensive early uranium mining activity took place in the Temple Mountain vicinity. In 1910, Castle Valley residents Joe Swasey, Oscar Beebe and "Long" Chris Jensen discovered uranium on the mountain and staked claims there. According to a Daughters of Utah Pioneers history of Emery County, the three prospectors received an offer of $30,000 for their claim from a man named Dempster; a Swasey family member could not verify or elaborate on this information.

A remarkably similar story indicates that Joe Swasey and an associate Wyatt Bryant located an area near South Temple Wash they thought was ripe for working while they were riding through the wash one day. There they dug and left as waste ore that a Huntington outfit headed by Byron Howard later hauled off and processed for a reported $40,000 profit.

The Swasey family's diggings for uranium in the Temple Mountain area also included an unsuccessful attempt between North Temple and Old Woman Washes at a location known both as Swazys Seep and Coyote Wash. [Coyote Wash could be what this author is calling "Farnsworth

A huge stack of wood still stands at the Copper Globe Mine.

MINING AREAS OF THE SAN RAFAEL SWELL

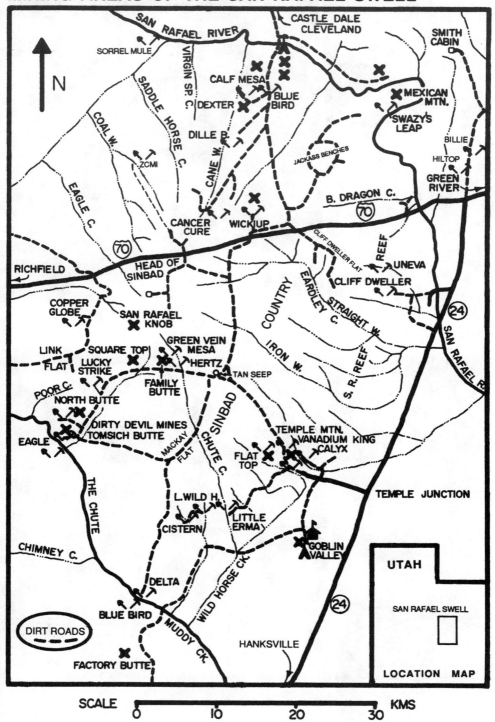

N

SORREL MULE

SAN RAFAEL RIVER

CASTLE DALE
CLEVELAND

SMITH
CABIN

VIRGIN SP. C.

SADDLE HORSE C.

COAL W.

CALF MESA

DEXTER

BLUE
BIRD

MEXICAN
MTN.

SWAZY'S
LEAP

EAGLE C.

ZCMI

DILLE B.

CANE W.

JACKASS BENCHES

BILLIE

HILTOP

GREEN
RIVER

B. DRAGON C.

70

CANCER
CURE

WICKIUP

CLIFF DWELLER FLAT

REEF

UNEVA

70

RICHFIELD

HEAD OF
SINBAD

CLIFF DWELLER

EARDLEY C.

STRAIGHT W.

24

SAN RAFAEL R.

COPPER
GLOBE

SAN RAFAEL
KNOB

COUNTRY

IRON W.

S. R. REEF

LINK
FLAT

SQUARE TOP

GREEN VEIN
MESA

HERTZ

LUCKY
STRIKE

FAMILY
BUTTE

TAN SEEP

POOR C.

NORTH BUTTE

DIRTY DEVIL MINES
TOMSICH BUTTE

MACKAY
FLAT

CHUTE C.

SINBAD

TEMPLE MTN.
VANADIUM KING
CALYX

EAGLE

FLAT
TOP

THE CHUTE

L. WILD H.

CISTERN

LITTLE
ERMA

TEMPLE JUNCTION

CHIMNEY C.

GOBLIN
VALLEY

WILD HORSE CK.

DELTA

BLUE BIRD

DIRT ROADS

MUDDY CK.

HANKSVILLE

24

UTAH

SAN RAFAEL SWELL

LOCATION MAP

FACTORY BUTTE

SCALE
0   10   20   30

KMS

One of half a dozen or so mine tunnels around the Copper Globe Mine complex.

Still another miner's cabin at the Copper Globe Mine. This one is south of the wood pile.

This is a water catchment basin said to be used by miners at the Copper Globe to bathe in.

Behind the cedars a ways, is this "out house", but without a house.

Canyon", and what some others are calling Doorway Canyon?]

Monte Swasey described the family's mining operation:

> Dad (Royal Swasey) said when they first went in there to dig, there'd be these rooms they'd open up, and there'd be this powder. They'd just shovel it into sacks, and haul it out that way...and of course, they'd freight it to Green River.

Monte was uncertain about the family's profit from these workings. "I don't know what they made...if anything. It might have all gone for groceries and shovels."

The Swasey's mining efforts at Temple Mountain were not without cost. While mining this area, one of Joe Swasey's sons, Central, was killed by a falling derrick. A messenger rode all night from Temple Mountain to Ferron to report Central's death. [In addition to working locations in the Temple Mountain area, the Swasey's also prospected and mined on the west side of the Swell in Coal Wash. Their operation there, the Z.C.M.I. mine, is discussed in the Folklore chapter].

Though tales of these early prospectors and miners do not indicate that they experienced great success in their searches, "a considerable but unknown amount of ore" reportedly was shipped from the Temple Mountain district from 1914 to 1920.

Temple Mountain uranium mining history since 1920 is complex. The 1965 USGS Bulletin on the **Geology and Uranium Deposits of the Temple Mountain District** reports other activities:

> Between 1920 and 1948 only a small amount of ore was produced--"perhaps 135 tons or as much as 15 carloads" (F. M. Murphy, written commun., 1944). Extensive mining and production began in 1948 and accelerated owing to the development of processes enabling profitable extraction of uranium and vanadium from the asphaltic ores.
>
> From 1948 through 1956 the district produced about 240,000 tons of uranium ore that contained about 585,000 kg of uranium and 1,726,818 kg of vanadium. Most of this ore came from an area near Temple Mountain; a small amount came from Flat Top in the western part of the district. During this period the Calyx 8 Mine was the largest producer, contributing about 38,000 tons of ore containing 103,781 kg of uranium and 342,677 kg of vanadium. Other large mines were the Calyx 3 and Vanadium King 1.
>
> The history of mining operations, even since 1948, is complex. Before 1948 most of the mining was done by the Standard Uranium Co.; between 1947 and 1951 several operators were active in the district. In 1951 all claims except those in the Vanadium King group were leased by the Consolidated Uranium Co., and from 1951 through 1956 Consolidated was the chief producer in the district. In November 1956, the interests of Consoidated were sold to Union Carbide Nuclear Corp., and most of the recent production has been by Union Carbide or its lessees.
>
> Most of the production since 1948 has been from new mines. The ore bodies under the Calyx Bench, largely discovered and partly blocked out by U.S. Atomic Energy Commission drilling in 1951 and 1952 (A. H. Anderson and R. D. Miller, written commun., 1952), have yielded over half the total amount of ore produced from the district. Minor production has been from the older mines, including the Camp Bird 12 group, North Mesa group, and the mines of the Vanadium King group, or from their dumps.

In line with the history of uranium mining in the Temple Mountain area, a mining camp first pitched in 1910 at the base of the mountain has experienced a fluctuating existence. Following a uranium ore discovery in 1905, miners established a small village that operated until after World War I. With the Depression, the mines were closed and the miners left the village. In the 1950's, the mines were reopened, modern machinery was brought in, and miners moved in house trailers and prefabricated homes. Eleven kms east of the mine, off State Highway 24, Temple Mountain Junction offered a cafe, grocery store, and a pool hall to miners and motorists. In 1962, miners began to move out and the Junction survived only to 1968. [One of the hikes included in this book is a circle hike around Temple Mountain. See that map for more details. This area is one of the more interesting mining sites in the Swell. It's easily accessible by a paved road from Temple Junction, and there are a number of old buildings around. To the south of the mountain are three rock dwellings, and in two other locations there are old wooden frame buildings or homes. And there are many, many old mine tunnels and shafts circling the mountain. The geology and the formations where the uranium ores are found are in the section on geology. The little business at Temple Junction was built and operated first by Alma J. Marsing. Some say it began in the late 1940's, but Marsing didn't actually get the deed signed until June, 1958. Marsing used a diesel motor to run a small electric generator and hauled drinking water from Hanksville. He later sold the land to Milt Oman in 1963, who evidently ran the store-bar-gas station until it closed in 1968. Today the only thing left at Temple Junction is the old parking lot, some evidence of building foundations and 2 small struggling Chinese elm trees].

A second area of concentrated uranium activity in the San Rafael Swell was located in the Muddy

A stone cabin(perhaps built by the Swasey's) located just south of Temple Mountain(background).

Pictograph panels just down-canyon from Temple Mtn. ruins. Note the vandalism.

Drill core sample, as seen just north of Temple Mountain Mining District.

Remains of a more productive time and era. Ruins of Temple Mountain.

An old military half-track truck located on the upper west side of Temple Mountain.

One of several rock shelters located just south of Temple Mountain.

River--Reds Canyon vicinity. The most famous mine in the Swell, the Delta, was located along the Muddy Creek by an amateur prospector Vernon J. Pick in June, 1952. Pick reaped $1 million from the mine before he sold it two years later to Floyd Odlum's Atlas Corporation for $9 million. Odlum was certain the Delta was a rich find; his geologists had estimated the mine held 540,000 tons of uranium ore. But much to Odlum's displeasure, the Atlas Corporation extracted only 90,000 tons of ore from the mine before the corporation abandoned it in 1957. After Odlum's company left the mine, then known as the Hidden Splendor, others tried unsuccessfully to realize some riches from it. The Uranius Corporation took over the mine for a time in cooperation with Central Oil. Finally, however, the Hidden Splendor was sold for taxes.

Publicity following Pick's discovery was widespread, and reportedly, it greatly increased prospecting in the Swell and other areas of the Colorado Plateau. In November, 1954, **Life** magazine ran an eleven page article entitled "Vernon Pick's $10 Million Ordeal."

Other recent mines include the Blue Bird prospect, discovered in 1952 by Kay Hunt of Hanksville; the Little Susan Mine; and the Ryan 101 Mine. On Tomsich Butte are the Dirty Devil Mines. Ore was discovered on the butte by W. J. Hanrert and John Tomsich in 1951, and before 1956, the Dirty Devil 3 and 4 and the Dirty Devil 6 were producing a considerable amount of ore. The Lucky Strike Mine which was discovered in 1949, was dug 8 kms northeast of Thomsich Butte, near the head of a side canyon that enters Reds Canyon. Several small mines in the Green Vein Mesa area which includes the mesa and Family Butte have produced ore. The Consolidated Mine had produced more than 900 tons of ore through 1956; the Hertz Mine had produced more than 450 tons through 1955.

One long time San Rafael resident, Ben Naillon, now 80 years old, prospected for uranium by Link Hole and Jerry Flat in 1919 and was also hired to guide prospectors in the Tan Seeps area. Naillon claims that he took the first piece of commercial ore out of the Head of Sinbad west of the Wickiup in 1949. Several small mines including the Wickiup group, the Cancer Cure, and the Virginia Low were developed in this area.

Further north in the Swell at Calf Mesa other development activity occurred. The Dexter 7 Mine at the south end of the mesa produced more than 450 tons of ore from 1950 through 1957. [As for the geology of these different mining areas, information comes from the **Geological Survey Bulletin 1239**, 1968, entitled **"Altered Rocks and Ore Deposits of The San Rafael Swell."** Those geologists put the different mining area into belts. The South Belt includes the Delta, Cistern, Little Erma, Little Susan, Dirty Devil, Conrad, and Lucky Strike mines, and the mines on the Green Vein Mesa. These uranium deposits occur mostly in the Monitor Butte and Moss Back Members of the Chinle Formation. The North Belt, which is less well defined, includes deposits in the Moss Back Member at Calf Mesa and numerous

Work crew cabins along Muddy Creek and near the Delta or Hidden Splendor Mine.

From a high point in Sinbad Country, looking southwest at Tomsich and North Buttes.

Mine tunnel and storage cave at one of several locations known as the Conrad Mine.

Mine and loading chute at one of several of the Dirty Devil Mines.

A mining cabin just west of Tomsich Butte belonging to Torval Albrecht and Sons.

The Torval Albrecht cabin, located just west of Tomsich Butte.

Lucky Strike Mine, with the towering Wingate and Navajo Walls.

occurrences of mineralized rock in the Temple Mountain Member of the northern Swell. The Temple Mountain belt parallels the local structure of the Swell near Temple Mountain and can be traced for less than 3 kms. The ore in this belt is in the Moss Back Member of the Chinle Formation.]

In the 1950's, Emery County, in which the San Rafael Swell is located, was second in the state's uranium production. In the 1960's lower prices and changes in the Atomic Energy Commission (AEC) purchase program took a toll on the county's production. In 1960, Emery County uranium production was valued at $1,913,850, but it dropped in 1965 to $437,912.

However, in 1967, the AEC was predicting greatly increased activity in uranium within a few years and reporting prospecting by major companies on the increase. Current activity in the Swell appears to support that prediction.

FOLKLORE

Though the folklore of a region is not history, per se, it can be helpful in understanding historical events. Folklore provides the flavor of a region and the character of its people that is easy to miss in the simple review of documented history. There are many colorful stories that make up the folklore of the San Rafael Swell. Some of these stories can be verified, at least in part, by one means or another. Others are almost surely tall tales whose meaning lies in what they reveal of the land and the people. Place names, too, can tell quite a bit of history and of a region's character. In a place such as the San Rafael Swell place names and folklore are so closely intertwined that the two cannot be separated.

The family that stands foremost in the folklore of the San Rafael region is the Swasey clan. Home for them was the territory from Ferron east to Green River and south to Hanksville. Here they rounded up wild horses for trading, labored for uranium and other ores, ran herds of cattle, brewed moonshine, planned and built rough cabins and christened land forms with choice names. Four brothers--Sid, Charley, Joe, Rod (also known as De Grasse, which the Swaseys pronounced Digress) took part in these diverse activities and are the subject of numerous stories.

The exact circumstances surrounding the arrival of the Swasey family in Castle Valley and the San Rafael Swell are not clear. One source remembered, "It seems to me they came over from Juab Country," though most other sources suggest an origin from Sanpete County. One reference indicates that   Charley Swasey's livestock herds were brought into Castle Valley around the time the Mormons first settled east of the Wasatch Plateau. (In 1875, Orange Seely and other Latter-day Saint livestockmen first brought stock over the mountains into the valley.) The same source also indicates a Swasey family moved into Wilsonville, on the Cottonwood Creek up from the confluence with the San Rafael River, in 1878 after wintering at Joes Valley.

Another source, great grandson of Joe Swasey, Lee Swasey had heard, though he's not certain, that Rodney D. Swasey, father of the four brothers came over into Emery County from Sanpete County in

Well preserved dynamite box in one of the Dirty Devil Mine tunnels.

At the Sorrel Mule Mine is a rather large mine dump and the rotting remains of an old log cabin. Copper was mined here along a minor fault line. The Sorrel Mule Mine is located along the upper San Rafael River Gorge not far below Fuller Bottom Draw. See Map 5, the Sids Mountain Hike for it's location.

An old army surplus truck stands idle, between Tomsich and North Buttes. Since this foto was taken, this truck has been dismantled and parts carted away.

Located near the center of the Swell, stands the prominent Square Top Butte.

A rare scene: A black dike along one wall of Chimney Canyon.

An old Ford Station Wagon (a Woody), from the 1940's (Chimney Canyon).

Family Butte, as seen from the south and atop the Moss Back M. of the Chinle F.

1869. "The old man left, and just the boys stayed," said the young Swasey.

Though the precise date of the arrival of the Swaseys is not documented in historical texts, several inscriptions on canyon walls in the Swell give evidence of the early presence of family member Joe Swasey:

> (Joe Swasey's name is located) in Red Hollow Draw on the south end of Belluvue Flats....south of the corral at the Red Ledge where Horn Silver Gulch breaks through the Entrada....north of the Red Ledge on white rocks....in Coal Wash in two places, one (this source has never seen it) near Stinking Springs where the trail goes from Coal Wash into Sinbad....

Though they spent considerable time camping in the rugged outdoors, the Swaseys planned and built cabins in the region. Construction plans called for cabins in Orchard Draw, Georges Draw, Rods Valley, Joes Valley, Long Valley (on the Green River) and near Eagle Canyon in the Head of Sinbad. Apparently, the first three never progressed past the planning stage, but cabins were built at Long Valley and the Head of Sinbad[Long Valley is actually Long Canyon on USGS maps. The cabin is located due north of Green River town, and just northeast of Gunnison Butte next to the Green River. This is at the very bottom end of Gray or Desolation Canyon].

At the Sinbad location, though evidence suggests the Swaseys first entered the area in the 1880's and kept cattle in Jackass Corral, which was constructed in 1905, it wasn't until March 1921 that the family built the cabin known as the Cliff Dweller. Up to this time, they had simply camped beneath overhangs in the nearby cliffs. According to early accounts, the Cliff Dweller Cabin was furnished with "two bunks with springs, a wood range, chairs and a table. It was quite comfortable at that time." But one visitor, Seeley J. Peterson, recalled, "When the old man (Joe) was alive, he took good care of it (the cabin), but after that, no one ever camped there much." Behind the cabin is a cave that, according to Joe Swasey's son Royal, stayed cool all year long and kept meat from spoiling. Cowman Peterson remembered using this refrigerator but "that by the time you'd get there with anything cold it would be warm."

Outside the cabin, the Swaseys fenced in a garden that according to grandson Monte Swasey was a hit-n-miss proposition with some years successful and some not. Great grandson Lee Swasey said the ground was wet enough to permit dry-farming a variety of vegetables. Lee added,

> Dad (Monte) said they had seven stallions there and the grass grew so high that the boys would go out and cut it with a pocket knife just as easy as let the fence down and let the horses out.

[Among local people, the Swasey Cabin at the Head of Sinbad is on the driving tour of the Swell (USGS maps spell the name Swazy). To get there, exit I-70 between mile posts 122 and 123 where Road Draw passes under the freeway. From there head south, southwest about 5 kms, always staying on the most used road. At that point, turn right or west for another km. The cabin is right on the road. The road continues on down Eagle Canyon, but it's steep and rough and for 4WD vehicles. A foot trail to the southwest of the cabin about 200 meters takes you to Cliff Dweller Spring, a very minor spring with a small discharge. Just to the west or southwest of the spring about 30 meters is the cave which stays cool the year round. And directly south of the cabin along the cliffs is an old corral, which must date way back in time. If you're travelling to the Swell in summer, the Head of Sinbad is a great place to camp, as the altitude is high, between 2100 and 2200 meters. The cliffs you see circling to the north, west and south of the cabin are of the Wingate Sandstone. If you plan to camp in the area, remember to take water with you as the spring doesn't give much. The road to the cabin is good for all vehicles.]

Stories about the Swaseys abound in Castle Valley with perhaps the best known being the story of Sids Leap. [This is usually referred to as Swaseys Leap, and on the USGS maps it's spelled Swazys Leap.] One of this tale's versions suggests Sid was being sought by lawmen and, feeling the pressure of a pursuing posse, jumped his horse across the Black Box of the San Rafael River, a 3 1/3 meter span with a 30 meter drop to the river. [Someone writing the book, **History of Emery County**, from the Emery County Historical Society,went up to the leap and took measurements. He found the distance across the top to be about 3 1/3 meters, but to jump the span it was closer to 4 1/4 meters. Below the bridge, the very narrowest point is about 2 1/2 meters wide and the river is actually about 17 meters below instead of the 30 meters suggested by many.] Lee Swasey rejects this version and said Sid and Charley "were kinda crazy," and for lack of anything better to do, bet a herd of cattle on Sid making the jump. The span "was not very wide, but scarey as heck," and with no area for Sid to take a straight running jump. Despite these odds Sid's leap was successful, but when his brother refused to bet on a return jump, Sid chose to ride around the canyon.

[To lend credibility to the story of the posse chasing Sid, Clyde Kofford says Sid was a little wild and a posse was indeed chasing him for stealing cattle. He made the jump then headed north and

The Swazy Cabin, located at the Head of Sinbad.

This is the cave the Swaseys used to store meat in.

Looking north from Swazy Cabin at the Wingate Walls circling the Head of Sinbad.

Wingate Walls found on three sides of the Head of Sinbad.

never stopped 'til he reached Canada. Kofford says he never returned and died somewhere in Canada.

If indeed this event ever did happen it must have taken place before about 1900. This according to Leah Defrieze Seeley of Castle Dale. She states that Paul C. Hanson and Hyrum Seeley put up the bridge at the same spot said to have been jumped by Swasey. That had to have been immediately after 1900 because Hanson was a young man at the time, having been born in 1882. Had the Hanson bridge been there the jump never would have taken place.

Concerning the bridge, Leah states that Hanson tied a rope to the horn of his saddle and managed to swing across the narrow gap. With Hanson on one side and Hy Seeley on the other, they proceeded to lay stringers(cottonwood logs) across the narrows. The next step was to lay brush on top of the saplings, then dirt on top of the brush. The reason they built the bridge in the first place was because it was spring time and the San Rafael River was running high. The sheep still had their winter wool and half the herd was on one side of the river, half on the other. They were afraid to run them through the water under those conditions. Later in time some cowboys improved the bridge by laying a wagon box across the logs].

A story about Sid's brother Joe highlights his fondness for teasing children. Great grandson Lee said Joe would ride along on his horse, his white beard and hair flying in the wind, and would snap a bullwhip at the feet of youngsters in front of him. Then when the child was about to cry, Joe would scoop him up, plop him on his horse and taxi him home.

Joe was totally at home in the desert environment of the San Rafael Swell. McLloyd Killpack, Castle Valley resident born in 1896, remembered Joe would take a bag of salt and live on the desert for days on end. When he wanted water, he knew where to find it. Camping one day with friend "Doc" Easley, Joe sent his associate looking for water. When the doctor returned empty-handed, Joe exclaimed, "Gad, Doc, even a coyote knows to dig for it."

As a livestockman, Joe was highly praised by Killpack. "Joe Swasey was one of the first real horsemen in the country...really outstanding." His brother Rod, who eventually settled in Wellington, was held in high esteem, too. Killpack remembered:

> They (the Swaseys) wrangled up a bunch of these (great) horses and one was a beautiful sorrel. Rod announced, "I'd give my right arm or a mighty good price for that horse."....and so brother Charley promised, "I'll tell you what...if you can lasso that horse and can hold the horse by the end of the rope...you can have him....he (Rod) held on to the horse...(all) through the brush and choked him down. Boy, they were really rough boys."

Chris N. Peterson recounted what is probably the most colorful tale of Joe Swasey's exploits:

> Me and Old Joe was ridin' the San Rafael Reef two years ago about now....As we come round a bend, Joe was kinda settin' on one laig and lookin' back at me talkin' when right over the top of his haid on a shelf of rock an' not more 'n 25 or 30 feet (8 to 10 meters) from him he caught sight of a wild cat.

When Joe discovered the wild animal, he moved to lasso it, but his throw missed. Joe then persuaded Peterson to follow the cat into a cave that it had "holed up" in.

> I crawled in, findin' it purty tight squeesin' in some places. I had my gun in my left hand an' my rope in my right. I caught a glimpse of them two eyes lookin' as big as two blue moons. The ol' cat gave a growl. I tried to git my rope up, but couldn't so aimin' the gun as near as I could in the dark, I let drive.

The cat scooted out of the cave and up a tree, where again Joe persuaded "Pete" to trail him.

> I moved up the tree very slow an' careful like, a little at a time. As I got near his last perch, he tried to turn. Like lightnin' I grabbed his laig an' jerked 'im off the limb an' held him yowlin' an' kickin' head down.

After the two cowmen landed the cat on the ground in a blanket, Joe announced, "We'll tame this baby an' make him a real good cat." Joe's associate soon discovered that he was appointed to begin the taming chores.

> I looked around t' where ol' Tom was a growlin' under his breath in the corner an' decided that as fur as I was concerned I'd jest as leave not have a cat around.

> But the next night when we come in off the range, Ol' Joe says: "Now Pete, it's time to tame the kitten. I've brought some meat fer 'im. You git 'im out an' pet 'im a while an' then we'll feed 'im."

When the cat's cage was opened,

From the San Rafael River, one has a unique view of the bridge spanning Swazys Leap.

Another look at Swazys Leap and the Hanson sheep bridge from the bluffs above the Black Box.

The ol' cat shot out of thet box an' at thet tent like a shot out of a gun. He bounced back when he struck the canvas. Then he looked around a minnit. Like a streak of gray lightnin' he flashed around an' around thet tent, up over the ceiling, up the sides and ends, over the bed, an' every which way.

Joe's attempts to tame the cat continued, but in the end,

About the fifth night Ol' Joe put his bag in through the bars an' wuz pushin' ol' Tom towards it with his stick when it seems as if the ol' cat went plumb crazy. He actually spit fire an' then with a lunge...he lit right on Ol' Joe's bosom....When thet cat saw the outdoors, with one bound he wuz gone. As he scooted across the desert I grabbed my gun an' started to pumpin' lead at 'im as he run.

But Joe would not permit shooting at the animal,

"Stop, for Lord's sake, stop. You ain't got no right to kill thet cat. Why thet sun-of-a-gun has licked us both, clean. Damned if I don't believe he could lick the whole United States Army."

A Swasey family exploit easier to substantiate than the tale of the cat concerns the family's mining location, the ZCMI Mine. The mine was located in the North Fork of Coal Wash a half km north of Stinking Springs. The initials ZCMI, Lee Swasey claimed, were an abbreviation for "Zion's Collection of Mormon Idiots." The mine was a weird formation according to Joe's grandson, Monte Swasey.

It had been an old extinct geyser, and they run this one tunnel--they were going to run it clear in through the mountain--...finally they went in there and the last shot hit the water spout in the chimney, and it went down. That's when they quit.

The mine had only produced a variety of trace elements--none of which were worth more than $10. Near the mine, the Swaseys built a house from the rocks quarried out of the workings. The whole family--Joe and all his boys--were involved in the project. They piled the stones up against a ledge and put a roof on. "It kept them out of mischief, I guess," said grandson Monte.

[The author actually counted 4 adits or tunnels into the round conical shaped hill which is the ZCMI Mine. One is vertical, one is just a prospect pit, another is caved in, and the main tunnel, which is just above the stone cabin. See Hike 3, North Fork of Coal Wash in the hiking section for details on how to get there.]

Other mining activity in the San Rafael region produced interesting stories. One of these invovles the Cancer Cure uranium deposit located in the Head of Sinbad. Ore from this deposit is reputed to have cured an individual who suffered from cancer.

Another mining related story of the San Rafael Swell deserves an honored place in any collection of American tall tales. In 1954 **Life** magazine published an 11 page story entited "Vernon Pick's $10 Million Ordeal," which supposedly reported the story of Pick's discovery of the Delta Mine. In the article Pick told of being tracked by mountain lions and of constant danger from rattlesnakes as he prospected the area. He spoke of camping alone beside the "ominous" Muddy River, "a nasty stream...and that...he found it necessary to ford this raging torrent a total of 27 times, holding clothing and scintillometer aloft as the waist deep water, heavy with silt, tried to suck him under." Finally, Pick reported that after discovering the Delta Mine, he made a raft by burning a log in half, lashing it together with boot laces and belt, and riding it on a "harrowing trip down the raging torrent."

Conflicts in Pick's version of his discovery were discussed by Samuel W. and Raymond W. Taylor in **Uranium Fever**. According to the authors, "a professional hunter from Gunlock said, in all his life (in the area), he had never seen a cougar until his dogs jumped one up." As for the violent Muddy, "everybody (local residents) knew that the normal flow of the Muddy in June (the month of discovery) is a mere trickle....Anyone attempting to ford it during (flash) flood would be patently insane, first because he would certainly drown, and second, because by waiting just a few hours the flash flood would subside." By the time the Taylors finished their review of Pick's tale it is exposed as being almost entirely fiction. Yet Pick's account contributed substantially to creating the 1950's "boom" in uranium prospecting in southern Utah.

Place Names

The naming of locations in the San Rafael Swell was a very practical matter. Most places in the Swell received either descriptive names, names that related to an event or use, or names memorializing an individual associated with the area.

The Swasey clan frequently bestowed their names on land forms. Just south of the Head of Sinbad Rod Swasey supposedly found what he thought was the most beautiful valley he had ever seen and named it Rods Valley. Brother Sid's name was given to a huge table mountain located just south of the San Rafael River, known ever since as Sids Mountain. Sids Draw is located a few kms away just north of the Head of Sinbad, and Charley Flat probably named for Charley Swasey is found in the Head of Sinbad.

Crawford Draw, just southwest of Charley Flat, was named for another early cattleman family that ran stock in the area. In Rods Valley is Tan Seeps, named for Nathaniel "Tan" Crawford, while George Crawford is remembered in the name of Georges Draw.

Also in the Head of Sinbad is Reid Nielsons Draw, which according to Royal Swasey, was named for an early sheepherder. Justensen Flats, north of the San Rafael Knob, was named for sheepherders Orson and Buck Justesen. The addtional "n" in the name was most likely an error on early maps and the revised spelling continued. North of Interstate 70, about a km east of Ghost Rock is the Dutchmans Arch, named for a Dutchman who worked with early cowman John Seely. Earls Draw gets its name from Earl Seely who frequently camped there while running cattle. Reds Canyon derives its name from red bearded "Red" Blackum.

The use of an area often inspired a name, too. Bullock Draw is a canyon that was fenced off and used to hold bulls when they were separated from the herd. Saddle stock was kept apart from other livestock in Saddle Horse Canyon. Cowboy Pasture Spring was a popular camping spot for cattlemen in the North Fork of Coal Wash because water was available and a nearby box canyon was a convenient place to pasture stock overnight. Home Base, just south of Georges Draw was named by wild horse chasers who used this area as their headquarters.

Specific events or unusual occurrences also generated a number of place names. The location of Sid Swasey's jump over the San Rafael River Canyon has been known ever since as Swaseys [Swazys] Leap. Eagle Canyon got its name when one day Rod and Joe Swasey rode up to the point where the canyon suddenly boxes, and Rod exclaimed "God, an eagle couldn't fly out of here!" Baptist Tanks and Baptist Draw in the south end of the Swell was where Joe Swasey and another cowboy stopped to take a drink and "baptized" an accompanying old shaggy dog by throwing him into the tanks. In nearby Blizzard Flat, early cowman Chris N. Peterson and company weathered a fierce winter storm.

Descriptive place names varied from strictly practical to the highly imaginative or whimsical. Sagebrush Flat had sagebrush "about as high as a horse;" and appropriately, in Salt Wash the water has a high salt content. The Black Box Canyon of the San Rafael River is a narrow slot with dark colored rock walls. Black Dragon Canyon is named for an Indian pictograph figure resembling a big bat or dragon found on a canyon wall. The next canyon to the south, Spotted Wolf Canyon, is home for "...when the sun is just right...a spotted wolf in the rock formation."

Many of the descriptive names in the Swell were suggested by the appearance of rock formations. One of the most obvious is Temple Mountain which resembles a church building (the Salt Lake Temple according to some). Likewise, Window Blind Peak, known first as Window Blind Castle, has shapes like big windows with the blinds drawn. The names for Lone Man Butte and Old Woman Wash are also derived from the appearance of rock formations. Swasey brothers Sid and Charley inspired the name of a rock formation, known as Sid and Charley, in North Salt Wash on the western edge of the Swell. The formation resembles the brothers, a big, heavy man and a tall, thin man. Similarly the formation Joe and His Dog, which resembles a dog sitting up and begging next to a big man, reminded early cowboys of Joe Swasey and a pet dog--perhaps the same dog that took a bath at Baptist Tanks.

Hondoo Country and Hondoo Arch along the Muddy River derive their names from the likeness of the arch to the small loop knot on the end of a cowboy's lariat.

Ghost Rock was named one day when fog in the Head of Sinbad hid the base of the rock from view and gave it the appearance of a ghost floating in the air. Because it often stood out in bad weather the Ghost Rock was an important landmark. "On the Swell, if you could see the Ghost Rock, you knew it was to the west," said Monte Swasey. Not far from Ghost Rock, behind Swasey's Sinbad cabin, stands the Broken Cross named by cowman Seeley Peterson, a fractured rock formation resembling a cross.

Royal Swasey indicates that Coal Wash was probably named because of an exposure of tar sand that could have been mistaken for coal, but his son Monte had a different idea. "A lot of people think it's Coal Wash, but if you've spent a night down there in the winter, you'd known damn well it's Cold Wash."

There are also two variations regarding the naming of Secret Mesa. Some say the name was applied because access was difficult to find and only a few people knew the way to it. Seeley Peterson described Secret Mesa as:

> a place not too many people knew about...with three routes out of it...through Eagle Canyon....by the South Fork of Coal Wash....and on the trail by Ghost Rock....We had cattle in there one winter and thought we were alone...and in the morning we turned around and found a sheep herd....it wasn't so secret!

Royal Swasey went beyond the remoteness of the mesa to indicate that because of its isolation it was sometimes used as a secret hiding place for stolen livestock.

One of the most intriguing names assigned to an area of the San Rafael Swell is the name "Sinbad Country." It seems reasonable to assume that the name was bestowed because the rock formations in the Head of Sinbad reminded someone of scenes or castles described in **The Arabian Nights**. Who among early visitors to the Swell would make such a comparison raises an interesting question. Local folklore attributes this name to early Spanish influence in the region, but that seems very unlikely for a number of reasons. The branch of the Old Spanish Trail used by Spaniards and Mexicans passed well north of Sinbad Country, few Spanish or Mexican travelers were able to read, and it is doubtful those who were literate would be familiar with **The Arabian Nights**. Finally, with the exception of the Anglicized San Rafael, none of the many other Spanish place names in the region remained in use much beyond the 1850's.

A miners trash dump, typical of many locations throughout the Swell.

Native Americans of Eastern Utah

Before ranchers, before prospectors, before government surveyors, before the U.S. Army, and before the mountain men--Indians had created the Rocky Mountains' first civilizations, following very different patterns from those that later colonizers would use. The diverse cultures of these Native Americans had all grown out of accommodation to the land; their technology was largely of the Stone Age, and their religion revered the many forces of nature.

The red men's ancestors had come to the continent thousands of years before from Siberia. During the last glacial advance of the Ice Age, ice absorbed much of the earth's waters, ocean levels fell, and submerged land appeared. A land bridge at least five hundred kms wide linked Siberia and Alaska. Warmed by temperate Pacific breezes and covered with willows, alders and grasses, this rolling plain must have offered lush pasturage for Ice Age mammals like the big horned bison and the hairy mammoth. As the huge beasts browsed across the Bering Land Bridge and down into North America, primitive hunters of Mongolian stock followed their prey southward along the flanks of the continent's western mountain ranges. During a three thousand year migration, some fanned out over the high plains to the east of the Rocky Mountains; others settled the Great Basin and the Colorado Plateau between the mountains and the Sierra Nevada. The westerly group subsisted on the small game and plants they found in this relatively dry area; the plains dwellers continued to hunt big game. Today, the high plains are arid shortgrass land, but in the moist late Ice Age, they, were a hunter's paradise.

Scanning the plains from Rocky Mountain foothills, Ice Age nomads easily spotted herds of mammoth and large bison; trailing them on foot through the tall grass, they drove the animals over bluffs or surrounded them, slaying them with stone-tipped spears. Probably their kill provided them with most of life's necessities: food, shelter, clothing, and tools of bone and sinew. So many large mammals flocked on the plains that the Indians probably gathered few plants; at least, they left behind no implements for grinding berries and chopping roots. They lived like this until, about 10,000 years ago, the glaciers began to recede, water became scarce, and their big prey died out. Out of necessity, the big game hunters began to live in the Desert Culture way; like the peoples of the Great Basin and the Colorado Plateau, they learned a highly flexible way of life, geared to exploiting the whole specrum of food resources their rigorous climate offered. Since the rain fell in different places from season to season and year to year, the concentrations of plants and animals varied greatly, and Indians moved often. They combed the land for antelope, rabbits, reptiles, plants--even insects; a locust plague was a feast for them.

Although the Desert Culture people had to be extremely mobile, their technology was more varied and sophisticated than that of the big game hunters. They made seed grinders, scrapers, and choppers from stone; digging sticks, fire drills, and spear throwers from wood. From grasses they wove some of the earliest known basketry of the world.

They roamed their territory in small families. Occasionally, when berries, rabbits, or fish abounded in a certain place, word passed from family to family, and groups gathered to harvest or hunt together. Families of the region's colder areas formed bands for the fall nut harvest, and during the winter, lived together off the food, which they stored in baskets.

About 9,600 years passed between the glaciers' retreat and the white man's arrival on the continent; during this time, three distinctive cultures arose in the Rocky Mountain region: Great Basin and Colorado Plateau Indians lived much as they had since coming to the area. Plains Indians, borrowing from their neighbors to the south and east, added farming to their hunting and gathering economy and lived a semi-sedentary life; the men hunted on foot for buffalo and small animals, and the women planted crops and made crude pottery. Pueblos of the southwest learned from tribes farther south to farm maize and to irrigate; they built permanent adobe houses, and became skilled potters and basketmakers.

Closer to home, in Emery County and the San Rafael Swell, we know the area was inhabited until about 1,500 years ago by people described as being of the Desert Culture or Desert Archaic Culture. These people lived together in small bands of five or six families. They lived a nomadic life style in which they followed a seasonal migration pattern, moving regularly to take advantage of the location of animals and wild plants which they hunted and gathered for their survival. The desert people lived entirely from what their environment supplied them. The shelters in which they lived were typically caves, or simple lean-tos constructed of brush and poles. The countryside was also their food source; rabbit appeared to have been the most important meat in their diet, with antelope, deer and desert bighorn sheep also common staples. Their main source of food was such wild plants as sego bulbs, piñon nuts, grass seed, and numerous other varieties of plants--their knowledge of which reveals the intimate familiarity of nature they necessarily possessed to survive in a desert environment without agriculture. The natural environment also provided the materials the desert people needed for tools, utensils, clothing, ritual gear, and medicine.

From approximately 500 A.D. to about 1300 A.D., Emery County was inhabited by people whom

One of the best pictograph panels around is found on the north side of Head of Sinbad.

This is part of the Cattle Guard Petroglyph panel, located in Buckhorn Wash.

anthropologists now describe as part of the Fremont Culture. Apparently because of contact with peoples living in southwestern New Mexico and northern Mexico, the style of life of the Fremont Culture was significantly different from the Desert Culture pattern. Most important, the Fremont people began to rely on agriculture to provide a major part of their food. They grew a strain of maize which was resistant to drought, adapted to wide extremes of climate, and required a short growing season. Despite their agricultural lifestyle however, the Fremont people also continued to hunt wild game and gather wild plants to supplement their food supplies of maize. Instead of being nomads, the Fremont peoples lived in villages which were often located on flat, nearly inaccessible buttes. The typical village had two or three dwellings called pit houses, which were dug to a depth of about one meter below the earth's surface, then lined with rock or adobe. Poles served as roof beams, and were covered with brush. A slab-lined fireplace was usually in the center of the pit. Maize granaries or storage rooms were also part of the Fremont village. Another advancement which characterized the Fremont Culture was the use of ceramic pottery. The blue clay which is found so abundantly in the area (Castle Valley) was used to fashion pots, bowls, vases, and interesting figurines.

About 1300 A.D., all of Utah was abandoned by the Fremont peoples. Anthropologists suggest two possible reasons why this may have occurred. A long period of drought may have made the normally arid region too dry for them to grow their crops. It is also likely at this time, new pressure on the limited resource of the area was created by the migration of new peoples into the region. For these, and perhaps other reasons, the Fremont peoples withdrew from the area, leaving it to the new arrivals--Shoshoni speaking bands that in historic times came to be called the Paiutes and Utes.

The Paiute and Ute Cultures more closely resembled that of the Desert Culture peoples than the Fremonts. They were highly skilled hunters and foragers, not farmers. Instead of establishing villages, they traveled in small, nomadic bands in a pattern dictated by the location of game animals and edible wild plants. The preferred shelters of the bands were caves or overhangs if they were available. If not, short-term huts or wickiups were constructed from sagebrush or tree branches.

Although we cannot be sure about earlier periods, during the first half of the 19th century, the mountains in the county were a summer campground for the Utes whose headquarters were in Sanpete County to the west. Also by this time, the Spanish had established the Old Spanish Trail as a major route connecting its New Mexico and California colonies. The trail passed through Emery County, and the Utes took advantage of this fact by grazing large herds of horses in the area to trade with the Spanish and Mexican merchants. By the late 1840's, however, Utah became United States territory, and use of the Spanish Trail as a trade route ended. Mormon settlers were moving into Sanpete, and the Indian era of Emery County was near its end.

Within the San Rafael Swell there are few remains of pit houses or other shelters used by either the Desert, Fremont or Ute Indian Cultures. But there have been some digs by **archaeologists** in Castle Valley to the east. This valley runs from Price to I-70. However, there are evidences of habitation within the Swell by the dozens of panels of Indian rock art left there. This consists of two kinds: petroglyphs, which are pecked into the rock; and pictographs, which are painted figures.

Rock art is scattered throughout the Swell, but most seems to be in the San Rafael River Gorge, the canyons along the eastern Reef, or the cliffs circling the Head of Sinbad. You'll often find rock art panels at the mouths of canyons, either on large boulders with lots of desert varnish, or at the base of high walls, also with dark desert varnish (petroglyphs). The painted on variety (pictographs) are in similar locations, but they are by necessity on lighter colored rock faces and are protected by overhanging cliffs. Almost all panels, whether pictographs or petroglyphs, face south and are either on a well traveled route and/or near a good permanent, or semi-permanent water source.

As you travel about the San Rafael Swell and read through this book, look for the PIC or PET letters on the hiking maps indicating the locations of Indian rock art. Another thing to keep in mind is that all rock art and other Indian artifacts are protected under law. The *Archaeological Resources Protection Act* passed in October, 1979, states among other things that, "No person may excavate, remove, damage, or otherwise alter or deface any archaeological resource located on public lands or Indian lands....." And of course there are stiff penalties for anyone caught defacing pictographs or petroglyphs. Let's all be thinking about the vandalism that has taken place on the Buckhorn Wash Pictographs and try our best to prevent further damage to other rock art panels.

Portions of the above have been adapted from **The Magnificent Rockies; Crest of a Continent**, American West Publishing Co., Palo Alto, California; and from **Emery County History**, Michael Peterson, Emery County Hitorical Society.

Petroglyph panel on a large boulder on the north side of Buckhorn Flat.

A part of the vandalized Buckhorn Wash pictograph panel.

Hiking the San Rafael Swell

Introduction

This book is centered on one rather small and until recently nearly unknown region of eastern Utah known as the San Rafael Swell. The Swell is an egg shaped anticline or uplift, measuring about 125 kms by 65 kms, which runs roughly north-northeast to south-southwest. The land is dry and has scant vegetation, therefore the geology is exposed and open and the land barren for the most part. Throughout millions of years, the uplift and erosion(which have occurred simultaneously), have created rings around the Swell, with the oldest rocks exposed in the center, while the younger rocks are found on the outer edges of the structure. One of the more prominent features of the Swell is the San Rafael Reef, which is made up mostly of the Navajo, Kayenta and Wingate Sandstone Formations. This forms a huge cliff completely circling the Swell making movement difficult but scenery magnificent. It's these cliffs and the deep and narrow canyons cutting through the Reef, which make this part of Utah so fascinating. The geology is covered in greater detail later on in this book.

Location

The San Rafael Swell is located due south of Price, southeast of Castle Valley and the towns of Cleveland, Huntington, Castle Dale, Ferron and Emery. It's northeast of Capitol Reef National Park, north of Hanksville and west of Green River. Interstate Highway 70 runs right through the middle of the Swell, which provides the single best access route to the heart of the uplift.

Emergency Kit for Your Car

One of the first things you should be aware of when visiting this region is that some parts are very isolated and it's a long way to the nearest garage. It's recommended you take a good running vehicle and one you can depend on. Always have a full tank of fuel, and always more than you think you'll need it. Also take extra water, food, tools, battery jumper cables, a tow rope or chain, a shovel and any other items you might think would come in handy in an emergency in a far away place. In recent years and with improved roads, there is a lot more traffic in the Swell, especially on weekends in the spring, summer and fall, but you'll want to go as well prepared as possible. A little time planning your trip may prevent a bad experience in the long run.

Road Report and Driving Conditions

For the most part the main roads in the San Rafael Swell are well maintained and in good condition. All, with the exception Interstate Highway 70, are dirt and/or gravel and can be used by any car during dry weather. In recent years traffic has increased throughout the Swell, therefore the need for better road maintenance. Road crews from Emery County maintain the main roads in the San Rafael(Wayne County maintains the Factory Butte Road). They are as follows: The roads from Castle Dale and Cleveland to Buckhorn Flat, then down Buckhorn Wash to the San Rafael River. This same road runs south to I-70, then continues south past Tan Seep and through MacKay Flat in the center of the Swell. From MacKay Flat it branches--one goes to the Delta Mine, the other to Tomsich Butte. From near Tan Seep another main road heads southwest to the Tomsich Butte area via Reds Canyon.

Another main road runs from Temple Junction west past Temple Mountain and to Tan Seep. South of Temple Mountain is a road to Goblin Valley and to the mouth of Little Wild Horse Canyon, while another runs from Temple Mtn. to the head of Chute Canyon. In the western part of the Swell is the Moore Road running from mile post and Exit 114 on I-70 to the little town of Moore. In the northern regions, the Green River Cutoff is another county road, as is the road to the Cleveland--Lloyd Dinosaur Quarry and to the top of Cedar Mtn. The Mexican Mtn. road is maintained by the county to as far as Red Canyon.

These main roads are graded occasionally and attempts made to upgrade them for better drainage so that heavy rains leave the road bed high and relatively dry. Portions of each road are made of clay, and can be slick after rain storms, but other parts are gravely or sandy and generally good no matter what the weather. Roads not mentioned above may be graded occasionally by the BLM, while others are never maintained.

Weather Conditions--Hiking Season

The San Rafael Swell sits in the rainshadow of the Wasatch Plateau to the west, therefore the area is moderately dry. In the San Rafael Desert, which is the lowlands east of the eastern San Rafael Reef, the amount of moisture received each year is about 12 to 15 cms(5 or 6 inches). But near the center of the Swell around Ghost Rocks and the San Rafael Knob, it's likely to be from 35 to 40 cms(14 to 16 inches) annually, which is similar to that of Salt Lake City. Elevation makes the difference; the desert is about 1300 meters altitude, while Ghost Rocks are over 2200 meters.

Precipitation is heaviest in August and September, followed by July and October. The winter months of December and January have the most rain or snow during the cooler months. June is generally the driest month of the year, not only in the San Rafael, but throughout the state of Utah.

Because this is a semi-desert region with relatively low elevations and warmer temperatures, the best time of year to hike, travel or camp is generally in the spring or fall months. The three months of summer aren't too bad in the middle part of the San Rafael where it's higher and cooler, but in most other parts it's uncomfortably warm. The author prefers to hike from the end of March, through April and May. September and October have comfortable temperatures too, but in the fall season the days are very short and the nights long compared to springtime.

You can of course hike or tour in the area in summer, but it's normally hot and you consume lots of water. Each winter is different, but when the fog ties up traffic in northern Utah valleys, the San Rafael can be rather pleasant. Nights in winter are always crispy cold because of the dry climate, but around mid-day it can be pleasant out in the sun. One advantage of driving around the San Rafael in winter is there are no insects or crowds. On the other hand, the lack of traffic means you'll have no help in case of a breakdown.

If you intend to hike in any of the narrow slot-type canyons, be sure and have a good weather forecast. There might be only one gully-washer or cloudburst-type storm a year in these canyons, but you don't want to be there on that one particular day.

Equipment for Day-Hikes

Here's a list of clothes and other items the author usually takes on day-hikes in the San Rafael Swell. Maybe this will give the reader some ideas. A day-pack, a one liter bottle of water, camera and lenses, extra film, short piece of nylon parachute cord or rope, toilet paper, pen and small notebook, map, chapstick, compass, pocket knife, a walking stick(made of a ski pole or aluminum shaft with a camera clamp on top which substitutes as a camera stand or a probing or walking stick on the river hikes), a cap with a "sun shield" or "cancer curtain" sewn on around the back, and usually a lunch.

In warmer weather, he wears shorts and a "T" shirt; in cooler weather, long pants and a long sleeved shirt, plus perhaps a jacket and gloves. In cooler weather and with more things to carry, a larger day-pack is required.

While there are longer hikes in this book and in the San Rafael, few people get involved with overnight hikes.

Boots or Shoes

Most of the hikes discussed in this book are along the canyon bottoms with sand or gravel and boulders. Therefore, there is usually no need to wear heavy duty mountaineering boots. Most people, including the author, wear some kind of simple running shoe. These are light weight and comfortable and seldom if ever cause blisters. Most people have a pair of these shoes already in their closet, so there's no need to go out and buy a new pair. If you decide to buy a pair of boots or shoes for hiking the canyons, then the best ones are the new light weight nylon and leather hiking boots. These are the perfect boots for the San Rafael--inexpensive, light weight, comfortable and normally no blisters.

If you're planning to do any of the hikes along the river bottoms such as through the Black Box, The Chute, or the Upper Muddy Creek, you'll need a boot or shoe for wading in water. The very best would be the canvas and rubber Converse All Star basketball shoe which is unaffected by water. For most people however, the best thing to do is take an older pair of running shoes which are already near the end of life anyway.

Insects

For the most part insects are not a problem in the San Rafael Swell. However, along the river bottoms, especially at the San Rafael Campground on the San Rafael River there are mosquitos in the warmer 5 or 6 months of the year. This is the only place you might consider taking and using insect repellent, because mosquitos hardly exit away from the rivers. In the months of May, June and July there are large gray horse flies in some canyons, especially in areas with moisture and tamarisk bushes. These pests will bite the back of your legs if you're wearing shorts, otherwise they aren't usually bothersome.

In the summer months you may encounter some very small gnats which get in your hair and bite hard, but if there's a breeze or you're in a tent or car, they're no problem. In fact, the author doesn't recall ever being annoyed by these insects in the San Rafael. The last insect you may encounter is the common house fly. The only time you'll see these is when you're in areas where cattle hang around and leave piles of manure; or if you're using someone else's trashy campsite where they have left food scraps lying around. Keep a clean camp and you won't attract flies!

Water

Even though the San Rafael is dry, and appears even drier to people from wetter climates, there is water around and in almost every canyon. Sometimes water flows for a short distance then seeps back into the ground. In other places you have nice springs, many of which are piped to a nearby stock tank. You just have to know where to look. The San Rafael River and Muddy Creek are permanent year-round flowing streams, but you'll have to treat, filter or boil this water. The best way to solve the water shortage problem is to carry plenty in your car for your trip plus some extra for emergencies. The author always has 5, one gallon(3.78 liters) jugs full in his car and fills them up at ever opportunity. Incidentally, the San Rafael Campground in the past has had a truck-in water supply, but as of 1989 the storage tank was in need of repairs. Just when that tank is to be fixed is uncertain(with the BLM it's always a money problem), so if you plan to camp there take your own water.

As you scan through the maps in the hiking section, flowing water is shown as heavy black lines while springs are small circles. For each hike, the water situation is discussed. In many canyons what flowing water there is has a sulfur, salty or mineral taste. These streams or springs generally come from the Chinle Formation. Coal Wash is a good example of sulfur tasting water, and Salt Wash at the southern end of the Swell has water tasting like it's from the sea. On the other hand, if you arrive at a spring coming from the Wingate, Kayenta or Navajo Formations, it will always taste good.

When it comes to actually drinking the water, old timers always used to say; if it's clear and it's a fast flowing stream, then it's normally safe to drink. In the San Rafael Swell and other canyon areas, the author often drinks from springs which have not been muddied up by cattle or from small streams without any sign of beaver or cattle and as near as possible to the spring source itself.

It's important to choose your drinking water carefully because it's possible to get an intestinal disorder called Giardiasis, caused by the microscopic organism, Giardia Lamblia(early day fur trappers used to call this ailment Beaver Fever). Giardia are carried in the feces of humans and some domestic and wild animals, especially cattle and beaver. The cysts of Giardia may contaminate surface water supplies. The symptoms usually include diarrhea, increased gas, loss of appetite, abdominal cramps, and bloating. It is not life threatening, but it can slow you down and make life miserable.

BLM and national park rangers constantly harangue hikers about its deathly possibilities(which is a little overdone in the authors opinion), but since many hikers haven't the experience to determine what water is safe to drink as is and what is not, here are some tips. If you're on a day-hike, simply carry your own water. On longer trips, perhaps overnight hikes, take water directly from a spring source(or perhaps from a pothole with clear water) which is out of reach of cattle. Or boil water for one minute, treat with iodine, or filter. Remember, the carriers of Giardia are cattle and beaver, so when you see sign of either of these animals take care. There are cattle grazing throughout the Swell sometime during the winter months, and beaver can be found along the San Rafael River and Muddy Creek.

Off Road Vehicles(ORV's and ATV's)

In recent years with increased traffic of all kinds in the Swell, there's also been a dramatic increase in the number of off road vehicles. Since these are called "off road vehicles", naturally the owners want to test drive them "off the road". This indiscriminate use and destruction of public land has caused a backlash from people(tree huggers, or environmentalists) who want to protect the land, especially lands that are as special as the San Rafael Swell. This is the primary reason why there's been a move in recent years to protect the more scenic areas. The more wild and scenic parts of the Swell have been set aside as Wilderness Study Areas(WSA's). The 6 WSA's in the San Rafael are shown on a map at the end of the hiking section. The boundaries of these areas are supposed to be set by 1990, but the final decision could be delayed for years. Just one last word-- it's you ORV owners who have used the public lands as test tracks for your fun machines which has caused the opposition to put the lock on some of the more scenic places in the Swell!

As of 1989, the official policy of the BLM concerning ORV's is that they always stay on existing roads. This goes for all vehicles, including the mountain bikes. Incidentally, mountain bikes cease to function in deep sand, so they have to stay on roads out of necessity.

Pack It In, Pack It out

Another reason some people are becoming alarmed at the destruction of the San Rafael Swell and want to lock it up into wilderness areas, is because of the trash left behind by a few thoughtless individuals. Around more heavily used campsites and along the roads one can see the sign of the times, the aluminum soda pop and beer cans. At no place in this region is there a garbage collection service(except on I-70), so it's up to all of us who use the Swell to pick up our own garbage, and in some cases the trash of our less-concerned neighbors, and dispose of it properly. The author always arrives home with a sack of aluminum cans. How about you?

Metrics Spoken Here

As you can see from reading thus far, the metric system of measurement is used exclusively in this book. It's not meant to confuse people, but surely it will do that to some. Instead, the reason it's used here is that when the day comes for the USA to join the rest of the world and change over to metrics, the author won't have to change his books. The author feels that day is fast approaching. Ha

In 1975, the US Congress passed a resolution to begin the process of changing over to the metric system. They did this because the USA, Burma, and Brunei were the only countries on earth still using the antiquated British System. This progressive move ended with the Reagan Administration in 1981.

Use the Metric Conversion Table on page 6 for help in the conversion process. It's easy to learn and use once you get started. Just keep a few things in mind: one mile is just over 1.5 kms, 2 miles is about 3 kms, and 6 miles is equal to 10 kms. Also, 2000 meters is about 6600 feet, and 100 meters is about the same as 100 yards. A liter and a quart are roughly the same, and a US gallon jug is 3.78 liters. One pound is 453 grams and one kilogram is about 2.2 pounds.

As you read this book.....

be aware that the author is a full-time hiker-climber-traveler. If he is hiking a canyon or climbing a mountain and has gathering information in mind, he sometimes walks much faster than the average person.

In the hiking section of this book you will notice there are 10 sub-titles under each hike. Two of these are; *Hike Length and Time Needed* and *Author's Experience*. In some cases the actual length of the hike is stated, however, terrain varies greatly so the number of kilometers(kms) sometimes has little meaning. The time it actually takes is more important. In some cases it will take you about twice as long to do a given hike as the author. An attempt has been made to calculate the *Time Needed* for the average hiker. Instead of putting the time needed in hours, it's put in terms of half a day or all day. A half-day hike will take maybe 4 hours(round-trip), a full-day means about 8 hours, and a long day-hike might take 9 or 10 hours or longer.

Under each hike the author's experience is given, stating exactly where he went and the actual time taken. People who only have but a few days each year to see and enjoy the San Rafael Swell may want to take twice as much time as he took.

Take a Map

The author has done his best to make good maps in this book, but no matter how careful the drawing is done, these sketch maps are no substitute for a real good USGS topographic map. Always buy and use the USGS or BLM maps of the region. The two maps which cover almost all the San Rafael Swell are Huntington and the San Rafael Desert at 1:100,000 scale.

Respect the Land

Although the San Rafael area may look rough and barren, it supports a fragile desert ecology that can easily be damaged by careless actions. It's a great place for outdoor fun, but keep a few things in mind(a summary of what has been stated above):

1. Protect fragile soils and vegetation by keeping vehicles and bikes on designated roads and trails.

2. If you camp some place other than a campground with toilets, bury all solid human body waste at least 30 meters from water sources.

3. Carry out what you carry in. While packing up, show your appreciation of the area by picking up trash left by others.

4. Use existing fire pits and clean them after you're through. If you make a fire, let it burn to ashes rather than burying charred stubs.

5. Leave prehistoric and historic artifacts as you find them.

This is in what the author calls 1st Canyon, which is just southwest of Bell Canyon along the Southern San Rafael Reef.

Lone Rock (author's name), found just northwest of Mexican Mountain.

INDEX MAP OF HIKES

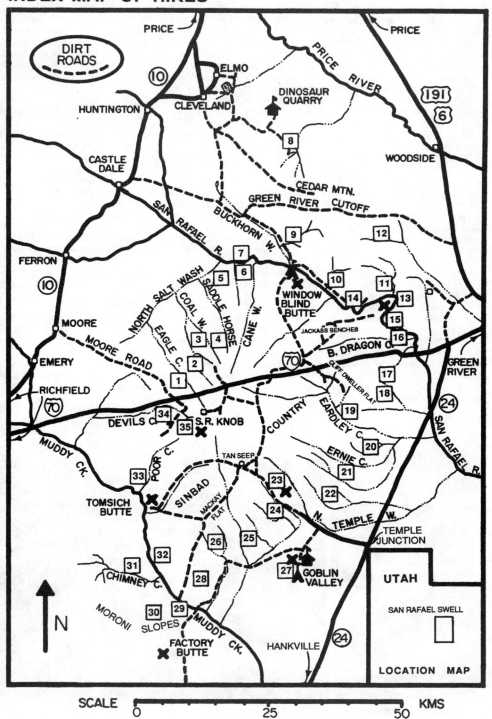

DIRT ROADS

PRICE

PRICE

PRICE RIVER

⑩

ELMO

DINOSAUR QUARRY

HUNTINGTON

CLEVELAND

191

6

8

WOODSIDE

CASTLE DALE

CEDAR MTN.

GREEN RIVER CUTOFF

BUCKHORN W.

SAN RAFAEL R.

9

12

FERRON

⑩

7

6

10

11

5

NORTH SALT WASH

EAGLE C.

COAL W.

SADDLE HORSE

CANE W.

WINDOW BLIND BUTTE

14

13

15

JACKASS BENCHES

16

MOORE

MOORE ROAD

3

4

B. DRAGON C.

GREEN RIVER

24

EMERY

2

70

CLIFF DWELLER FLAT

17

RICHFIELD

70

1

COUNTRY

EARDLEY C.

18

SAN RAFAEL R.

DEVILS C.

34

35

S.R. KNOB

19

ERNIE C.

20

TAN SEEP

21

33

POOR C.

SINBAD

23

22

TOMSICH BUTTE

MACKAY FLAT

24

N. TEMPLE W.

TEMPLE JUNCTION

32

26

25

31

CHIMNEY C.

28

27

GOBLIN VALLEY

UTAH

MUDDY CK.

30

29

SAN RAFAEL SWELL

N

MORONI SLOPES

MUDDY CK.

HANKVILLE

24

LOCATION MAP

FACTORY BUTTE

SCALE

0   25   50

KMS

Eagle Canyon

Location and Access Eagle Canyon is located in the western part of the San Rafael Swell. Interstate 70 runs across the area and it crosses Eagle Canyon between mile posts 117 and 118. There will be two of the most spectacular bridges in America crossing this canyon by 1990. There are several entry points into Eagle. To reach the middle sections, drive to mile post and Exit 114, and leave I-70 across the road from the rest area. This puts you on the Copper Globe Road. Drive eastward about 2 kms to Justensen Flat and look for a side road running north under the freeway. Cars must be parked near I-70 as it's a 4WD-type road beyond. If you exit I-70 between mile posts 118 and 119, you can reach the middle part of the canyon on the north side. With a 4WD, you can drive to the bottom end of the canyon marked 1825 meters, but locating the side track off from the Moore Road is difficult. You can reach the head of the canyon by exiting I-70 between mile posts 122 and 123, and driving south and west to the Swazy Cabin and walking down in from there.

Trail or Route Conditions There are no trails into Eagle Canyon, but in the upper sections 4WD's or ORV's occasionally use the dry creek bed. There's a problem for hikers trying to get down the entire length of Eagle. As the creek bed crosses the Kayenta Formation, it narrows and there's a big drop-off(marked *falls-2000*). One will need a climber's rope to make it over this obstacle. The best way to get to the short narrows section below the dryfalls is to park on the Moore Road as shown, and route-find down into the canyon just below the falls. There may be water in the potholes in the shaded narrows. Horses can go down Eagle Canyon from the Swazy Cabin to the falls.

Elevations Swazy Cabin, 2195 meters; the dryfalls, 2000; bottom end of canyon, 1825 meters.

Hike Length and Time Needed From the middle sections of the canyon to Swazy Cabin is an easy day-hike, round-trip. From the area of Justensen Flat, down to the falls and back, about half a day . From the car-park on Moore Road, down into the narrows below the falls and back, another easy half-day hike.

Water Carry water in your car and in your pack. However, there may be pothole water below or just above the dryfalls at 2000 meters. Also, there is a sulfur spring in the upper end of the canyon, as well as a very minor seep not far from the Swazy Cabin.

Maps USGS or BLM map San Rafael Desert(1:100,000), or San Rafael Knob(1:62,500).

Main Attractions The narrows, dryfalls, and potholes in lower Eagle Canyon, and Swazy Cabin in the upper end(read about its history and how to get there under the chapter on *History, and Folklore*).

Ideal Time to Hike Spring, fall or in the morning hours in summer.

Hiking Boots Any dry weather boots or shoes.

Author's Experience Once the author camped at Justensen Flat and walked down to the dryfalls, but was turned back(about 4 hours round-trip). Another time he climbed down into the area below the falls from the Moore Road in less than half a day. Still another time he walked down to the bridge from Swazy Cabin and back in less than half a day.

A view of the middle parts of Eagle Canyon from near the rest stop at Exit 114.

MAP 1, EAGLE CANYON

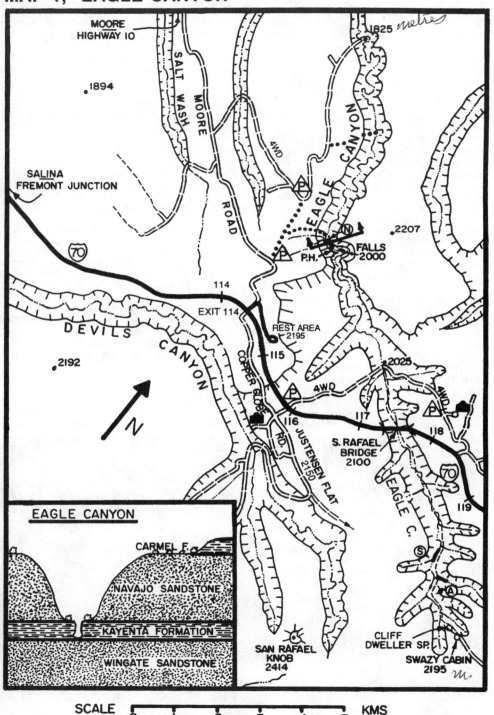

MOORE
HIGHWAY 10

SALT WASH

MOORE ROAD

1825 metres

EAGLE CANYON

•1894

SALINA
FREMONT JUNCTION

4WD

P

N

•2207

P

FALLS
2000

P.H.

70

114

EXIT 114

REST AREA
2195

DEVILS

CANYON

•2192

•2025

4WD

115

N

P

4WD

COPPER GLOBE RD.

116

117

P

118

JUSTENSEN FLAT
2150

S. RAFAEL
BRIDGE
2100

70

119

EAGLE C.

S

A

EAGLE CANYON

CARMEL F.

NAVAJO SANDSTONE

KAYENTA FORMATION

WINGATE SANDSTONE

SAN RAFAEL
KNOB
2414

CLIFF
DWELLER SP.

SWAZY CABIN
2195

SCALE   0   1   2   3   4   5   KMS

South Fork of Coal Wash

Location and Access Coal Wash is located in the northwest quadrant of the San Rafael Swell. This suggested hike includes its South Fork, Bullock Draw and East Fork. Interstate 70 runs through the area just to the south of the head of South Fork. There are basically 2 trailheads you can use. The first is right at the Ghost Rock Rest Stop on the Interstate between mile posts 120 and 121. To reach the second, exit I-70 between mile posts 122 and 123, open and close a gate, then drive in a northwest direction past Dutchman Arch and to the car-park marked 2134 meters. At that point the road steepens and it's a very rough track beyond.

Trail or Route Conditions From the rest area on I-70, walk to the northwest along the left-hand canyon rim. After a short distance, route-find down into the head of South Fork. From there you can walk down canyon as far as you like. From the 2134-meter car-park, walk up the 4WD road a ways, then veer left or west and route-find down into the upper end of East Fork. Once into this canyon you can head west and into the South Fork and exit at the rest area or at the head of Bullock Draw. The third alternative, is to walk up the 4WD road beyond the 2134-meter car-park about 2 or 2 1/2 kms, and again route-find down a rock slide into the head of Bullock Draw. You could then walk down-canyon and return to the car-park via East Fork or exit at the rest area in the upper end of South Fork. If you're making one of the loop hikes, you could also park at Dutchman Arch. In places in the bottoms of these canyons you will see the faded remains of some old 1950's mining exploration tracks. Horses would have a hard time getting down into the canyon from the top, but can come up from the bottom easily.

Elevations Ghost Rock Rest Area, 2200 meters; confluence of Bullock Draw and South Fork, 1828; car-park north of Dutchman Arch, 2134 meters.

Hike Length and Time Needed To walk from Dutchman Arch down Bullock Draw, then up to Ghost Rock and back to Dutchman is about 32 kms, or one very long day-hike. From the 2134-meter car-park, down Bullock and up East Fork is about 24 kms; an easy day-hike. From the car-park at 2134-meters, down East Fork and return via Ghost Rock, is an easy or short day-hike(including the walk cross-country back to your vehicle).

Water Always have plenty of water in your car and in your day pack. There are however a number of minor springs in the bottom of South Fork and Bullock Draw, but some have a sulfur taste. Sometimes right after a wet spell you'll be able to find good drinking water in some potholes as well.

Maps USGS or BLM map San Rafael Desert(1:100,000), or San Rafael Knob(1:62,500).

Main Attractions Deep canyons, huge Navajo blocks, dramatic scenery, easy access, and wilderness solitude near a national highway.

Ideal Time to Hike Spring, fall, or early mornings in summer.

Hiking Boots Any dry weather boots or shoes.

Author's Experience The author hiked down Bullock Draw, then up to Ghost Rock and finally cross-country back to Dutchman Arch in a long 8 hours. On the same trip he explored and found the route down into the East Fork. This was 4 days after a heavy rain and he found lots of pothole water.

The Navajo Bluffs rise above the creek bed in Bullock Draw, a tributary to Coal Wash.

MAP 2, SOUTH FORK OF COAL WASH

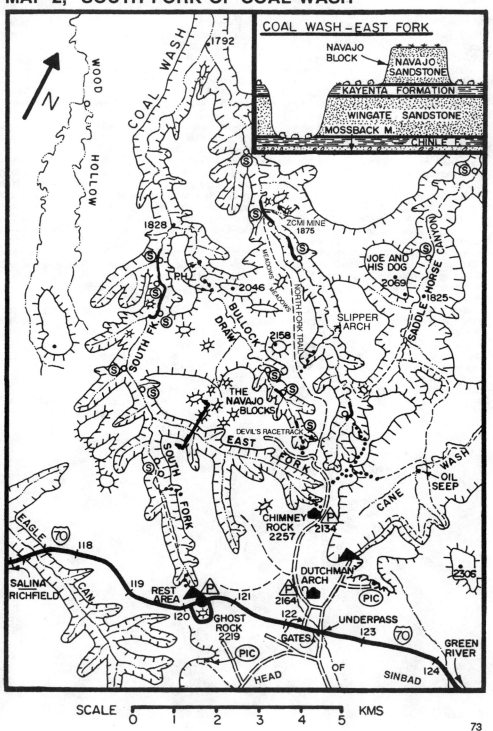

COAL WASH – EAST FORK

NAVAJO BLOCK
NAVAJO SANDSTONE
KAYENTA FORMATION
WINGATE SANDSTONE
MOSSBACK M.
CHINLE F.

1792

WOOD HOLLOW

COAL WASH

N

ZCMI MINE 1875

1828

P.H.

MEADOWS

2046

NORTH FORK TRAIL

BULLOCK DRAW

SOUTH FK

2158

SLIPPER ARCH

JOE AND HIS DOG
2069
1825

SADDLE HORSE CANYON

THE NAVAJO BLOCKS

DEVIL'S RACETRACK

EAST FORK

SOUTH FORK

CANE WASH
OIL SEEP

CHIMNEY ROCK 2257

P 2134

EAGLE CAN

70
118

SALINA RICHFIELD

119

REST AREA

P

120

GHOST ROCK 2219

121

122

GATES

DUTCHMAN ARCH

P 2164

PIC

UNDERPASS
123
70

2306

GREEN RIVER
124

PIC

HEAD   OF   SINBAD

SCALE   0   1   2   3   4   5   KMS

North Fork of Coal Wash and the ZCMI Mine

Location and Access Coal Wash is located in the northwest portion of the San Rafael Swell and just north of Interstate Highway 70, which runs east-west through the area. This hike centers on the North Fork of Coal Wash and the ZCMI Mine(read more about it in the mining history section of this book). To get there, exit I-70 between mile posts 122 and 123. Drive through a gate on the south side of I-70 and head in a northwest direction past Dutchman Arch and to the car-park marked 2134 meters. At that point the road become steep and very rough.

Trail or Route Conditions You can use one of three routes down into the North Fork of Coal Wash. First is the North Fork Trail. This is an old stock trail once used to take cattle from Castle Valley to the Head of Sinbad. Walk from the 2134-meter car-park up the 4WD road to where the main track veers to the left. Locate and follow the faded one to the right(look for stone cairns), walking in a northwest direction. In the beginning you'll find that dirt bikes and ORV's have used it illegally(this being in a WSA), so it's easy to follow. In the middle parts the stock trail is evident as it runs along a ridge called the Devil's Racetrack. In the lower end it's occasionally used by 4WD's and dirt bikes. This North Fork Trail passes through some very pretty meadows in the northern end. Half way down the trail, you can enter the North Fork via a short side canyon just south of Slipper Arch as shown on the map. Once in the canyon bottom, you can walk up-canyon to the south and exit via a rock slide in the upper end of North Fork. Two hundred meters north of where the North Fork Trail reaches the bottom of the canyon, turn right or east onto a track in the bottom of a wash and follow it 500 meters to a brown cone-shaped hill and the ZCMI Mine. It's located about 2 kms due west of Joe and His Dog spire. Horses can enter North Fork from the bottom end and from along the North Fork Trail, but they can't use the southerly entry points.

Elevations Car-park, 2134 meters; bottom of North Fork Trail, 1800; ZCMI Mine, 1875 meters.

Hike Length and Time Needed From the car-park to the ZCMI Mine is about 13 kms. It's about the same distance back up the canyon bottom to the upper canyon exit, so count on 26 kms, round-trip. This would be an all day hike. To walk down to the arch and return via the canyon bottom would be a half day hike.

Water Always carry plenty of water in your car and in your pack. There are some seeps in the bottom of North Fork, but they are mostly sulfur tainted and there are cattle grazing there in the winter season.

Maps USGS or BLM map San Rafael Desert(1:100,000), or San Rafael Knob(1:62,500).

Main Attractions An old historic stock trail, deep canyons, one large arch, and the old ZCMI Mine which has 4 openings and an old stone cabin. It's located in the Kayenta Formation.

Ideal Time to Hike Spring, fall, or morning hours in summer.

Hiking Boots Any dry weather boots or shoes.

Author's Experience Once the author walked down the North Fork Trail and tried to locate the ZCMI Mine, but failed. On another trip, he explored the middle parts of the canyon via the Slipper Arch exit and found the mine. Both trips took about 6-6 1/2 hours round-trip.

The old rock cabin built by Joe Swasey just below the ZCMI Mine.

MAP 3, NORTH FORK OF COAL WASH & ZCMI MINE

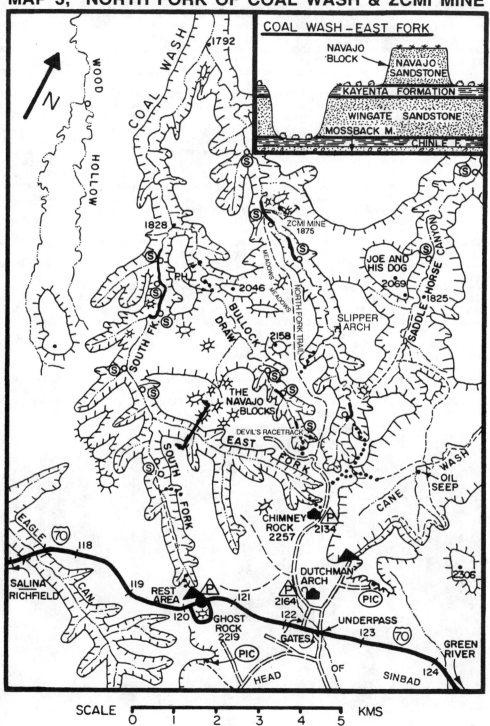

COAL WASH – EAST FORK

NAVAJO BLOCK

NAVAJO SANDSTONE

KAYENTA FORMATION

WINGATE SANDSTONE

MOSSBACK M.

CHINLE F.

N

WOOD HOLLOW

COAL WASH

1792

1828

PH

2046

MEADOWS

MEADOWS

NORTH FORK TRAIL

ZCMI MINE 1875

JOE AND HIS DOG

2069

1825

SADDLE HORSE CANYON

SLIPPER ARCH

SOUTH FK.

BULLOCK DRAW

2158

THE NAVAJO BLOCKS

DEVIL'S RACETRACK

EAST FORK

SOUTH FORK

CHIMNEY ROCK 2257

2134

CANE WASH

OIL SEEP

2306

EAGLE CAN

70

118

SALINA RICHFIELD

119

REST AREA

P

121

DUTCHMAN ARCH

P

2164

PIC

120

GHOST ROCK 2219

122

GATES

UNDERPASS

123

70

GREEN RIVER

124

PIC

HEAD

OF

SINBAD

SCALE

0   1   2   3   4   5   KMS

Upper Saddle Horse Canyon and Cane Wash

Location and Access The upper ends of Saddle Horse Canyon and Cane Wash are both immediately east of the North Fork of Coal Wash and in the north central part of the San Rafael. These canyons drain to the north and into the San Rafael River Gorge just south of the Wedge Overlook. This hike begins in the area of Dutchman Arch, which is just north of Interstate 70. To get to the trailhead, exit I-70 between mile posts 122 and 123. Open, then close a stockman's gate, and drive northwest past Dutchman Arch and to a steep rocky place in the road marked 2134 meters. Park and/or camp there.

Trail or Route Conditions From the 2134-meter car-park, walk up the road about a km, then veer to the right or northeast. Walk past the southern-most end of North Fork and to a point where you can scramble down into the upper canyon as shown on the map. At the bottom, walk north another km and you'll see the faded remains of a 1950's uranium mining track. Walk on this as it zig zags up through a notch in the eastern wall. On the other side is the head of Saddle Horse Canyon. Continue down Saddle Horse for a couple of kms, then if you like, veer to the right on another old track and walk over yet another pass or break in the wall. On the other side is the head of Cane Wash. Follow the same old track, which is presently used by an occasional 4WD vehicle or dirt bike. About 2 kms into Cane Wash you can either go down the creek bed or continue up-canyon. If you go up-canyon another 2 kms, you'll be at the bottom of another rock slide where you can exit Cane Wash and return to your car. Horses would have a hard time getting up and down the routes mentioned.

Elevations Car-park, 2134 meters; upper Saddle Horse Canyon, 1825; the oil seep in Cane Wash, about 1935 meters.

Hike Length and Time Needed The walk into upper Saddle Horse and Cane Wash and back to one's car, is about a 20 km hike; an all day outing for the average person.

Water Carry plenty of water in your car and in your pack, even though there is one minor seep in the upper end of North Fork.

Maps USGS or BLM map San Rafael Desert(1:100,000), or San Rafael Knob(1:62,500).

Main Attractions Little known canyons and an oil seep. The upper end of the North Fork is the most impressive part of this hike. Another interesting place to visit is to the east of Dutchman Arch. Drive due north from the freeway to the Wingate Cliffs on the north side of the Head of Sinbad. There you'll find a fine panel of pictographs high on a wall and an overlook down into Cane Wash.

Ideal Time to Hike Spring, fall, or in the mornings in summer. Because of the higher altitude of this area, summers aren't as hot as elsewhere in the Swell.

Hiking Boots Any dry weather boots or shoes.

Author's Experience The author camped at the car-park(2134 meters), then explored the upper part of East Fork of Coal Wash, but came right back out. He then found and walked down the rock slide route into North Fork. Later he went as far as Joe and His Dog spire, and returned to his car via the oil seep in Cane Wash, all in about 7 hours.

An oil seep right in the creek bed of upper Cane Wash.

MAP 4, UPPER SADDLE HORSE C. & CANE WASH

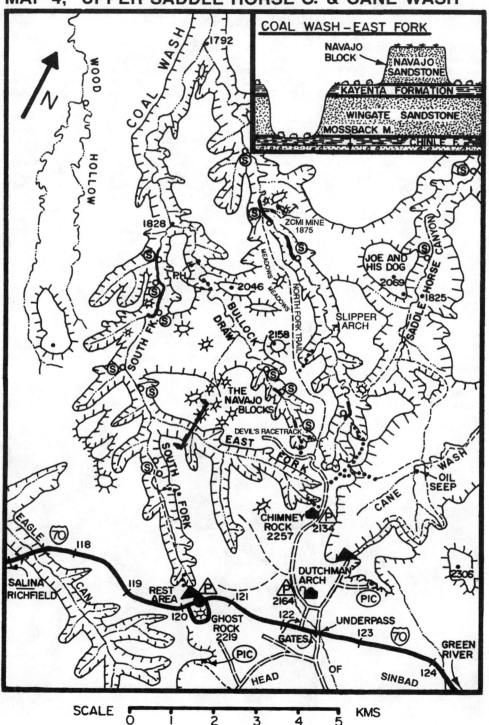

COAL WASH—EAST FORK

NAVAJO BLOCK

NAVAJO SANDSTONE

KAYENTA FORMATION

WINGATE SANDSTONE

MOSSBACK M.

CHINLE F.

WOOD HOLLOW

COAL WASH

1792

1828

P.H.

SOUTH FK.

BULLOCK DRAW

MEADOWS

2046

NORTH FORK TRAIL

2158

ZCMI MINE 1875

JOE AND HIS DOG 2069

1825

SLIPPER ARCH

SADDLE HORSE CANYON

THE NAVAJO BLOCKS

DEVIL'S RACETRACK

EAST FORK

SOUTH FORK

CANE WASH

OIL SEEP

CHIMNEY ROCK 2257

2134

DUTCHMAN ARCH

2164

PIC

2306

EAGLE

70

118

SALINA RICHFIELD

CAN

119

REST AREA

P

120

GHOST ROCK 2219

121

122

GATES

PIC

HEAD

OF

UNDERPASS 123

70

SINBAD

124

GREEN RIVER

N

SCALE 0 1 2 3 4 5 KMS

Sids Mountain and North Salt Wash

Location and Access This hike is along the lower end of North Salt Wash and to the top of Sids Mountain. This area is in the northwest part of the San Rafael Swell. To get there, head south out of Price on Highway 10. Drive to the Cleveland turnoff between mile posts 56 and 57, or between 49 and 50, and turn southeast; or continue on Highway 10 to a point just north of Castle Dale, and turn east from between mile posts 39 and 40. Follow the signs toward Buckhorn Wash. After a few kms, you'll arrive at a place called Buckhorn Flat and the Buckhorn Well. The well is at a 4-way junction and includes a large metal tank, small pump house and watering trough. At that point turn right into Fuller Bottom Draw. Drive this good road about 10 kms to the San Rafael River where you can park and/or camp.

Trail or Route Conditions From the San Rafael River bottom, simply start walking down-stream. You will occasionally cross the river, but it is normally shallow except maybe during the spring runoff which is in late May or early June. A walking stick is good when wading. Soon the walls of the canyon will begin to rise and the river enters a gorge. About half way through, there are petroglyphs on the left and further on the Sorrel Mule Mine on the right. By the time you come to the mouth of North Salt Wash, you will be in a very deep canyon. Walk southwest up North Salt Wash which should have a small stream year-round. As you go up this canyon, you will see at least one old set of ruins(likely Fremont Indians), 2 petroglyphs panels and one interesting side canyon with a very high dryfall. About half a km before you arrive at the mouth of Saddle Horse Canyon, look for a trail to the left heading upon Sids Mtn. Sids Mtn. Trail ends at two old cabins built in the late 1930's by Rex Kofford who homesteaded most of one section near the middle of the mountain. The author didn't locate it, but there's another old stock trail to the top of the mountain roughly southeast of the cabins and from the area known as Mexican Seeps in Cane Wash. Horses can be taken to the top of Sids Mountain.

Elevations Trailhead, 1625 meters; junction of San Rafael River and North Salt Wash, 1600; Kofford Cabins, about 1900 meters.

Hike Length and Time Needed The distance to the cabins on Sids Mtn. is about 18 kms one way, or about 36 kms round-trip. That's a long all-day hike, but the walking is easy and fast. Some may want to camp one night in North Salt Wash.

Water Carry water in your car and in your pack. North Salt Wash is likely drinkable, but there are cows there in the cooler months of each year. There's also one minor spring as shown on the map.

Maps USGS or BLM map Huntington(1:100,000), or Wilsonville SE and Red Plateau SW(1:24,000).

Main Attractions Petroglyphs, deep canyons, rincons, historic old cabins, a mine and a wild mesa with good views from on top.

Ideal Time to Hike Spring or fall.

Hiking Boots Wading boots or shoes.

Author's Experience The author did the hike suggested in about 8 hours round-trip, but others will need more time, perhaps 2 days.

The Rex Kofford Cabin built in the late 1930's. Building it on poles or stilts was supposed to keep the mice and rats out.

MAP 5, SIDS MOUNTAIN AND NORTH SALT WASH

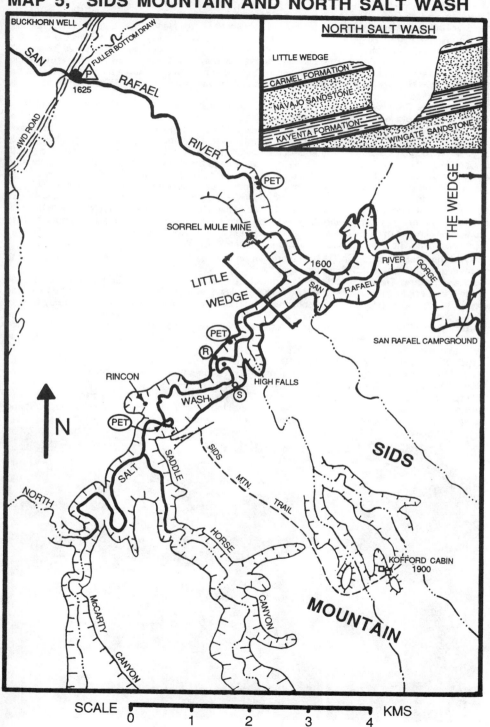

SCALE

0   1   2   3   4   KMS

Virgin Spring Canyon and Lower Cane Wash

Location and Access These canyons are located in the northern part of the Swell just west of the San Rafael Campground. Both are immediately south of The Wedge Overlook and both drain into the San Rafael River. To get there, drive south out of Price on Highway 10. Leave this highway and head southeast from between mile posts 56 and 57 or 49 and 50, or between mile posts 39 and 40. Drive in the direction of Buckhorn Wash and the San Rafael Campground. You can also arrive at the campground by exiting I-70 at mile post and Exit 129 and drive south. About a km southwest of the San Rafael Bridge, turn west onto a side road heading for the Johansen Cabin. Park somewhere near the cabin and corrals.

Trail or Route Conditions From the Johansen Cabin, walk west into the Upper San Rafael River Gorge along an old mining and stockmans road. After a short distance you pass the ruins of another old cabin while the road gradually fades. Further on you walk along an old cattle trail on the south side of the river. After about 6 kms of easy walking, you arrive at the mouth of Cane Wash. Immediately to your left and just inside the canyon under an overhang will be some pictographs. From the mouth of Cane Wash you can either follow the river around a large bend or walk up-slope to the west through a notch in the Wingate Sandstone. From the notch walk down to the northwest and on the west side of a small butte is another good panel of pictographs. Just before you arrive at the mouth of Virgin Spring Canyon, locate and use an old stock trail which zig zags to the top of the Moss Back Bench, thus avoiding the need to wade in the river. On top of the bench you can then drop down into the half-km-long lower end of Virgin Spring Canyon which holds a pool of water and some pictographs high on the west wall about half way between the river and the spring. Adventurous hikers can walk up Virgin Spring C., cross the pass marked 1875, drop down into Cane Wash and return to the trailhead.

Elevations Johansen Cabin, 1560 meters; Virgin Spring, 1590; the pass between Virgin Spring Canyon and Cane Wash, 1875 meters.

Hike Length and Time Needed To do a round-trip hike up Virgin Spring Canyon and down Cane Wash then back to the car-park would be walking at least 30 kms. Many people couldn't do it in one day. A shorter hike up to the pictographs near Virgin Spring and return would be an easy day-hike for most people. Horses can be taken along the San Rafael River and into Cane Wash.

Water Virgin Spring should have good water anytime, but water from Cane Wash and the river should be treated first. Always carry plenty of water in your car and in your pack. Don't expect to find water at the San Rafael Campground!

Maps USGS or BLM map Huntington(1:100,000), or Wilsonville SE and Red Plateau SW(1:24,000).

Main Attractions Deep canyons, several pictograph panels and petrified wood in Cane Wash.

Ideal Time to Hike Spring or fall.

Hiking Boots Dry weather boots or shoes are OK if you stay on the south side trail.

Author's Experience The author camped near the Johansen Cabin, then walked to Virgin Spring Canyon, over the pass at 1875 meters, down Cane Wash and back to his car in 9 hours.

Near the mouth of Virgin Spring Canyon is Virgin Spring and its crystal clear pool.

MAP 6, VIRGIN SPRING C. & LOWER CANE WASH

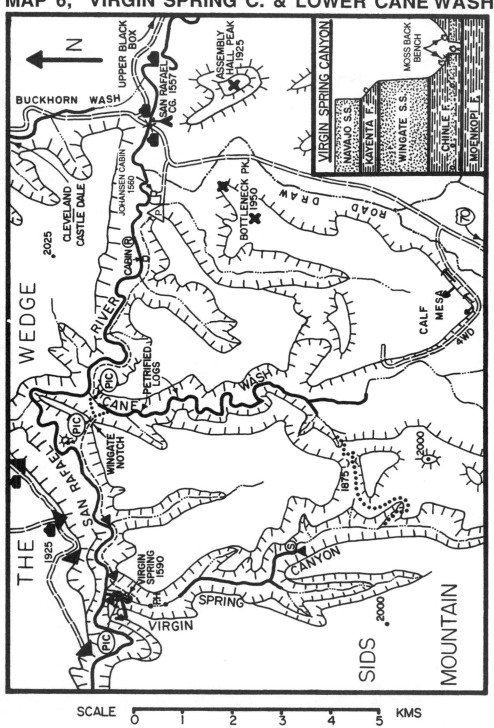

SCALE

0   1   2   3   4   5   KMS

Upper San Rafael River Gorge

Location and Access The canyon country shown on this map is found in the northern part of the San Rafael Swell. This entire mapped region is north of Interstate 70. To get to the area, you can leave I-70 at mile post and Exit 129, and drive north to the San Rafael River and campground. Or drive south out of Price on Highway 10. Between mile post 56 and 57, or between mile posts 49 and 50, turn southeast toward Cleveland and the Buckhorn Wash. Or continue south on Highway 10 to a point just north of Castle Dale and turn east from between mile posts 39 and 40. After a few kms on either road, you'll come to Buckhorn Flat and Buckhorn Well which is a 4-way junction. At the well is a large metal tank, small pump house and a watering trough. Turn right at that point and drive 10 kms down Fuller Bottom Draw on a good sandy road to the San Rafael River where you can park and/or camp.

Trail or Route Conditions This hike begins at the end of Fuller Bottom Draw and ends at the San Rafael Campground at the junction of the San Rafael River and Buckhorn Wash. In the beginning, you will be walking in a shallow valley with a meandering small stream, but soon the river enters a gorge and the walls get higher and higher. At the deepest point, the Little Grand Canyon(as some call it) is nearly 500 meters deep. Along the way you'll be crossing the stream many times but will also be walking on cow trails much of the way. The deepest part of the gorge is in Sids Mtn. Wilderness Study Area, but some ORV's continue to run up and down the canyon bottom illegally. Along the way you will pass at least 4 panels of petroglyphs or pictographs as shown on the map. Horses can be taken all along the San Rafael River.

Elevations Trailhead 1625 meters; highest part of The Wedge, 2025; San Rafael Campground, 1557 meters.

Hike Length and Time Needed From Fuller Bottom Draw to the campground is about 28-30 kms. This can be done in one day, but camping one night can be enjoyable. To do this one-way hike you'll need two cars. With just one car you'll have to walk into the gorge from either end and return.

Water Always carry water in your car and in your pack because the San Rafael River water must be boiled or treated. Virgin Spring at the bottom end of Virgin Spring Canyon has the only drinkable-as-is water along the way. Don't expect to find drinking water at the San Rafael Campground!

Maps USGS or BLM map Huntington(1:100,000), or Wilsonville SE and Red Plateau SW(1:24,000).

Main Attractions A deep rugged gorge with petroglyphs, pictographs and the Sorrel Mule Mine.

Ideal Time to Hike Spring or fall, but if the snowpack is heavy in the mountains, then the spring runoff could make the river a little deep for wading. Normally high water comes in late May or early June. In October water levels are low, plus you'll have fall colors.

Hiking Boots Wading boots or shoes.

Author's Experience Because he's always alone, the author has walked into the middle of the gorge from both ends many times, as well as having seen the canyon from The Wedge Overlook on several occasions.

A view of the San Rafael River Gorge looking east from the Wedge Overlook.

MAP 7, UPPER SAN RAFAEL RIVER GORGE

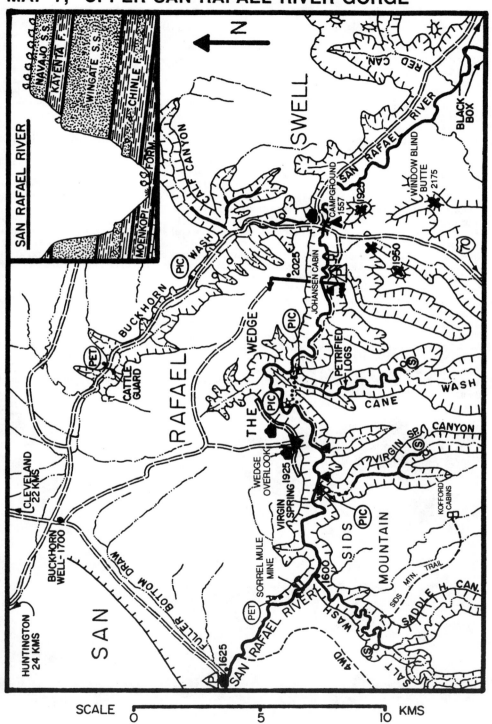

SCALE

0   5   10   KMS

83

Humbug Canyon and the Jump Trail

Location and Access Humbug Canyon and the Jump Trail are located due east of the small towns of Huntington, Cleveland and Elmo, and just southeast of the Cleveland--Lloyd Dinosaur Quarry. To get there, make your way to Highway 10, the main road linking Price and Huntington and the rest of Castle Valley. Turn east and south from between mile posts 56 and 57, or between 49 and 50 and drive in the direction of Elmo or Cleveland(see the access map to the Cleveland--Lloyd Dinosaur Quarry). From either of these towns head east and follow the signs toward the dinosaur quarry. The Utah Travel Council Map *Northeastern Utah* is a good one to have if you're unfamiliar with the access to this area. The distance from Cleveland or Elmo to the quarry is about 20 kms. Just before you arrive at the quarry turn east and drive another 10 kms to the beginning of the Jump Trail. Most of the time the road will be good for any car, but part of it has a clay base, so during wet weather, it's best to stay away for a day or two.

Trail or Route Conditions Once at the trailhead, locate a small sign on the edge of the canyon rim. This points out the beginning of the Jump Trail. The trail was apparently constructed to take cattle from Lucky Flats down to the lowlands and perhaps as far as the Price River. Today it's still used to move cattle around, but it's also often used by hikers. It's in good condition and you can use it to get into Humbug Canyon. At the bottom of the dugway the trail fades, so from there you're on your own. Walking up the canyon bottom is normally easy. Horses can be taken down the Jump Trail.

Elevations The Cleveland-Lloyd Dinosaur Quarry, 1750 meters; the trailhead, 1800 meters.

Hike Length and Time Needed The trail itself is only about half a km long, but there are several kms of walking up Humbug Canyon, or even around the base of the cliff to the east. One can hike here for an hour or two or all day. It's recommended you do this hike in conjunction with a visit to the dinosaur quarry visitor center. The two together make a fine one-day outing. The quarry is open on weekends from Easter to Memorial Day, then throughout the summer from Memorial Day to Labor Day it's open daily except it is closed on Tuesday and Wednesday. It's closed from Labor Day through Easter weekend. The hours are from 10 am until 5 pm.

Water Only at the Cleveland--Lloyd Dinosaur Quarry visitor center, so for any hiking take all the water you'll need in your car and in your day-pack.

Maps USGS or BLM map Huntington(1:100,000), or Cow Flats and Flattop Mtn.(1:24,000).

Main Attractions The dinosaur quarry and an old livestock trail into a red rock canyon.

Ideal Time to Hike Spring or fall. Sometimes you can hike during warm spells in winter, but only if the roads are dry. Summers are warm.

Hiking Boots Any dry weather boots or shoes.

Author's Experience The author first visited the dinosaur quarry, then drove out to the trailhead. He spent a couple of hours in the area walking into Humbug Canyon a short distance.

This is the top part of the Jump Trail, which gives access to Humbug Canyon.

MAP 8, HUMBUG CANYON AND THE JUMP TRAIL

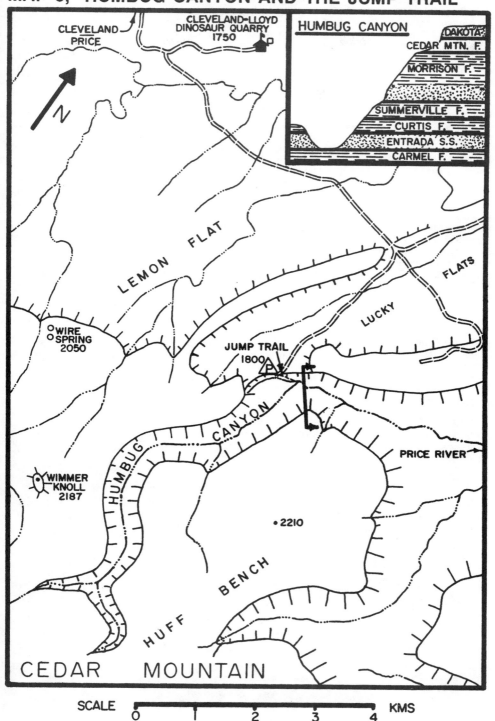

CLEVELAND PRICE

CLEVELAND-LLOYD DINOSAUR QUARRY 1750

HUMBUG CANYON

DAKOTA
CEDAR MTN. F.
MORRISON F.
SUMMERVILLE F.
CURTIS F.
ENTRADA S.S.
CARMEL F.

N

LEMON FLAT

FLATS

LUCKY

WIRE SPRING 2050

JUMP TRAIL 1800

P

HUMBUG CANYON

PRICE RIVER

WIMMER KNOLL 2187

• 2210

BENCH

HUFF

CEDAR MOUNTAIN

SCALE   0   1   2   3   4   KMS

Calf, Cow and Pine Canyons

Location and Access The drainage here, which is one main canyon and two side canyons, lies in the northern part of the San Rafael Swell just south of the Cedar Mountain Overlook and north of the San Rafael Campground. To get there, drive south out of Price on Highway 10. Between mile posts 56 and 57, or between mile posts 49 and 50, turn southeast and drive past Cleveland toward Buckhorn Wash. Or you can get there from Highway 10 just north of Castle Dale and from between mile posts 39 and 40. Turn east at that point and follow the signs to Buckhorn Wash and the San Rafael Campground. You could also leave I-70 at mile post and Exit 129 and drive north to the San Rafael Campground, then continue north into the Buckhorn Wash. You could also get there via the Green River Cutoff and from between mile posts 283 and 284 on Highway 191-6. The bottom end of Calf Canyon is about 3 kms north of the San Rafael Campground. You can drive into the canyon a short distance to a campsite or car-park. You'll need one of the USGS maps of the area to locate the right turnoff in order to reach the Big Flat car-park.

Trail or Route Conditions There's a trail-of-sorts into Calf and the walking is easy. Mostly you just walk in the dry creek bed. Above where there's a spring and campsite, you walk on cattle trails. Another short hike would be to head up Pine Canyon which is easy walking. The upper end of Calf is known as Cow Canyon. Another way to get into the head of the drainage would be from Big Flat and the car-park marked 1875 meters. From there, locate a north-south gully and walk down in from the top. The upper part is more rugged but walking is still not difficult. Horses can go up from the bottom.

Elevations Canyon mouth, about 1600 meters; Big Flat car-park, 1875 meters.

Hike Length and Time Needed From the mouth of the canyon to the car-park on Big Flat is about 8 or 9 kms. If one were to explore Pine Canyon, then walk up to the Double Caves and back to the canyon mouth it would take the average hiker most of one day. But half-day or one or two hour hikes are probably more common.

Water Always take water in your car and in your pack. There is however a small stream in the bottom of Calf and Pine Canyons, as shown by the heavy dark lines on the map. But be aware there are cattle in the canyon during some winter months. In drier years, there will be less water than is shown.

Maps USGS or BLM map Huntington(1:100,000), or Red Plateau SW, Bob Hill Knoll, Chimney Rock(1:24,000).

Main Attractions A deep canyon, easy access, big caves, and at least one good campsite.

Ideal Time to Hike Spring or fall, but some winter warm spells can be pleasant. Summers are hot.

Hiking Boots Any dry weather boots or shoes.

Author's Experience The author parked at the mouth of Calf and walked into Pine Canyon. Later he went up to the Double Cave in upper Calf Canyon and returned to his car, all in about 4 hours. On another trip he came down into Cow Canyon part way from the Big Flat car-park to check out the route.

An early spring Cub Scout campout in Calf Canyon.

MAP 9, CALF, COW AND PINE CANYONS

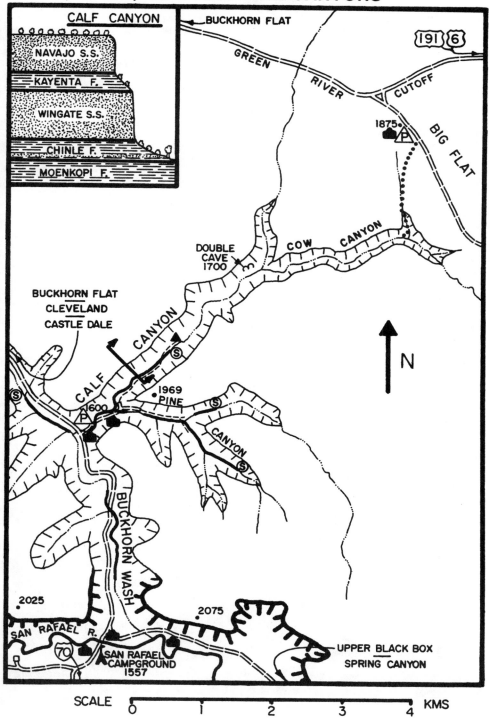

CALF CANYON

NAVAJO S.S.

KAYENTA F.

WINGATE S.S.

CHINLE F.

MOENKOPI F.

BUCKHORN FLAT

GREEN RIVER CUTOFF

191 6

BIG FLAT

1875

COW CANYON

DOUBLE CAVE 1700

BUCKHORN FLAT
CLEVELAND
CASTLE DALE

CALF CANYON

1969 PINE

CANYON

N

1600

BUCKHORN WASH

2025

2075

SAN RAFAEL R.

70

SAN RAFAEL CAMPGROUND 1557

UPPER BLACK BOX
SPRING CANYON

SCALE 0 1 2 3 4 KMS

Red Canyon and the Black Box Overlook

Location and Access The hiking area featured here is in Red Canyon and a minor drainage known as White Horse Canyon; plus the mesa top country in between and what the author is calling the Black Box Overlook. This place is found due east of the San Rafael Campground and about half way between the campground and Mexican Mountain. To get there, leave I-70 at mile post and Exit 129, and drive north to the campground. Immediately across the river to the north, turn east on the Mexican Mtn. Road. If you're coming from the north, drive south out of Price on Highway 10. Turn southeast from between mile posts 56 and 57, between 49 and 50, or between 39 and 40 and drive down into Buckhorn Wash to the San Rafael River, then turn east on the Mexican Mtn. Road. Drive along this usually-good road for about 8 kms, then turn north into the dry creek bed of Red Canyon and continue for another 2 kms to a campsite at or near the mouth of East Fork. Normally any car can make it to that point.

Trail or Route Conditions There are no trails anywhere on this map, but some ORV's have been into each canyon a short distance in the dry creek beds. The recommended hike is to walk due east up East Fork, then turn south in the upper end and exit as shown on the map. From there walk south and a little east to the rim of the mesa, called here the Black Box Overlook. So you don't have to back-track on the return trip, walk west from the overlook to the upper part of White Horse Canyon, and look for an easy route down, as shown on the map. From there make your way down-canyon to the Mexican Mtn. Road then walk back to your car. The shortest and fastest way to the overlook would be to climb up White Horse Canyon and return the same way. Horses can't make the routes described.

Elevations The car-park in Red or White Horse Canyons, 1600 meters; the Black Box Overlook, about 2000 meters.

Hike Length and Time Needed To make this loop-hike would be to walk about 20-21 kms, or about 13 or 14 kms if you had two vehicles. To just walk up White Horse to the rim and return, would be about 10 kms round-trip. Some people will need to spend an entire day doing the round-trip hike, but about half a day would get you up and down via White Horse Canyon(not doing the loop-hike).

Water Take plenty of water in your car and in your pack. You may find a small seep in the East Fork which cattle can't get to.

Maps USGS or BLM map Huntington(1:100,000), or Red Plateau SE(1:24,000).

Main Attractions Two wild and easily accessible canyons with fine views of Mexican Mtn. and the Upper Black Box from the rim.

Ideal Time to Hike Spring or fall, but sometimes warm spells in winter can be pleasant. Summers are very warm and unpleasant down low, but on top of the mesa it's much cooler.

Hiking Boots Any dry weather hiking or climbing boots.

Author's Experience The author walked up the East Fork and found the route out the upper end. He then walked to the overlook and later went down White Horse Canyon and back to his car via the Mexican Mtn. Road, all in about 5 hours.

A view from the Black Box Overlook. Lone Rock is in the upper left, Mexican Mtn. to the right.

MAP 10, RED CANYON & THE BLACK BOX OVERLOOK

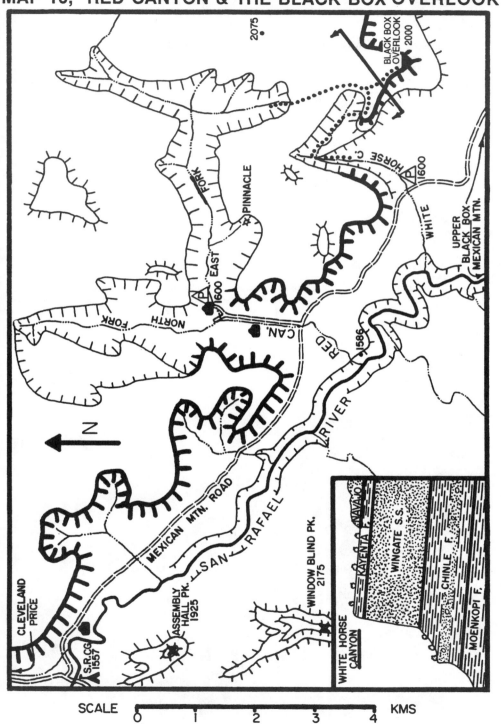

SCALE 0 1 2 3 4 KMS

Spring and Nates Canyons

Location and Access Spring and Nates Canyons, are located north of Mexican Mountain in the northeast part of the Swell. To get there, drive south out of Price on Highway 10. Between mile posts 56 and 57, or 49 and 50, or between 39 and 40, turn southeast or east, and follow the signs into Buckhorn Wash and to the San Rafael River with the campground on the south side. If you're coming to the area from I-70, turn south at mile post and Exit 129, and drive north to the San Rafael Campground. On the north side of the river, turn east on the Mexican Mtn. Road and drive about 22 or 23 kms. In the past, there has been a road running to the airstrip at Mexican Bend, but in recent years the BLM has blocked off the road because the entire area around Mexican Mtn. is part of a Wilderness Study Area. However, some ORV's continue to circumvent the road block illegally.

Trail or Route Conditions Park at the road block and walk into the mouth of Spring Canyon. There's a blocking dryfall in Nates, but if you walk up the north fork of Spring, you can exit as shown on the map(Old timers in the region claim that Butch Cassidy, Elza Lay and Joe Walker came down this route after the robbery at Castle Gate on their way to Robbers Roost. It is perhaps possible to get horses down this route, but not back up. They call it the Walker Trail. Awhile before the payroll holdup, Joe Walker was once pursued by Sheriff Tuttle of Castle Dale for stealing a horse. Walker ended up shooting Tuttle in the leg just inside the mouth of Spring Canyon). If you're out for a really good hike, route-find southwest to the rim of the mesa for a good look down on Mexican Mtn. Instead of back-tracking, you can then find a moderately easy route down into the head of Sulphur Canyon and return that way to your vehicle. Horses can only go up to just below the Walker Trail.

Elevations Mouth of Spring Canyon 1375 meters; the viewpoint, 1800 meters.

Hike Length and Time Needed If one were to park at the road block, and walk to the upper end of Spring or Nates Canyon, then return the same way, it would take most people the better part of a day for the round-trip. To made the circle route suggested above will take fit hikers all-day as well. That would be about a 26 km hike and/or climb.

Water Always carry water in your car and in your pack, but there is some running water in both upper Spring and Nates. There are also cattle there during the cooler months each year. If you take water from an up-canyon location at or near the spring source, it's likely drinkable as-is.

Maps USGS or BLM map Huntington(1:100,000), or Beckwith Peak SW(1:24,000).

Main Attractions An isolated and wild canyon complex, excellent views from the rim, and some good petroglyphs on south-facing boulders at the mouth of Spring Canyon.

Ideal Time to Hike Spring or fall, or maybe warm spells in winter. Summers are hot.

Hiking Boots Any dry weather boots or shoes. More rugged boots are needed for the loop-hike.

Author's Experience The author parked and camped near the road block, then hiked to the upper end of Nates and Spring, and returned to his car all in under 6 hours. On a second trip, he walked the circle-route in about 7 hours.

At the very mouth of Spring Canyon are several large boulders with petroglyphs.

MAP 11, SPRING AND NATES CANYONS

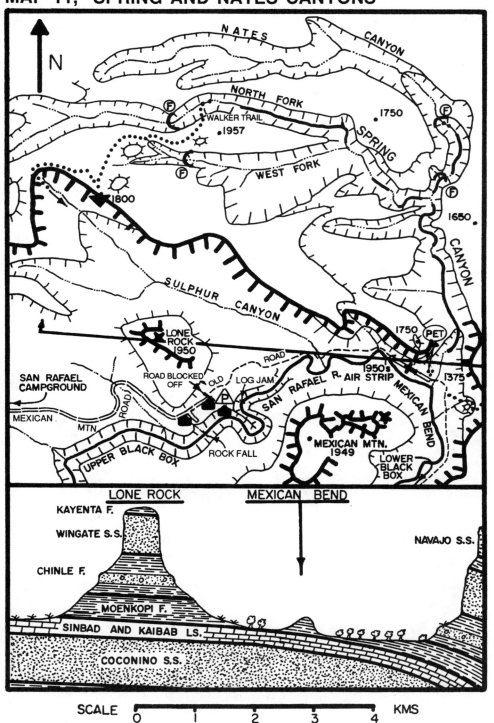

Cottonwood Draw

Location and Access Cottonwood Draw is located in the extreme northeastern part of the Swell and immediately north of Nates and Spring Canyons. It's in a part of the Swell that's almost unknown and seldom visited. To get there, drive along Highway 191-6 west of Green River and to between mile posts 295 and 296. At that point is an electrical substation. Turn west and drive about 4 kms or until you come to the power lines, then turn north. About 300 meters before you pass under the same power lines, turn to the right and proceed to follow the power lines on a 4WD type road until you reach the mouth of the canyon. If you don't have a 4WD, then continue on the most-used road to the Smith Cabin in the Tidwell Draw, which is about 11 kms from Highway 191-6. From there you can drive a short distance north but will have to park and walk the rest of the way(it's about 8 kms from Smith Cabin to the mouth of Cottonwood). You can also get to the same location by driving north from the Hanksville exit on I-70. If you take this well-used graveled road, drive until you reach the power line before turning north.

Trail or Route Conditions Cottonwood Draw is a well watered canyon with many cottonwood trees. It has high Navajo Sandstone walls and some with petroglyphs. In the bottom end of the draw are some tracks of ORV's, but otherwise there are no trails in the canyon. About 1/4 the way up there is no more ORV abuse and the way becomes more rugged. There are dryfalls and steep walls in all the side canyons, but with some scouting around, you can probably get out of the top end of the main canyon. Horses can go most of the way up Cottonwood Draw.

Elevations Smith Cabin, 1375 meters; petroglyphs, 1550; head of canyon, about 1850 meters.

Hike Length and Time Needed If you make it to the canyon mouth in a vehicle, then you can see most of the sights in about half a day; but if you park at Smith Cabin and walk the 8 kms to the mouth of the canyon, the round-trip will take all day. The canyon is about 7 or 8 kms long.

Water Always have water in your car and in your pack, but in the lower end of the canyon is a small year-round stream. Take water from its source and it should be good. There are cattle in the canyon during some of the winter months.

Maps USGS or BLM map Huntington(1:100,000), or Dry Mesa(1:24,000).

Main Attractions A crystal clear stream and many cottonwood trees and good campsites. About one km up-canyon on the north side is a huge Navajo wall with several panels of petroglyphs. Between Smith Cabin and the mouth of Cottonwood Draw is the faded remains of the old 1883 railway grade of the Denver & Rio Grande Western Railroad.

Ideal Time to Hike Spring or fall, and perhaps some warm spells in winter. Summers are hot.

Hiking Boots Any dry weather boots or shoes.

Author's Experience The author camped near the Smith Cabin and in the morning drove a ways north on the short road along the foot of the Reef. He then walked along the power line road to the mouth of Cottonwood Draw and 3/4 the way up. The round-trip hike from his car took about 5 hours.

Some of the best petroglyph panels in the Swell are found in Cottonwood Draw.

MAP 12, COTTONWOOD DRAW

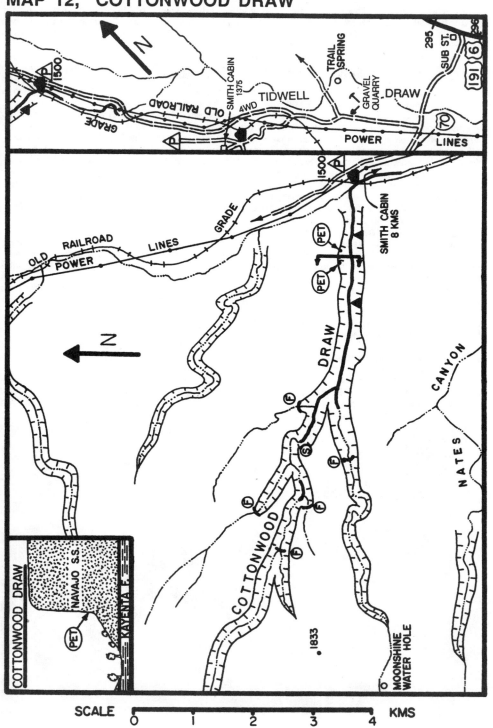

SCALE 0 1 2 3 4 KMS

The Horse Thief Trail

Location and Access The Horse Thief Trail is located directly east of Mexican Mountain. It was apparently built to take horses from the Tidwell Bottom or Draw to Mexican Bend on the San Rafael River. One story says rustlers used to take horses stolen from Rio Grande Railroad crews, across the northern part of the Reef into Mexican Bend. It's a constructed trail part way, which you can hike from Mexican Bend to Smith Cabin(or vice versa). To get there, drive east from the San Rafael Campground on the Mexican Mtn. Road to very near Mexican Bend. To reach the Smith place, drive to the electric substation between mile posts 295 and 296 on Highway 191 & 6, the main road between Price and Green River(see the map on the Cottonwood Draw for a better look at that route). Drive about one km south of the Smith place and walk west up a minor draw.

Trail or Route Conditions Park at the road block at the end of the Mexican Mtn. Road and walk east past the old air strip and to the drill hole site with the metal post sticking out of the ground. From there walk due east again and into a minor canyon on the north side of a rincon(abandoned meander). Half way around the rincon, look for one small stone cairn, then head straight up the slope to the east. The author left several trail cairns. The trail is evident as it passes through the Moss Back Member of the Chinle, then disappears. Further up-slope, you'll see more cairns to the left side. It's the steep part of the slope where the trail was actually constructed. From the pass, just go down-canyon to the east. Eventually you'll have to turn north, then east again, to reach the flats south of the Smith Cabin. It will be easier to find the trail from the Mexican Mtn. side than from the east. Horses can make it all the way along this route and trail.

Elevations Air strip, 1375 meters; the pass, 1625; Smith Cabin, 1375 meters.

Hike Length and Time Needed The time needed will depend on where you're able to park along the Mexican Mtn. Road. It should take all day to walk from the area of the Black Box to the Smith place, and back. To hike to the top of the pass at 1625 meters and return either way will be about a half-day walk.

Water Always have water in your car and in your pack, because you'll have to treat or boil water from the San Rafael River or the spring at the Smith Cabin. The water in Spring Canyon might be safe to drink higher up-stream near the spring.

Maps USGS or BLM map Huntington(1:100,000), or Beckwith Peak SW and Desert(1:24,000).

Main Attractions Great views of the Mexican Mtn. area along an old historic stock trail.

Ideal Time to Hike Spring or fall, but warm spells in winter can be pleasant. Summers are warm.

Hiking Boots Any rugged dry weather boots or shoes.

Author's Experience The author left his car at the road block and hiked up Spring Canyon a ways, then returned south and found two routes up through the Moss Back. He got to the pass and went down the other side to within about 3 kms of the old Smith place and returned. He had a dip in the river on the way back. Hike-time was about 7 1/2 hours round-trip. On a second trip, he walked from the Smith Cabin to the pass and back in 2 hours.

From the top of the Horse Thief Trail, one has fine views of Mexican Mtn. and Bend.

MAP 13, THE HORSE THIEF TRAIL

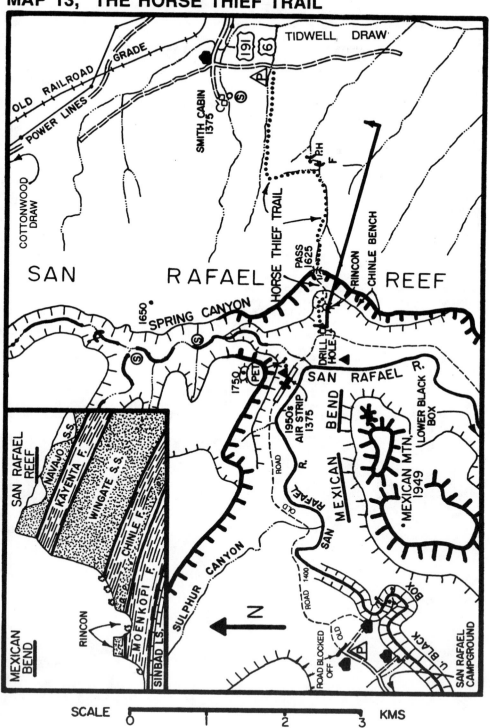

SCALE 0 1 2 3 KMS

95

Introduction to the Black Box

In the fall of 1988, the author received a letter from several hikers who had had a tough time getting through the Upper Black Box. As it turned out, sometime between late 1986 and mid-1988, there was a big storm which sent a flash flood through the canyon. That flood left a huge pile of logs in the bottom end of the Upper Black Box. As a result, this log jam has created a major delay and inconvenience at the end of a long and tiresome hike. In the spring of 1989, the author returned to the area and reconnoitered the scene and discovered several exits or entry points one can use to get around the log jam. This edition does a better job of explaining this new problem in greater detail.

Location and Access The normal way for people from northern Utah to reach the Upper Black Box, is to drive south from Price on Highway 10 in the direction of Huntington and Castle Dale. Between mile posts 56 and 57, or between mile posts 49 and 50, turn southeast and drive to Cleveland, then turn south towards Buckhorn Wash and the San Rafael Campground on the San Rafael River. Another alternate route is to drive Highway 10 to between mile posts 39 and 40, and turn east toward the same Buckhorn Wash.

From the north side of the San Rafael River bridge, turn east onto the Mexican Mtn. Road. Drive about 16 kms until you arrive at a point where you have a small butte on the left or north, and a small old stock pond with tamarisks on the right or south. You can park and camp there, or you could drive a newly created track running southeast as shown on the map. The author believes it's best to park on the road, and walk southeast to the river. If it's a really long hike you want, you could begin further upstream at what some people call the Lockhart Box. But that part of the gorge isn't as impressive as the lower end.

You can also drive I-70 to mile post and Exit 129, then turn north and drive down Cottonwood Draw to the San Rafael Campground and the bridge. From there drive east on the Mexican Mtn. Road.

To get to the Lower Black Box, either drive south from the San Rafael Campground and up Cottonwood Draw; or leave I-70 at mile post and Exit 129 and drive north. About 9 kms from Exit 129, you'll come to Sinkhole Flat, as shown on the **Area Map.** From the north end of the flat, turn east for 3 kms, then turn northeast for another 5 kms. At the Jackass Benches, turn right and drive 6 kms. At that point you can drive with a HCV to the lower end of the Lower Black Box. There are two rough spots at the beginning of this road, but it's pretty good after that.

If you continue around to the north side of the Jackass Benches, you can get on another HCV road which leads to the northern or upper end of the Lower Black Box. This road also has several rough spots, but with a shovel, most higher clearance vehicles can make it to or near Swazys or Sids Leap and the Hanson sheep bridge.

For people with nice cars, you could also park at the rest area between mile posts 140 and 141 on I-70, and walk cross-country from there across the upper part of Black Dragon Canyon to the lower end of the Lower Black Box. You could also drive to the mouth of Black Dragon Canyon from near mile post 145 on I-70, and get in from there. The author used this route when he hiked all the way through the Lower Black Box.

From the top of the log jam looking down stream at the 10-15 meter-long floating mess below(1989).

ACCESS ROADS TO THE BLACK BOX--AREA MAP

SCALE 0 _____ 5 _____ 10 KMS

97

Upper Black Box

Trail or Route Conditions When hiking the Upper Black Box.one must walk in the river up to 50% of the time(during years with high water levels). To do this hike successfully, you must have an *inner tube or life jacket* for each person, as there are many deep holes along the way. From the car-park, walk southeast for about one km. When you reach the canyon rim, you should see the river below and a shallow drainage coming in on the right. Look for stone cairns marking an old stock trail down into the Box. About 3/4 the way through, you'll come to a rockfall which has dammed the river. At that point you'll need a *short rope* to get yourself, cameras, packs, etc., over the short drop-off in a dry condition. If you have nothing to damage in the water, then you could jump or slide down the 3 meters, but there may be rocks under the murky water! You could also swim through a narrow opening on the right side avoiding a jump. If you have to, you could exit at that point by climbing a steep ravine up the north wall, but that's for more experienced climbers or hikers. Down-stream from the rockfall there are 3 other entry/exit places and a large log jam as shown on the small insert map. The 2nd exit is easy, but it would put you on the south side of the canyon. The 3rd exit is also easy and this is the recommended way out if the log jam is too difficult. It begins where there's a second and smaller rockfall in the river. Just beyond the 3rd exit, is another easy way out, but on the south side of the gorge. About 300 meters below the 4th exit, is a narrowing and a large log jam. You can easily climb up on top of it, but there are 10-15 meters of floating logs on the other side you'll have to swim through or crawl over. This is not so difficult unless you're trying to keep a camera dry. Not far below the log jam you'll walk out the bottom end of the Box and can then walk back to your car. Two cars would eliminate a long road-walk. Horses have no chance in any part of the Black Box.

Elevations Car-park, 1650 meters; bottom of the Upper Black Box, 1400 meters.

Hike Length and Time Needed From the entry car-park to the bottom of the Box is about 14 kms. If you have to walk all the way back to your car it's about 28 kms round-trip, a very long all-day hike. You can shorten it by leaving at the 3rd exit, or having two cars.

Water Carry water in your car and in your pack. River water must be treated before drinking.

Maps USGS or BLM maps Huntington and San Rafael Desert(1:100,000), or Red Plateau SE & Beckwith Peak SW(1:24,000) and The Wickiup(1:62,500).

Main Attractions A steep-sided, deep and dark canyon, where you'll need an inner tube and short rope to get all the way through. For experienced and tough hikers only.

Ideal Time to Hike Warm or hot weather; from June through September.

Hiking Boots Wading boots or shoes.

Author's Experience The author walked, waded and swam down to the rockfall and had to exit(no rope and alone), then made it back to his car in 7 hours. For this 2nd Ed. he entered the canyon at the rockfall and climbed up and out at all 3 entry/exits as shown. He was worried about getting his camera wet on the down-stream side of the log jam, so he left the canyon at the 2nd exit and returned to his car which was parked above the rockfall.

You'll need an inner tube to get through the Upper Black Box safely and dry.

MAP 14, UPPER BLACK BOX

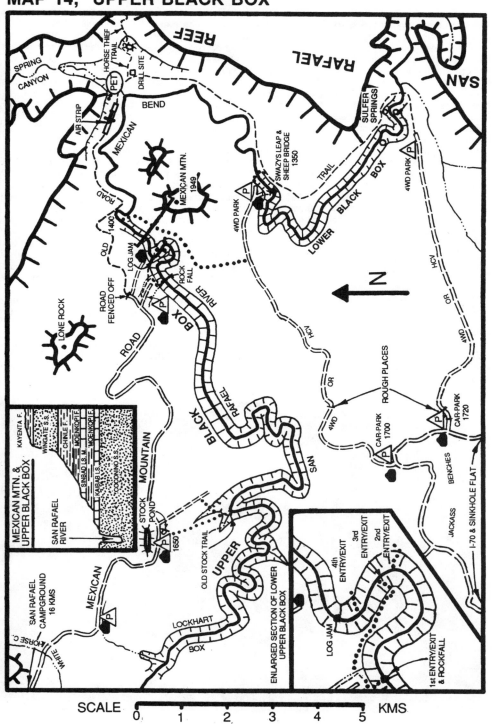

SPRING CANYON

HORSE THIEF TRAIL

PET

DRILL SITE

REEF

SAN RAFAEL REEF

AIR STRIP

MEXICAN BEND

MEXICAN MTN. 1949

SULFER SPRINGS

SWAZYS LEAP & SHEEP BRIDGE 1350

TRAIL

4WD PARK

LOWER BLACK BOX

4WD PARK

OLD 1400 ROAD

LOG JAM

ROCK FALL

ROAD FENCED OFF

LONE ROCK

RIVER

BOX

N

ROAD

RAFAEL

BLACK MOUNTAIN

SAN

HCV OR 4WD

HCV OR 4WD

ROUGH PLACES

CAR-PARK 1700

CAR-PARK 1720

BENCHES

JACKASS

I-70 & SINKHOLE FLAT

MEXICAN MTN. & UPPER BLACK BOX

KAYENTA F.
WINGATE S.S.
CHINLE F.
MOENKOPI F.
MOENKOPI F.
SINBAD LS. M.
KAIBAB LS. M.
COCONINO S.S.

SAN RAFAEL RIVER

STOCK POND

P 1650

OLD STOCK TRAIL

UPPER

SAN RAFAEL CAMPGROUND 16 KMS

WHITE HORSE C.

MEXICAN

P

LOCKHART

BOX

ENLARGED SECTION OF LOWER UPPER BLACK BOX

4th ENTRY/EXIT

3rd ENTRY/EXIT

2nd ENTRY/EXIT

LOG JAM

1st ENTRY/EXIT & ROCKFALL

SCALE 0 1 2 3 4 5 KMS

Lower Black Box & Swazys or Sids Leap

Trail or Route Conditions In order to successfully get through the Lower Black Box you will need an *inner tube or life jacket,* because you'll pass through many deep swimming holes(during years with abundant precipitation). Drive, ride a mountain bike, or walk to the end of the road at or near Swazys Leap, then walk to the upper end of the narrows and get down into the river just as it begins to dive into the Lower Black Box. Soon you will walk and/or float under the old Hanson sheep bridge at the narrowest place in the gorge called Swazys or Sid's Leap. It's about 3 meters wide at the top and 17 meters above the river. You can walk across this bridge, but it's pretty rickety these days. Read more on the history of this bridge on page 55. As you head on down the canyon, you will find several minor rockfalls and places with deep channels. You must swim or float through these places. This canyon is similar to the Upper Black Box, only it's a bit shorter and without major obstacles. It's also a bit more narrow. When you reach the bottom end, turn left and walk back to the sheep bridge along an old stock trail on the east side of the Box. If you walk or drive to the lower end of the Box, walk the trail to the upper end of the Box first, then walk down-canyon in the water. Don't attempt to walk up-stream against the current. It's best to have at least one experienced hiker along on this trip, in case the river channel changes. For emergency purposes, also take along a *short rope.* Stay out of this gorge if the weather looks bad. Horses can't go through this canyon.

Elevations Swazys or Sids Leap, 1350 meters; the bottom end of the Lower Black Box, about 1300; the two Jackass Bench car-parks, about 1700 meters.

Hike Length and Time Needed The distance through the Box is about 8 kms. If you must leave your car at one of the Jackass Bench car-parks and make the round-trip hike from there, it'll be 28-30 kms--a very long day. This is about the same distance as if you were to start at the rest stop on I-70 or at the mouth of Black Dragon Canyon, the two other alternative routes in. It's best to take a shovel and try and drive to Swazys Leap or to the lower end of the Box. There are two or three bad spots along each road. This would be a great place to try out a mountain bike, if you have a normal car. Drive with care and any car should have no trouble getting to and around the Jackass Benches.

Water Always carry water in your car and in your pack, but there are several minor freshwater seeps within the Box. The springs at the lower end are sulfur tainted and undrinkable. The river water would have to be treated before drinking.

Maps USGS or BLM map San Rafael Desert(1:100,000), or Tidwell Bottoms(1:62,500).

Main Attractions A deep, dark canyon with an interesting old historic sheep bridge.

Ideal Time to Hike In warm or hot weather(June through September).

Hiking Boots Wading type boots or shoes.

Author's Experience The author has been there several times, but when he did the complete Lower Black Box hike, he did it from Black Dragon Canyon with a total walk-time of 9 1/2 hours.

An unusual look at Swazys Leap, from the river, 17 meters below.

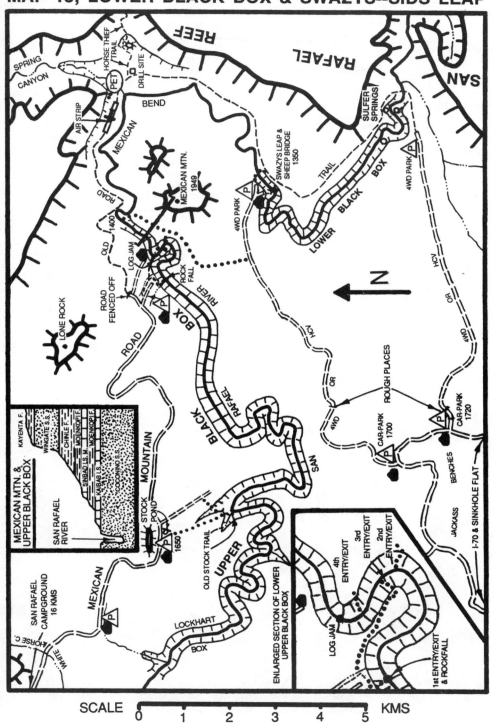

SCALE 0 1 2 3 4 5 KMS

Black Dragon C. and the Lower San Rafael River Gorge

Location and Access Black Dragon Canyon and the lower part of the San Rafael River where it cuts through the eastern Reef, are both located in the northeastern part of the San Rafael Swell just north of I-70. To get there, drive along I-70 on the east side of the San Rafael Reef to between mile posts 144 and 145. Locate a minor dirt road on the north side of the freeway, then go through a gate(close it behind you). Drive about 2 kms north, then turn left or west, and drive another km in the bottom of a dry creek bed into the mouth of Black Dragon Canyon. Low clearance cars will have to go slow, but most can make it to a large overhang which makes a fine campsite.

Trail or Route Conditions This hike involves walking up Black Dragon, turning north, walking over a pass and down along the San Rafael River as it cuts through the Reef, then back to one's car in Black Dragon. In the bottom end of Black Dragon, you'll be walking along an old mining exploration track. Further up and as the canyon widens, the road splits. Turn right and walk until you're around the big Wingate cliffs, then route-find over a pass and walk northeast down to the lower end of the Lower Black Box. Once you're at the river, turn east and head down-stream. The author tried walking along the sides, but the tamarisks are thick in places, so he got out in the water and waded much of the way through the Reef. The river water is ankle to knee deep and you shouldn't need an inner tube, although a *walking stick* will be handy to probe for deep holes in the murky water. As the river emerges from the canyon walls on the east side of the Reef, one must leave the stream channel and head south. Look for an old vehicle track to take you back to the mouth of Black Dragon. Horses can go through either canyon, but would have a hard time getting over the pass marked 1650 meters.

Elevations Mouth of Black Dragon Canyon, 1325 meters; high point on the hike, 1650 meters.

Hike Length and Time Needed The loop-hike up Black Dragon and down the San Rafael River is about 24 kms, or an all-day hike for strong hikers. For some this can be very long and tiresome, but there's plenty to see.

Water Always carry water in your car and in your pack. The springs in the lower end of the Lower Black Box are sulfur tainted and undrinkable.

Maps USGS or BLM map San Rafael Desert(1:100,000), or Tidwell Bottoms(1:62,500).

Main Attractions Deep canyons cut in the up-turned beds of sandstone, and about 200 meters up-canyon from the campsite in Black Dragon is a good panel of pictographs.

Ideal Time to Hike Because you'll be in water much of the time, it's likely best to do this hike in warm weather after the spring runoff--June through September. If you're just out to hike up Black Dragon, then spring or fall would be best.

Hiking Boots Wading boots or shoes for the river part of the hike.

Author's Experience The author has camped at the Black Dragon site several times. On one occasion, he walked up the canyon and went over the pass as suggested, then down the river and back to his car in about 6 1/2 hours.

From the bluffs at the mouth of Black Dragon Canyon, looking west and up canyon.

MAP 16, BLACK DRAGON CANYON AND THE LOWER SAN RAFAEL RIVER GORGE

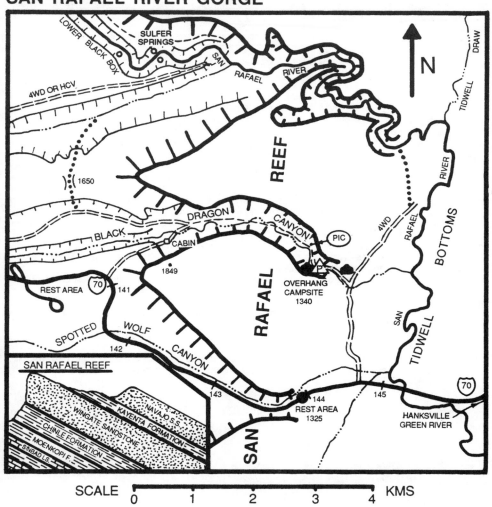

LOWER BLACK BOX

SULFER SPRINGS

SAN RAFAEL RIVER

4WD OR HCV

N

TIDWELL DRAW

REEF

1650

DRAGON CANYON

BLACK

CABIN

PIC

4WD

SAN RAFAEL RIVER

BOTTOMS

1849

RAFAEL

OVERHANG CAMPSITE 1340

REST AREA (70) 141

SPOTTED

WOLF CANYON

142

143

SAN

144 REST AREA 1325

145

SAN TIDWELL

(70)

HANKSVILLE GREEN RIVER

SAN RAFAEL REEF

NAVAJO S.S.
KAYENTA FORMATION
WINGATE SANDSTONE
CHINLE FORMATION
MOENKOPI F.
SINBAD LS.

SCALE

0   1   2   3   4   KMS

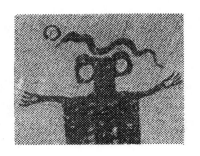

San Rafael Reef--North

Location and Access The San Rafael Reef runs completely around the San Rafael Swell where the Wingate and Navajo Sandstone Formations are exposed, but the one place where it really becomes prominent is on the eastern side of the Swell. From about I-70 south to the mouth of Straight Wash(Eardley Canyon) the reef stands virtually on end--that is, the rocks which were at one time lying in a horizontal position, are now very near vertical. Walking along this Reef is one of the more unique hikes in the San Rafael. For those with low clearance cars, the best place to park and start hiking is at or near the rest area on I-70 located at the eastern base of the Reef and at mile post 144. If you'd like to start near the center of the Reef, drive along Highway 24(the road running south to Hanksville) to between mile posts 153 and 154, and turn west, then north, and finally west again. This public access road runs to the mouth of both Three Fingers and Second Canyon(the author's name). It also runs onto I-70 and it's in pretty good condition most of the time. You can also come in from Hatts Ranch, but you should let those people know you're in there or they might lock the gate on you(the Hatts have a small parcel of private land right where their gate is).

Trail or Route Conditions It's recommended you begin at I-70. Park at the restrooms, then hike west up the freeway until you can walk up a short side canyon to the southwest. From there you're on your own as you walk south in the Chinle-Moenkopi Valley(author's name). Between Spotted Wolf(where the freeway now runs) and Little Spotted Wolf Canyons, you must look for a route up and over some ledges, but that's not difficult. South of Little Spotted Wolf, the route becomes easy as you walk up and down within this little hidden valley west of the Reef all the way to Three Fingers Canyon. You can pass through the Reef at several of the other canyons enroute to Three Fingers, so go as far as your own fitness and time will allow. The return trip north is along the eastern base of the Reef. This would be a rugged area for riders on horseback.

Elevations Rest area, 1340 meters; high point in the Chinle-Moenkopi Valley, 1600 meters.

Hike Length and Time Needed The loop-hike suggested above(between I-70 and Three Fingers) is about 23 kms long, and will take most hikers all day.

Water Always carry water in your car and in your pack, but you can usually find seep or pothole water in the canyons, especially where the Navajo Sandstone is exposed.

Maps USGS or BLM map San Rafael Desert(1:100,000), or Tidwell Bottoms(1:62,500).

Main Attractions Petroglyphs at the mouth of Three Fingers Canyon, several old mines in the Chinle Formation, potholes, great geology and easy access.

Ideal Time to Hike Spring or fall, but some winter warm spells can be nice. Summers are hot.

Hiking Boots Any dry weather boots or shoes.

Author's Experience The author walked the same route as described above from I-70, and did some exploration of each canyon. To Three Fingers Canyon and back took him 7 1/2 hours.

From near I-70, a look at the San Rafael Reef, a most unusual geologic feature.

MAP 17, SAN RAFAEL REEF--NORTH

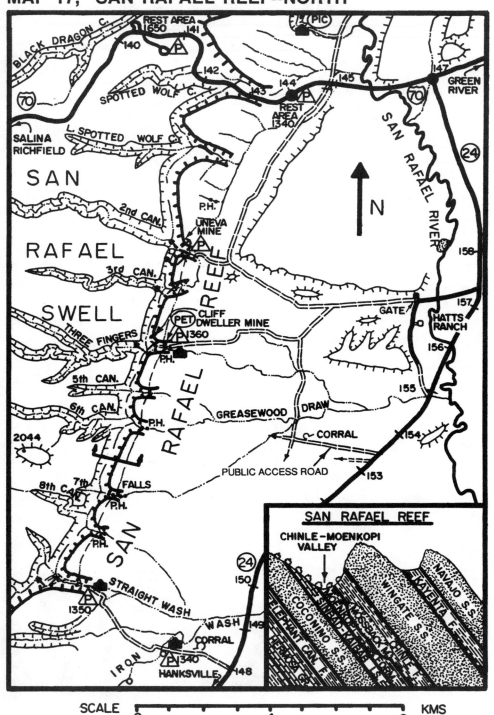

SCALE

0   4   8   KMS

San Rafael Reef--South

Location and Access The previous map covered the northern half of this mapped area; this page covers the southern half, that part of the San Rafael Reef between Three Fingers Canyon and Straight Wash(Eardley Canyon). This section has the same vertical standing cliffs formed mostly by the Wingate and Navajo Sandstone Formations. There are two basic access routes to choose from. First, drive along Highway 24, the road connecting Hanksville and I-70. Between miles posts 153 and 154, drive west to just beyond the corral, then turn north, and finally to the west again, and head for the mouth of Three Fingers Canyon. The last km or so is rough, but with a shovel, you can prepare the road across small gullies so that cars with higher clearance can be taken across. The other option is to turn west right at mile post 148. This is a good well-used road to the bottom of Iron Wash. At that point, decide whether or not you can take your vehicle across without getting bogged down in the sand. If you can get across the wet sandy bottom, then you should have no trouble getting to the mouth of Straight Wash as it cuts through the Reef.

Trail or Route Conditions If you begin at the mouth of Three Fingers Canyon, walk west into the canyon, while observing the petroglyph panel at the mouth. Once well into the canyon you'll come to a valley behind the Reef. The author calls this the Chinle-Moenkopi Valley, because these two formations have formed this depression. From there, head south in an up-and-down fashion along this valley. At one or more convenient places, climb up to the top of the Wingate cliffs for outstanding birds-eye views of the Reef. At Straight Wash, head down-canyon then turn north and walk along the base of the Reef back to your car. If you have the time, you might explorer one or more of the many little canyons cutting through the Reef. Parts of this area would be difficult for horses.

Elevations Mouth of Three Fingers Canyon, about 1360 meters; the highest point along the Chinle-Moenkopi Valley, about 1600 meters.

Hike Length and Time Needed Round-trip for the above suggested hike is about 20 kms. Most people can do this in one full day of walking.

Water Always carry plenty of water in your car and in your pack, but you will likely find some pothole water in the many mini-canyons, especially as they cut through the Navajo Sandstone.

Maps USGS or BLM map San Rafael Desert(1:100,000), or Tidwell Bottoms(1:62,500).

Main Attractions Interesting geology, large potholes and petroglyphs at the mouth of Three Fingers Canyon. You might also see some desert big horn sheep in the area of Straight Wash.

Ideal Time to Hike Spring or fall, and maybe some warms spells in winter. Summers are hot.

Hiking Boots Any dry weather boots or shoes.

Author's Experience The author did this round-trip hike from Three Fingers Canyon, up through the Chinle-Moenkopi Valley, south to Straight Wash, then back along the eastern face of the Reef to his car in about 8 hours. For some this could be a very long day.

From a high point atop the San Rafael Reef looking north.

MAP 18, SAN RAFAEL REEF--SOUTH

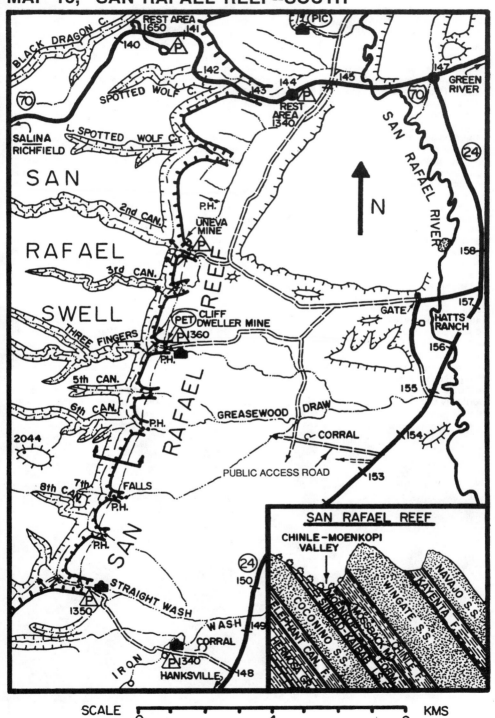

SCALE   0   4   8   KMS

Eardley Canyon and Straight Wash

Location and Access This canyon is located in the eastern part of the San Rafael Swell and between Interstate 70 and Highway 24. One can get to the upper parts of the canyon by exiting I-70 at mile post and Exit 129. Head west first, then south to Charley Holes; or exit 1-70 near mile post 133, and drive southeast to the landing strip between Red and Hyde Draws called Cliff Dweller Flat. To reach the bottom end of Eardley, drive south from I-70 on Highway 24 about 20 kms to mile post 148, then turn west on a good dirt road. Any vehicle can make it to Iron Wash, but first look over the wash and perhaps with the aid of a shovel, get across. The road beyond is good, but the sandy bottom of Iron Wash may stop some vehicles.

Trail or Route Conditions From the car-park at the mouth of Straight Wash, there's the faded remains of an old mining exploration road running into the canyon, but as one gets into Eardley, there is no trail(Eardley Canyon actually begins just west of the Reef). The bottom of this canyon is totally untouched and a real gem. Right at the bottom of Eardley are some large potholes and falls, which cannot be passed. You must therefore walk up the slope on either side of the bottom narrows, until a descent route can be found. The author entered, then exited, just below and just above the geology cross section arrow. Above the rincon, there are no route problems and there's a number of exit possibilities. Perhaps the best part of Eardley lies the upper end which can be entered from the Red Draw area. Look for one of several routes down into the Coconino Narrows. This part has some potholes in side canyons, but is otherwise a dry hike. One of the best parts of this hike is walking through the Reef along Straight Wash, then into the almost hidden mouth of Eardley. The other good part is the narrow section below Red Draw. Horses can't be taken into either end of Eardley Canyon

Elevations Elevations range from 1350 meters at Straight Wash, to 1980 in the upper canyon.

Hike Length and Time Needed To walk the entire length Eardley would likely take two days, unless you have 2 cars. One-day hikes are best however, from either end of the canyon, and into the best parts.

Water Always carry water in your car and in your pack. However there is normally some water in potholes throughout the canyon.

Maps USGS or BLM map San Rafael Desert(1:100,000), or Tidwell Bottoms(1:62,500).

Main Attractions The San Rafael Reef, huge potholes and narrows in the upper and lower end of the canyon, and solitude in a canyon that can't be seen from the highway. You may also see wild burros in the Cliff Dweller Flat area or big horn sheep along the Reef.

Ideal Time to Hike Spring or fall. Summers are very warm down low, but cooler in the upper canyon. Sometimes you may be able to hike in the lower end of the canyon during winter warm spells.

Hiking Boots Any dry weather boots or shoes.

Author's Experience The author camped on Iron Wash, then walked into Straight Wash and eventually into Eardley on the north side, exiting just south of the rincon. The round-trip took 8 hours. He also spent 5 hours in the upper canyon and Red Draw on another hike.

The upper part of Eardley Canyon (Straight Wash) has some fine narrows.

MAP 19, EARDLEY CANYON AND STRAIGHT WASH

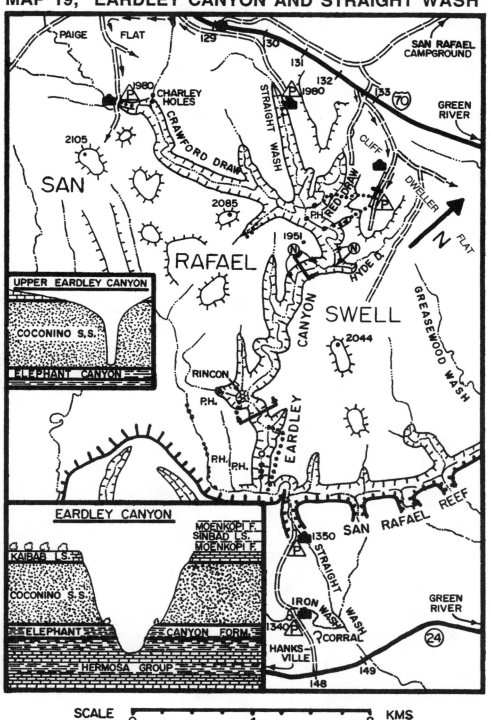

SCALE

0   4   8   KMS

North Fork of Iron Wash

Location and Access On the USGS maps this canyon has no name, but the author is calling it the North Fork of Iron Wash. It's located along the eastern San Rafael Reef about half way between I-70 and Temple Mtn. To get there, drive along Highway 24, which runs between Hanksville and I-70. Right at mile post 148, turn west onto a good dirt road. This runs due west past a corral, then drops down into the bottom of Iron Wash, which seems to have a year-round stream of water along with some shade trees. Park and camp along the creek bed. This is the same access route you would use to reach the mouth of Straight Wash and Eardley Canyon.

Trail or Route Conditions From the car-park walk up the bottom of Iron Wash which is just a shallow valley at that point. It will likely have flowing water, but you can walk around it without getting your feet wet. About a km above the car-park turn right into the North Fork. Immediately look for a route out of this mini box canyon, as about 400 meters upstream you'll come to a dryfall you cannot pass. Once you skirt this first obstacle, you again walk in the sandy and rocky creek bed. Further along, the canyon deepens with Navajo bluffs soaring above. This part is very similar to the canyons of the Escalante River further to the south. At the next major junction, turn left and walk southwest. After about 3 kms the canyon turns abruptly west. It's here you'll come to some narrows which are about half a km long. At the upper end of the narrows is a 15 meter-high dryfall you cannot pass. You'll have to search for a route to the upper part of this canyon. Besides the canyon with the narrows, there's another major fork just to the north. It isn't so interesting, but you may be able to reach the top for some fine views out into the Swell and the lower part of Eardley Canyon. Horses can traverse most of this canyon.

Elevations Car-park, 1340 meters; the high point on the Reef, 1947 meters.

Hike Length and Time Needed The length of this hike from the car-park to the big dryfalls and narrows is only 7 or 8 kms. It can be hiked in about half a day round-trip, but some may want a full day to do some exploring. There are good campsites with water and shade trees in the North Fork for those who may want to stay overnight.

Water Always carry water in your car and in your pack. But there is a crystal clear stream of water in the canyon and it should be good to drink if you take if from the spring source. There are cattle in the drainage during some of the winter months each year.

Maps USGS or BLM map San Rafael Desert(1:100,000), or Tidwell Bottoms(1:62,500).

Main Attractions Easy access, pretty good water, and some short but interesting narrows.

Ideal Time to Hike Spring or fall, but hiking in some winter warm spells is possible. Summers are very warm.

Hiking Boots Any dry weather boots or shoes.

Author's Experience The author camped at the car-park, then with an early morning start he hiked up to the narrows. He then backtracked and hiked into the middle canyon shown on the map. It took about half a day for this round-trip hike.

Another fine narrows section, this one is in the North Fork of Iron Wash.

MAP 20, NORTH FORK OF IRON WASH

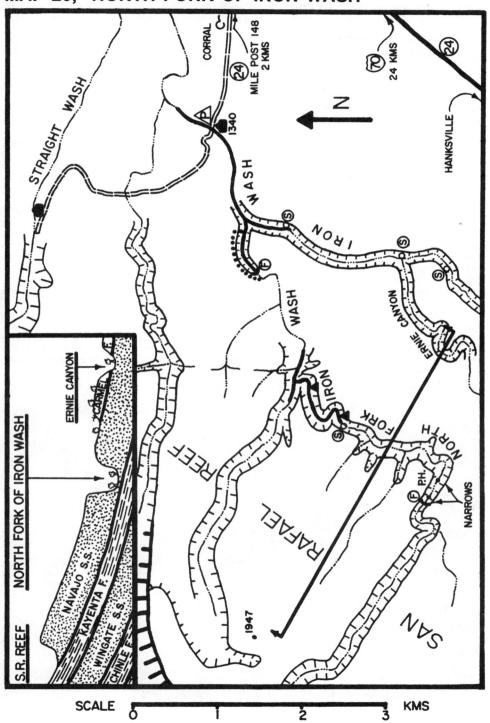

Iron Wash and Ernie Canyon

Location and Access Iron Wash and Ernie Canyon are found on the eastern side of the San Rafael Swell and along the eastern Reef. They are about half way between Interstate Highway 70 and Goblin Valley, which is north of Hanksville. The head of each of these drainages is near the center of the Swell, but the canyons aren't impressive until they dive through the Reef. To get there drive along Highway 24, the main road linking I-70 to Hanksville. Look for a moderately good road leading west from between mile posts 142 and 143. Drive west down into and out of lower Iron Wash, past Lost Spring, then proceed to the southwest 3 or 4 kms. Just before you reach Iron Wash for the second time, turn northwest a short distance until you reach a stock pond. You can camp and/or park at the pond. A road not used by the author and not on any of the USGS maps, is the one running from near Lost Spring to the mouth of Ernie Canyon. The route of the road as shown on the map is unconfirmed. The road running to the stock pond at the mouth of Iron Wash is good for any car. The road running to the mouth of Ernie appeared to be less traveled.

Trail or Route Conditions From the mouth of Iron Wash simply walk up the dry creek bed in the canyon bottom. At the first major junction turn right into Lone Man Draw. Further up canyon and after you pass the Wingate Cliffs on your right, look for an easy route over the pass and down into Ernie Canyon. When you reach the mouth of Ernie, turn right again and walk either cross-country along the base of the Reef, or along the road back to your car. Horses could be taken into the lower parts of each canyon.

Elevations Each canyon mouth, about 1500 meters; the pass between the two canyons about 1730.

Hike Length and Time Needed To do the full loop-hike as suggested is to walk about 22-23 kms. This means it will take all day for the average person.

Water Always carry water in your car and in your pack, but there are some minor seeps in both canyons. There are also cattle around from October through June each year. Take water from the source at Lost Spring and it should be drinkable as-is.

Maps USGS or BLM map San Rafael Desert(1:100,000), or Temple Mtn.(1:62,500).

Main Attractions Deep and seldom visited canyons with some water in places. The author didn't see any petroglyphs along the way but surely there are some around somewhere.

Ideal Time to Hike Spring or fall, but some winter warm spells may be pleasant. Summers are hot.

Hiking Boots Any dry weather boots or shoes.

Author's Experience The author camped near the stock pond at the mouth of Iron Wash. Next morning he walked up Iron and down Ernie, then cross-country back to his car; all in about 5 1/2 hours. This was about 8 days after a big storm, and there were a number of small seeps along the way. Most of the time there will be less water in the canyons than is shown on the map.

A view of the mouth of Ernie Canyon (looking west).

MAP 21, IRON WASH AND ERNIE CANYON

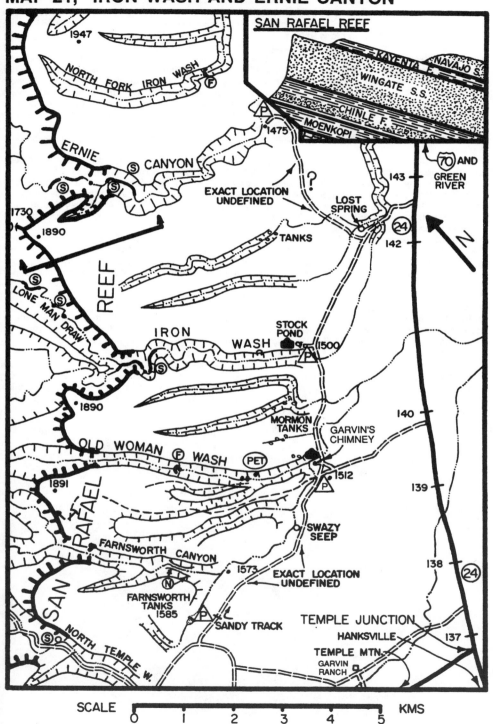

SAN RAFAEL REEF

KAYENTA
NAVAJO S.
WINGATE S.S.
CHINLE F.
MOENKOPI

1947

NORTH FORK IRON WASH

F

ERNIE

CANYON

EXACT LOCATION
UNDEFINED

?

1475

LOST
SPRING

143

GREEN
RIVER

70 AND

24

142

N

1730

1890

REEF

TANKS

LONE MAN DRAW

IRON

WASH

STOCK
POND

1500

140

1890

MORMON
TANKS

GARVIN'S
CHIMNEY

OLD WOMAN

F

WASH

PET

1512

139

1891

SAN RAFAEL

FARNSWORTH CANYON

SWAZY
SEEP

EXACT LOCATION
UNDEFINED

138

24

1573

N

FARNSWORTH
TANKS
1585

SANDY TRACK

TEMPLE JUNCTION

HANKSVILLE

137

NORTH TEMPLE W.

TEMPLE MTN.

GARVIN
RANCH

SCALE
0   1   2   3   4   5

KMS

Old Woman Wash and Farnsworth(Doorway) Canyon

Location and Access Farnsworth(sometimes called Doorway) Canyon and Old Woman Wash are found about half way between I-70 and Hanksville and just northeast of Temple Mountain. Old Woman Wash gets its name from an old woman named Nancy Virginia McCrery Harris who ran a freighting station near the mouth of the canyon sometime after about 1900. Apparently nothing remains of her old place. There is however an old chimney standing at the mouth of the canyon. According to one Hanksville resident it was built by a man named Garvin as assessment work to keep his claims alive. He's the same man who first built the ranch(now in ruins) west of Temple Junction. To get to the mouth of Old Woman, drive along Highway 24 to a point just south of mile post 140. Turn west and stop at the 4-way junction near the mouth of the canyon. Cars mus* be parked near there. The easiest way to reach Farnsworth is to drive along the Temple Mtn. Road to just west of the Goblin Valley turnoff, then turn north and park somewhere close to Farnsworth Tanks(see the map on Temple Mtn. Loop Hike). Unless you have a 4WD vehicle, you'd better park near the tanks, as the road beyond has deep sand in places.

Trail or Route Conditions If you go straight up Old Woman Wash you will pass some potholes and trees near where an old mining road on the left heads upon the Reef to the west. Stay in the canyon bottom and you'll eventually be confronted by a dryfall. If you take the track, it will lead to the top of the Reef and the old copper mine; as does another track which begins at the 4-way junction. Farnsworth Canyon has some short but pretty good narrows. You can walk all the way through this gorge, then climb over a pass to the south and return down North Temple Wash. Horses can only go a short distance up either canyon.

Elevations The mouth of each canyon about 1500 meters, the copper mine about 1790 meters.

Hike Length and Time Needed To walk up Old Woman to the dryfall and return would be an easy half-day hike. Another trip would be to walk up Farnsworth and come down North Temple Wash. This will take about half a day to complete. A third hike would be to the top of the Reef and the copper mine which will take a little over half a day.

Water Always carry water in your car and in your pack.

Maps USGS or BLM map San Rafael Desert(1:100,000), or Temple Mtn.(1:62,500).

Main Attractions Little known canyons with some petroglyphs near the mouth of Old Woman, a route to the top of the Reef, and the remains of Garvin's Chimney which dates from just after 1900.

Ideal Time to Hike Spring or fall, or perhaps in winter warm spells. Summers are hot.

Hiking Boots Any dry weather boots or shoes.

Author's Experience On one trip the author went up the bottom of Old Woman Wash and was stopped by the falls. On another trip, he parked near Garvin's Chimney and walked the old mining track upon the Reef to the old copper mine. This took about 4 1/2 hours round-trip. On a third occasion he parked at Farnsworth Tanks and walked up the canyon, then passed over to North Temple Wash and returned to his car in about 2 1/2 hours.

This is Garvin's Chimney at the mouth of Old Woman Wash. Apparently it was built by the same man who built the Garvin Ranch to the south.

MAP 22, OLD WOMAN WASH AND FARNSWORTH (DOORWAY) CANYON

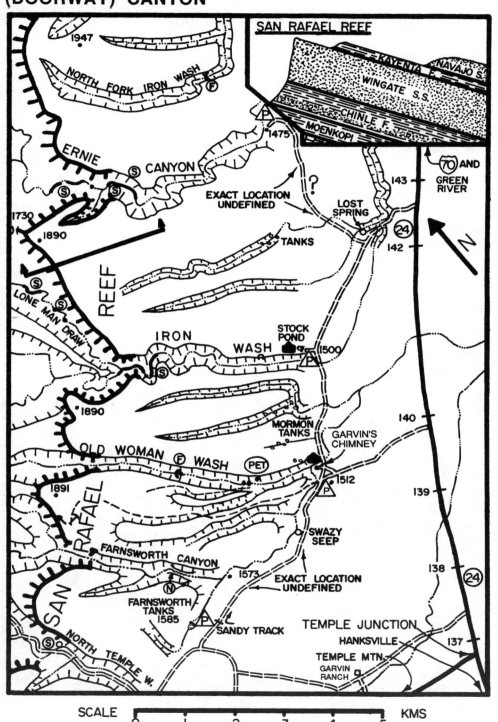

SAN RAFAEL REEF

KAYENTA F.
NAVAJO S.S.
WINGATE S.S.
CHINLE F.
MOENKOPI

1947

NORTH FORK IRON WASH

ERNIE CANYON

1475

EXACT LOCATION UNDEFINED

?

LOST SPRING

143 — GREEN RIVER

70 AND

24

142 —

1730
1890

REEF

TANKS

STOCK POND

IRON WASH

1500

LONE MAN DRAW

1890

OLD WOMAN WASH

140

MORMON TANKS

GARVIN'S CHIMNEY

PET

F

1512

139 —

1891

SAN RAFAEL

FARNSWORTH CANYON

SWAZY SEEP

138 —

24

1573

EXACT LOCATION UNDEFINED

N

FARNSWORTH TANKS
1585

SANDY TRACK

TEMPLE JUNCTION

HANKSVILLE

NORTH TEMPLE W.

TEMPLE MTN.

137 —

GARVIN RANCH

SCALE   0   1   2   3   4   5   KMS

Temple Mountain Loop-Hike

Location and Access Temple Mountain is located on the eastern side of the San Rafael Swell and just west of the main eastern Reef. It's about half way between I-70 in the north and Hanksville in the south. It's also not far north of Goblin Valley State Park. To get there, drive along Highway 24 to Temple Junction, which is between mile posts 136 and 137. Turn west onto a paved road. This leads to where Temple Mtn. mining camp or town site used to be located, and is paved nearly all the way. The car-park marked 1658 meters is at or near the main camp. At one time this place was called Magliaccio's, because a man by that name had so many claims in the area. This makes a good base if you'd like to walk around the mountain visiting the many mines and old camps. You can also drive up North Temple Wash to another encampment found at the car-park marked 1707, but that road may not be in the best condition for cars. The mines on Temple Mtn. are dug into the Temple Mountain Member of the Chinle Formation. It was uranium they were after and it was a rich mining area while it lasted. Temple Mtn. was first mined soon after 1900 and it lasted until after World War I. It began to boom again in the late 1940's with miners living in trailers. It died for the last time in about 1962.

Trail or Route Conditions There are many old and mostly abandoned mining roads in the area of Temple Mtn. Two of these roads make a complete loop around the mountain, one of which is higher up. The highest track isn't used by vehicles any more but it can be used as a walking trail. High on the west face of the mountain you can see a military half-track vehicle. On the north side an experienced hiker can scramble up above some old tunnels and reach the top of Temple Mtn. The lower circular road is very rough and is sometimes used by ORV's. At one point it is completely blocked by rock slides, so even ORV's can't make the loop. Riders on horseback can also make the loop around the mountain.

Elevations Car-parks are at 1658 and 1707 meters; top of Temple Mtn. is 2064 meters.

Hike Length and Time Needed The complete loop-hike around the mountain is about 10 kms in length and is easy walking all the way. The whole trip can be done easily in about half a day for some people, but if you're doing a lot of exploring and perhaps climbing the peak it may take an entire day.

Water There's no water anywhere, so always carry plenty in your car and in your pack.

Maps USGS or BLM map San Rafael Desert(1:100,000), or Temple Mtn.(1:62,500).

Main Attractions Good pictographs in South Temple Wash, hundreds of old mine shafts and tunnels, ruins of old buildings and piles of mine rubble including petrified logs.

Ideal Time to Hike Spring or fall, but some winter warm spells can be pleasant. Summers are hot.

Hiking Boots Any dry weather boots or shoes.

Author's Experience The author has visited this area on several occasions. He camped at the main camp site twice. Once he hiked around the mountain in 2 1/2 hours, round-trip. Another time he re-hiked the loop but on the upper track and climbed to the top. That trip lasted about 5 hours.

On the east side of Temple Mountain are several old abandoned miner's shacks.

MAP 23, TEMPLE MOUNTAIN LOOP-HIKE

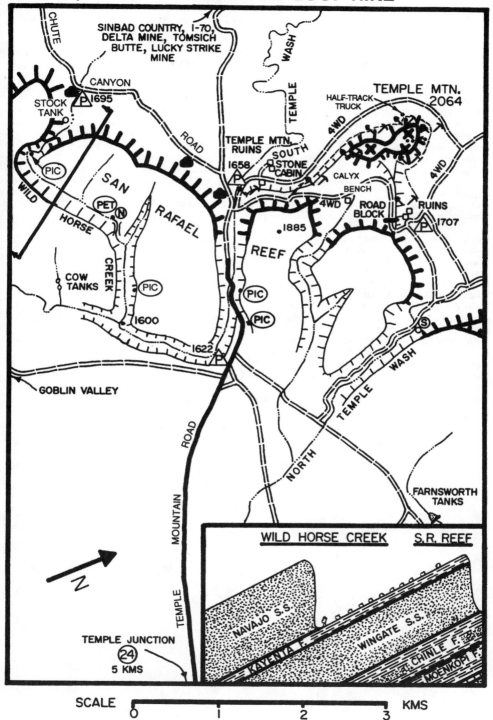

SINBAD COUNTRY, I-70, DELTA MINE, TOMSICH BUTTE, LUCKY STRIKE MINE

CHUTE

CANYON

STOCK TANK

1695

TEMPLE WASH

TEMPLE MTN. 2064

HALF-TRACK TRUCK

ROAD

TEMPLE MTN. RUINS

1658

SOUTH STONE CABIN

4WD

PIC

SAN

PET N

RAFAEL

CALYX BENCH

4WD

ROAD BLOCK

RUINS

1707

WILD

HORSE

CREEK

.1885

REEF

4WD

COW TANKS

PIC

PIC

1600

PIC

1622

GOBLIN VALLEY

ROAD

MOUNTAIN

TEMPLE

NORTH

TEMPLE WASH

FARNSWORTH TANKS

WILD HORSE CREEK   S.R. REEF

NAVAJO S.S.

KAYENTA F.

WINGATE S.S.

CHINLE F.

MOENKOPI F.

N

TEMPLE JUNCTION
24
5 KMS

SCALE 0   1   2   3 KMS

117

Wild Horse Creek Canyon

Location and Access The Wild Horse Gorge of Wild Horse Creek is located just south of Temple Mountain. This is not to be confused with the Little Wild Horse Canyon further to the southwest. This canyon has easy access and is a good hike for the whole family. It's possible to do this hike on the same day as hiking around Temple Mountain. To get there, drive along Highway 24, the road linking Hanksville to the south with 1-70 in the north. Just south of mile post 137, turn west at a place called Temple Junction. This is a good paved road to as far as the South Temple Wash pictographs, then it's a well maintained gravel road to the west and into Sinbad Country of the San Rafael. About half a km west of the old Temple Mtn. townsite, turn left or southwest onto the Chute Canyon Road. Drive about 3 kms along this good road until you come to a shallow drainage which is the upper part of Wild Horse Creek. Park and/or camp just off the road in the large cedar trees. You could also park near the bottom of the canyon a km or two along the Goblin Valley Road and walk into the bottom of the canyon.

Trail or Route Conditions If you park on the Chute Canyon Road, you just walk down the dry creek bed. Near the beginning, you can follow an old stockman's road to the right where it ends at a spring and an aluminum watering trough. Further down-canyon the walls get higher and higher, after which there are narrows in the middle part. Further down-canyon it slowly becomes more shallow. Keep an eye out for 3 sets of pictographs and petroglyphs, the best of which is high on the northern wall near the bottom of the canyon. Horses can't get past the narrows in the middle of the canyon.

Elevations Top of canyon, 1695 meters; bottom of canyon, about 1600.

Hike Length and Time Needed From the top to the bottom of the canyon it's about 6-7 kms and can be hiked in a couple of hours. But you'd need two cars; or go back out the same way you entered. You could also walk through the canyon, then road-walk back to your car which would be about a 14 km hike. This may last most of a day for some.

Water Always carry water in your car and in your pack, but there is one small fenced spring with a metal stock tank in the upper canyon less than a km from the Chute Canyon Road.

Maps USGS or BLM map San Rafael Desert(1:100,000), or Temple Mtn.(1:62,500).

Main Attractions A couple of short little narrows sections and some high Navajo walls. Also, the pictographs and petroglyphs in the canyon. One is in the upper end, another in the middle part just above the narrows, and the last is high above the canyon floor in a south facing alcove.

Ideal Time to Hike Spring or fall, but some winter warm spells can be pleasant. Summers are hot.

Hiking Boots Any dry weather boots or shoes.

Author's Experience The author camped at the old Temple Mtn. town site area, then walk along the Chute Canyon Road and down Wild Horse all the way. In the end, he road-walked along South Temple Wash back to his car in about 3 hours round-trip. Another time he walked into the bottom of the canyon and found the best pictographs near the lower end.

Sheer Navajo Walls with desert varnish rise above the creek bed of Wild Horse Creek.

118

MAP 24, WILD HORSE CREEK CANYON

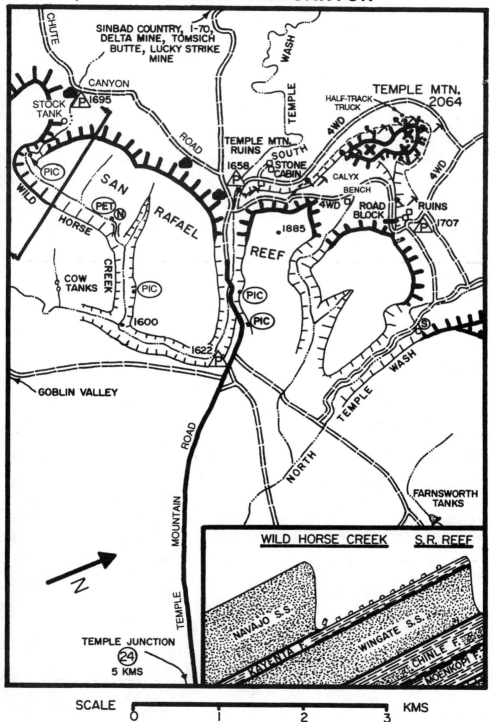

CHUTE

SINBAD COUNTRY, I-70,
DELTA MINE, TOMSICH
BUTTE, LUCKY STRIKE
MINE

WASH

TEMPLE

CANYON

STOCK
TANK

P 1695

ROAD

TEMPLE MTN. 2064

HALF-TRACK
TRUCK

4WD

PIC

SAN

WILD

RAFEL

TEMPLE MTN.
RUINS

1658

SOUTH
STONE
CABIN

CALYX
BENCH

4WD

4WD

4WD

PET

N

HORSE

.1885

REEF

4WD

ROAD
BLOCK

RUINS

P 1707

CREEK

COW
TANKS

PIC

PIC

PIC

1600

S

1622

P

GOBLIN VALLEY

TEMPLE WASH

ROAD

NORTH

FARNSWORTH
TANKS

WILD HORSE CREEK

S.R. REEF

MOUNTAIN

Navajo S.S.

Wingate S.S.

Chinle F.

TEMPLE

Kayenta F.

MOENKOPI

TEMPLE JUNCTION
24
5 KMS

N

SCALE

0 1 2 3 KMS

119

Crack and Chute Canyons

Location and Access These two canyons are found just north and northwest of Goblin Valley State Park, and along the southeastern part of the San Rafael Reef. To get there, turn off Highway 24 at Temple Junction, which is between mile posts 136 and 137, and drive west on a good paved road. After about 8 kms you can turn south toward Goblin Valley on a well maintained road. About 1 km before arriving at Goblin Valley, turn to the right or southwest and drive to the bottom of the Wild Horse drainage and park at the 1460 meter car-park as shown on the map. One problem with parking there is the deep sand which is at its worst during long dry spells. Therefore, it's recommended those with regular cars head for the west or upper side of the Reef. To get there, drive all the way to the old Temple Mtn. townsite(see the Temple Mtn. Loop Hike map), then about half a km past it, turn to the left or southwest onto the Chute Canyon Road. Drive this for about 13 kms to where it ends near the Erma Mine, a metal shack, and a rock house called "Morgan's Cabin." If you just want to hike Crack Canyon, then drive only 8 or 9 kms along this same road and park. There are good camp sites near Morgan's Cabin and near the beginning of the Chute Canyon Road.

Trail or Route Conditions If you start on the Goblin Valley side of the Reef, walk up Chute, then road-walk northeast to the head of Crack Canyon, then down Crack and back to your car. Some ORV's are using Chute Canyon, but thank goodness they can't get up or down Crack. There are three sets of good narrows in Crack making it one of the best narrow canyons around. Doing these canyons from the top end is by far the best way in, especially for people with cars. One reader wrote and complained about a big drop-off in Crack Canyon, but the author failed to see it as an obstacle. Climbing over minor falls or ledges is just part of the canyon hiking experience. Horses can be taken all the way through Chute Canyon but not through Crack.

Elevations Head of Crack Canyon, 1650 meters; head of Chute Canyon, 1550; bottom of both canyons, 1460 meters.

Hike Length and Time Needed To make a circle route of both canyons will be to walk about 25 km(a long all day hike), but hikers will be most interested in Crack Canyon. You can hike most of the way down from the Chute Canyon Road and return, in about 3 or 4 hours.

Water Carry water in your car and in your pack, as there are no springs around. If you need more water, drive to Goblin Valley State Park to replenish your supply. Goblin Valley is a fee-use area.

Maps USGS or BLM map San Rafael Desert(1:100,000), or Wild Horse and Temple Mtn.(1:62,500).

Main Attractions High cliffs, deep canyons, old mines and cabins, and good narrows.

Ideal Time to Hike Spring or fall, but some winter warm spells can be pleasant. Summers are hot.

Hiking Boots Any dry weather boots or shoes.

Author's Experience He once camped at the 1460 meter site, then went up Chute and down Crack in about 5 1/2 hours round-trip. Another time he walked down from the Chute Canyon Road past the narrows in Crack Canyon and back, in less than 2 hours.

This is the narrows of Crack Canyon as it cuts through the Kayenta Formation.

MAP 25, CRACK AND CHUTE CANYONS

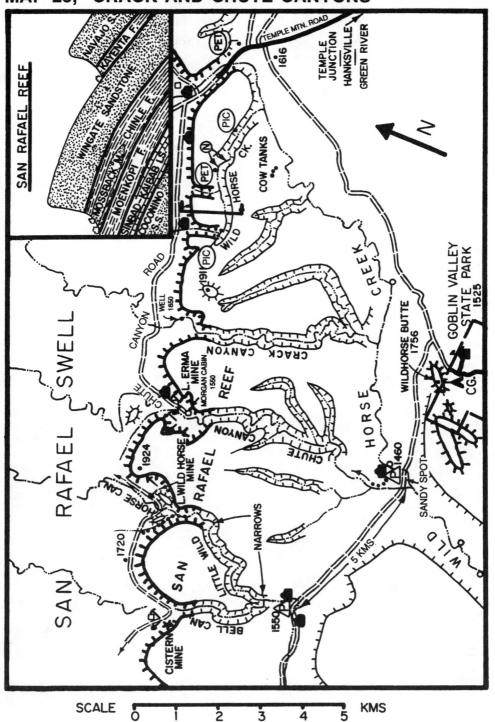

SAN RAFAEL REEF

NAVAJO S.S.
KAYENTA F.
WINGATE SANDSTONE
CHINLE F.
MOSSBACK M.
MOENKOPI F.
SINBAD L.
KAIBAB LS.
COCONINO S.S.

N

TEMPLE MTN. ROAD
1616
TEMPLE JUNCTION
HANKSVILLE
GREEN RIVER

PET
PIC
N
PET
WILD HORSE CK.
COW TANKS

191 PIC
WELL 1650

SAN RAFAEL SWELL

CANYON ROAD
CHUTE CANYON

CRACK CANYON

REEF CANYON

L. ERMA MINE
MORGAN CABIN 1550
1924

CHUTE CANYON

HORSE CREEK

WILDHORSE BUTTE 1756

GOBLIN VALLEY STATE PARK 1525

CG.

1460

SANDY SPOT

U. WILD HORSE MINE
L. WILD HORSE MINE
RAFAEL

1720

SAN RAFAEL SAN

HORSE CAN.

LITTLE WILD

NARROWS

BELL CAN.

WILD

5 KMS.

1550

CISTERN MINE

SCALE 0 1 2 3 4 5 KMS

Bell and Little Wild Horse Canyons

Location and Access These two popular canyons are located due west of Goblin Valley State Park and in the southeastern part of the San Rafael Swell. To get there, drive along Highway 24 between Hanksville and I-70. Between mile posts 136 and 137, turn west onto a paved road signposted for Goblin Valley and Temple Mtn. Drive this road for 8 kms then turn south toward Goblin Valley. After another 11 kms, or about one km before arriving at Goblin Park, turn right or southwest, and drive another good road down through the bottom of Wild Horse Creek. In the creek bed area, drive as fast as conditions will allow, because of the sand. The author has been there many times and hasn't had any trouble, but remember, drive fast through the sandy places and don't stop. Lately, this road has been maintained better than before so there's very little risk of getting stuck today. Also, wet sand is easier to drive through than dry. After Wild Horse Creek, continue west over a low divide for about 5 kms 'til you drop down into Little Wild Horse Canyon. Park just beyond the dry creek bed. Some people drive up the creek bed a ways and camp under shade trees.

Trail or Route Conditions The recommended hike is to walk up-canyon past some minor falls, then turn left into Bell Canyon. Walk through this one in the dry creek bed, then when you reach the west side of the Reef, road-walk to the right or northeast to the upper part of Little Wild Horse. Then return down this canyon to your car. Little Wild Horse is probably the best of the two canyons. It has about 2 kms of narrows, one km of which averages one to two meters in width. In one section, it would be difficult to take a frame pack through because of its narrowness. It is pocked with potholes, but one hiker told the author he went through a day after a big storm and the pothole water was no more than thigh-deep. Obviously, you don't want to be there during a big storm. This isn't a place for Horses.

Elevations Car-park at Little Wild Horse, 1550 meters; high point in the Swell, 1720 meters.

Hike Length and Time Needed From the car-park, up Bell, down Little Wild Horse, and back to one's car is about 13 kms. This loop-hike can be done in about half a day, but most people would want to spend the better part of a day in these canyons.

Water Always carry water in your car and in your pack. If you need more stop at Goblin Valley which is a fee-use campground.

Maps USGS or BLM map San Rafael Desert(1:100,000), or Wild Horse(1:62,500).

Main Attractions One of the best little narrow canyons on the Colorado Plateau and a fun hike for the whole family. You might also check out the Cistern Mine area.

Ideal Time to Hike Spring or fall, but some winter warm spells can be pleasant. Summers are hot, but in a shaded canyon, hiking is still possible.

Hiking Boots Any dry weather boots or shoes, except right after a storm, then waders.

Author's Experience The author camped at the mouth of Little Wild Horse Canyon, then walked up Bell and down Little Wild Horse in about 4 hours. On a second trip he did the same hike but in the reverse direction in under 4 hours.

In Little Wild Horse Canyon, you'll find about 2 kms of narrows similar to this.

MAP 26, BELL AND LITTLE WILD HORSE CANYONS

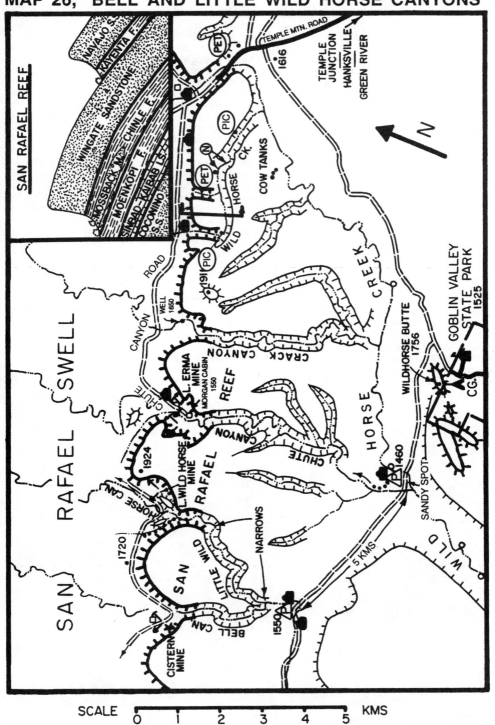

SCALE 0 1 2 3 4 5 KMS

123

Goblin Valley Hikes

Location and Access Goblin Valley is located about half way between I-70 and Hanksville and to the west of Highway 24. This small and rather obscure valley is found just outside the San Rafael Swell and the southeastern Reef, and near the mouths of Crack and Chute Canyons. The valley has been made into a Utah State Park because of its many grotesque formations and oddly shaped rocks carved out of the Entrada Sandstone. The park has a campground with a culinary water supply, a sanitary dump station and a ranger station, manned the year-round. The electricity for the rest rooms comes from photovoltaic cells and the water for the showers from a well. Water is heated by solar panels. There is a small fee for entry, plus a fee for camping and showers. It's one of the few places in the area to stock up on water. To get there, drive along Highway 24 and turn west at Temple Junction, located between mile posts 136 and 137. Drive 8 kms to the west on a paved road, then turn south and drive 12 kms on a well maintained sandy dirt road to the park.

Trail or Route Conditions There are but 2 maintained trails in the park. One is called the Carmel Canyon Trail. It begins at the end of the paved park road and at a viewpoint and picnic site. It heads off to the east and to the south side of Mollys Castle. About half way between the campground and the picnic site is the Curtis Bench Trailhead. The trail from that point heads south to the Henry Mountains Lookout, then turns east and ends at the picnic site at the end of the road. Both trails are short and moderately well used. If you prefer, you can wander through the park at will, using the picnic site as a base. Within the park boundaries all wheeled vehicles(including mountain bikes) must stay on the pavement. Horses aren't allowed on the trails in Goblin Valley State Park.

Elevations The campground and both trailheads are at about 1500 meters altitude.

Hike Length and Time Needed The Carmel Canyon Trail to Mollys Castle is about 5 kms, round-trip. Do this hike in less than a couple of hours. The Henry Mountains Lookout Trail is about 2 kms long from the Curtis Bench Trailhead to the picnic site. This hike will also take but an hour or two. In about half a day you can see all there is at Goblin Valley.

Water At the restrooms in the campground.

Maps USGS or BLM map San Rafael Desert(1:100,000), or Temple Mtn.(1:62,500).

Main Attractions Unique geologic features and a desert campground with solar heated showers. Some people use this campground as a base for the many other hikes in the nearby Reef.

Ideal Time to Hike Spring or fall, but some winter warm spells are pleasant. Summers are hot.

Hiking Boots Any dry weather boots or shoes.

Author's Experience He has been there on several occasions--to hike, get water and for information. If you're a public campground enthusiast, this is a nice place to camp, especially if you need a shower or water, but there are plenty of other primitive campsites elsewhere in the area.

Typical scene in Goblin Valley. The rocks are part of the Entrada Sandstone.

MAP 27, GOBLIN VALLEY HIKES

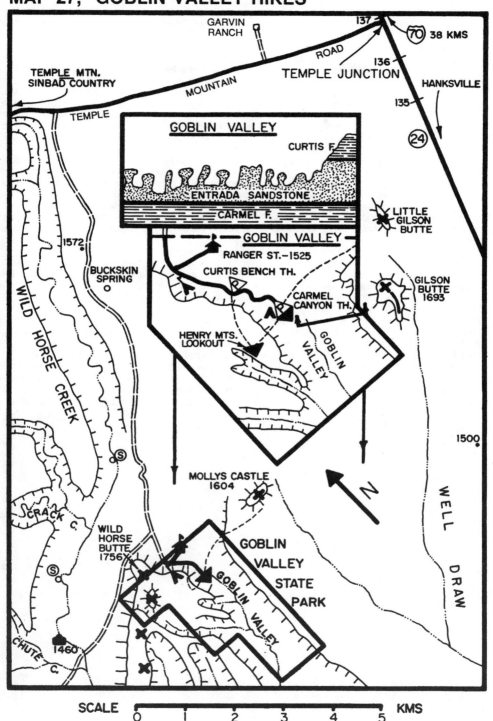

Cistern C. & Canyons of the Southern San Rafael Reef

Location and Access All 4 canyons on this map are located in the southern end of the San Rafael and between where Muddy Ck. and Little Wild Horse Canyons dive through the Reef. There are two ways you can get to this hiking area. First, drive along Highway 24 running between I-70 and Hanksville. Between mile posts 136 and 137, turn west onto a good paved road. Further along turn south at the sign toward Goblin Valley. When you're within one km of the Goblin, turn right or southwest and head for L. Wild Horse Canyon(see the previous map). When you reach L. Wild Horse, continue on for 2 more kms in the gravely stream channel. When the road turns south, you turn east and park near some trees, but beware of the *deep sand!* This place is close to what the author calls 1st and 2nd Canyons. The second car-park is 4 or 5 kms before you arrive at the Delta Mine. See the L. Muddy Creek Hike for driving instructions. Park about where the map indicates.

Trail or Route Conditions From the Little Wild Horse car-park, walk up the sandy creek bed to the west. After about one km, turn right and head up 1st Canyon and into some good Navajo Narrows. You can walk all the way through this canyon to the inside of the Reef. The author walked part way up 2nd Canyon, but isn't 100% sure you can get through it. Try walking up 2nd, and if you make it, you'll know for sure you can get down 1st. To get into 4th and Cistern Canyons, it's best to begin near the Delta Mine. From the road, walk almost due south and into 4th. This canyon has some pretty good Kayenta Narrows, then a large choke stone that some people may have a little trouble passing. Take a short rope to help the less-experienced members of your group. In the bottom end is a large dryfall. You can easily get around this minor obstacle by climbing up or down on either side. Cistern Canyon is another canyon with some good Navajo Narrows, but no obstacles. Horses can't make it into these canyons.

Elevations L. Wild Horse Car-park, 1500 meters; car-park near the Delta Mine, 1650.

Hike Length and Time Needed From Little Wild Horse, a loop-hike up 2nd and down 1st, and return is maybe 10 kms. Most people can do it in 3 or 4 hours. To do a loop-hike of Cistern and 4th Canyons is only slightly longer, but will take about the same length of time.

Water Always carry water in your car and in your pack. There's one minor year-round seep in Cistern Canyon called Bullberry Spring.

Maps USGS or BLM map San Rafael Desert(1:100,000), or Wild Horse(1:62,500).

Main Attractions Some of the best narrows around. Cistern Canyon appears to be the same as what G.K. Gilbert called Boulder Canyon during his 1875 expedition to the Henry Mountains.

Ideal Time to Hike Spring or fall, but some winter warm spells are pleasant. Summers are hot.

Author's Experience The author arrived late in the pm and made a quick hike up to the head of 1st Canyon in 2 1/4 hours. Next morning he hiked as far as the narrows of 2nd Canyon, then continued west and up Cistern, down 4th, and back to his car along the little valley below Little Wild Horse Mesa. Round-trip, just over 6 hours. Later he came down from the top end into 4th Canyon on a 2 hour hike.

One must do a little climbing at this point in what the author calls 4th Canyon.

MAP 28, CISTERN CANYON, AND CANYONS OF THE SOUTHERN SAN RAFAEL REEF

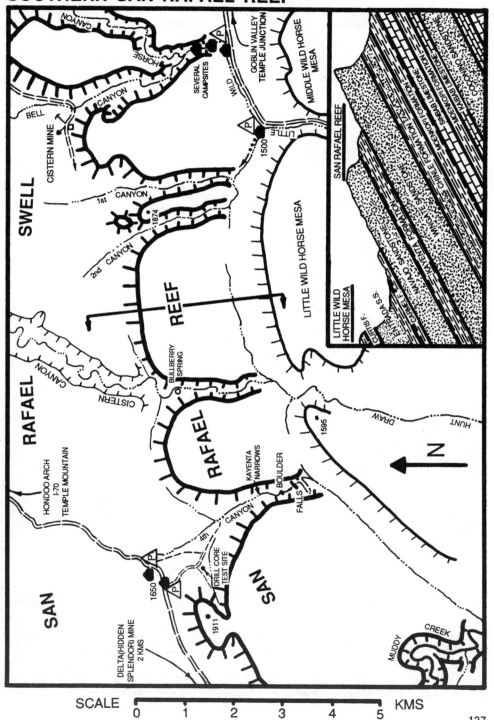

Lower Muddy Creek Gorge

Location and Access Muddy Creek flows from the mountains west of Emery and heads southeast across the southern part of the San Rafael Swell. As it flows through the inside of the Reef, it's deeply entrenched in a Coconino Sandstone canyon called The Chute. It then cuts through the south end of the Reef and soon joins the Fremont River to form the Dirty Devil at Hanksville. The hike here is where Muddy Creek flows through the Reef. To get there, drive along Highway 24 to between mile posts 136 and 137, and turn west onto a good paved road. Head west past Temple Mountain and Flat Top and to the center of the Swell, then turn south and head for the Delta(Hidden Splendor) Mine. If you're coming from I-70, leave the freeway at mile post and Exit 129, and drive almost straight south to the Delta Mine. All the roads up to that point are excellent for any car, except perhaps right after heavy rains. The county keeps these roads well maintained.

Trail or Route Conditions At one time there was a mining road cut down through the canyon below the mine, but it's almost totally gone now. You simply walk down-stream crossing Muddy Creek many times. The creek is always small, except just after big rain storms. Even then, all you have to do is wait an hour or two and the water level will come back to normal. In winter, or after a long dry spell the creek is as clear as a mountain stream; but after storms it's muddy as hell, thus the name. The water is normally ankle deep or less. Walking is easy in this spectacular gorge, perhaps the deepest in the San Rafael country. Head for the bottom and return the same way. Riders on horseback can go all the way through this gorge.

Elevations Delta(Hidden Splendor) Mine, 1463 meters; bottom of gorge, about 1432.

Hike Length and Time Needed From the old mining camp down to the mouth of the gorge is only about 7 kms, or 14 kms round-trip. This distance can be hiked in about half a day, but some may want more time.

Water Always carry water in your car and in your pack, but there is a minor seasonal seep below the high falls as shown on the map. There are also cattle in the area during the winter months and beaver year-round, which means you'll have to treat the water in Muddy Creek.

Maps USGS or BLM map San Rafael Desert(1:100,000), or Wild Horse(1:62,500).

Main Attractions A little known and isolated canyon with some of the highest and steepest walls found in the San Rafael Swell. Also, there are many old mine tunnels and a work–crew building last used when the Delta Mine was producing in the 1950's. Near the bottom of the gorge is an alcove and spring and a very high and impressive dryfall.

Ideal Time to Hike Spring or fall. Winter months would be too cold because you'll be wading so much. Summers are very warm, but you could at least cool off in the creek.

Hiking Boots Wading boots or shoes.

Author's Experience The author camped near the landing strip and old mining camp site. After visiting the mines and old buildings, he walked down to near the mouth of the canyon and returned, all in about 3 hours.

One of the deepest canyons in the Swell is where Muddy Creek cuts through the Reef.

MAP 29, LOWER MUDDY CREEK GORGE

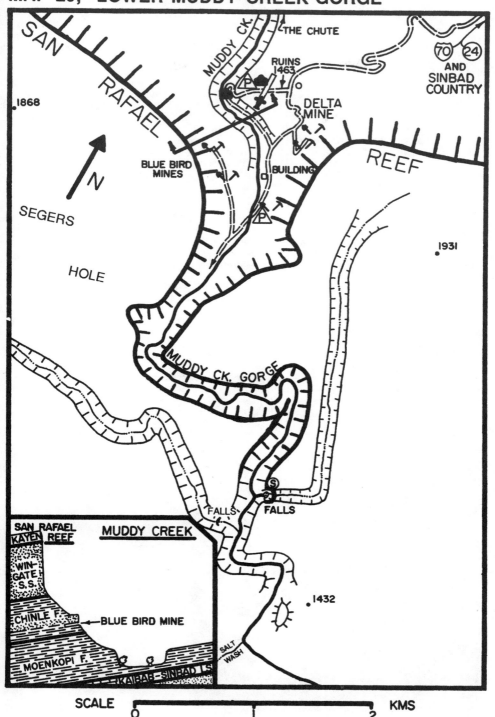

The Moroni Slopes and the North Caineville Reefs

Location and Access The Moroni Slopes and the North Caineville Reefs are located at the extreme southern end of the San Rafael Swell and just south and west of where Muddy Creek cuts through the main Reef. There are many hiking opportunities in this area, but for the most part you won't find the extremely deep and narrow slot canyons one sees further to the northeast. To get to the Moroni Slopes, drive along Highway 24 to between mile posts 106 and 107. This is about 16 kms west of Hanksville along the main road leading to Loa, Torrey and Capitol Reef National Park. Turn north onto a good gravel road which heads in the direction of Factory Butte. This is a well maintained road until the turnoff to the old Factory Butte Coal Mine, then it's less maintained to Muddy Creek. In dry conditions any car can make it to Muddy Creek, but this road runs across Mancos Clays all the way, so use it in dry weather only. The best place to park and/or start any hike would be at the viewpoint on top of the dugway marked 1500 meters.

Trail or Route Conditions There are no real trails in the area, but there are some old miners roads in the bottom part of Salt Wash. These tracks are for powerful 4WD vehicles only, and useable only in dry weather conditions. If you'd like to explore some of the un-named canyons across the face of the Moroni Slopes, park at the viewpoint and walk west down the clay road. You'll have to cross over or pass through about 3 cockscombs or minor reefs to reach the Slopes. All these little cockscomb ridges are known as the North Caineville Reef or Reefs. If you're a geology freak this is the place for you. All the formations are standing at about a 45 degree angle and it's literally an open geology textbook. There are a number of canyons cutting down into the Moroni Slopes, most of which cut into the Navajo Sandstone. You will find some narrows, but also lots of blocking dryfalls as well. There's plenty of room for exploring. Horses can be taken to parts of this area.

Elevations Trailhead, 1500 meters; top of the Moroni Slopes, about 2000 meters.

Hike Length and Time Needed You can spend an entire day or just a couple of hours in the area.

Water Take all the water you'll need for hiking or camping. Water from Salt Creek tastes just like sea water, but Muddy Creek above the confluence tastes pretty good(after treatment). Both streams are crystal clear during dry spells but muddy after storms.

Maps USGS or BLM maps Salina, San Rafael Desert, Hanksville and Loa(1:100,000), or Wild Horse, Factory Butte, Fruita(1:62,500), and Emery 4 SE(1:24,000).

Main Attractions An open geology museum, fine views from the higher slopes and solitude.

Ideal Time to Hike Spring or fall. Some winter warm spells are pleasant(beware of wet clay roads!).

Hiking Boots Any dry weather boots or shoes.

Author's Experience The author began at mid-day at the viewpoint. He walked down the road to the west and crossed the reefs, then headed for the high point marked 1986 meters. Later he returned to Salt Creek and walked north to where Muddy Creek cuts through the main Reef. He then returned to his car via the road from Muddy Creek. This took 6 hours non-stop.

From part way up the Moroni Slopes one has a good view to the south at the Henry Mtns., Factory Butte and the several ridges making up the North Caineville Reef.

MAP 30. THE MORONI SLOPES AND THE NORTH CAINEVILLE REEFS

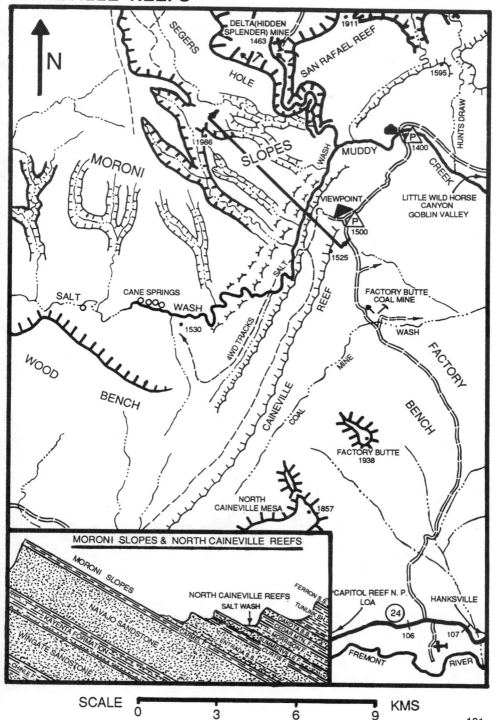

SCALE 0 3 6 9 KMS

131

Chimney Canyon

Location and Access Chimney Canyon is located in the extreme southern end of the San Rafael Swell. This canyon runs from west to east and empties into Muddy Creek not far north of the Delta or Hidden Splendor Mine. To get there leave I-70 at mile post and Exit 129 and turn south. Drive due south through the middle of the Swell to the Delta Mine. Or you could drive west from Temple Junction between mile posts 136 and 137 on Highway 24. Head for the middle of the Swell, then turn south and stop at the Delta Mine on Muddy Creek and park. All the above roads to this area are well maintained on a regular basis and good for any vehicle.

Trail or Route Conditions The normal way to get into Chimney Canyon is from the Delta Mine. From the old airstrip either walk or drive downhill to the stream channel, then simply walk up Muddy Creek and into the bottom end of The Chute. This could be done almost any time as the stream is usually small and insignificant. If you're there during the spring runoff(late May and early June), the water in some years could be high enough to make it difficult walking up stream. When you reach the mouth of Chimney Canyon, simply walk up the dry creek bed to the northwest. When you reach the confluence of the north and south forks, turn right and walk into the north fork. After 150 meters or so, you'll come to the washed-out remains of a track or trail on the left. You have to use this old trail in order to get upon a bench and into the upper canyons. From on top of the bench at the confluence you can make your way into the north or south forks.

Elevations Delta Mine, 1463 meters; confluence of north and south forks, about 1550.

Hike Length and Time Needed One can get into the middle parts of Chimney Canyon and back in one long day. The distance from the Delta Mine to the miners cabin in Chimney is about 11 kms one way. However, if you want to explore the upper sections of the canyon it would have to be done in two days. Horses can't make it past the lower end of Chimney.

Water There are good springs in both north and south forks and at the miners camp at the confluence. Take water from the spring source, as there are cattle in the area during the winter months each year.

Maps USGS or BLM maps San Rafael Desert and Salina(1:100,000), or Wild Horse(1:62,500), and Emery 4 SE(1:24,000).

Main Attractions Remote and wild canyon that is almost unknown, good water sources, an old miners cabin, good campsites and petrified wood(on a bench just above and north of the cabin).

Ideal Time to Hike. Spring or fall. Summers are hot.

Hiking Boots Use wading boots or shoes along the Muddy Creek, but dry weather boots are best for the rest of the hike.

Author's Experience The author made this hike on a cool spring day, but the water in Muddy Creek wasn't too cold. He made it to the confluence of the north and south forks and had lunch at the cabin(nearby is an old chicken coop, and further down canyon is an old Ford station wagon--which somehow must have come in from the Tomsich Butte side?), then went to the good spring in the south fork. He returned to his car in a total time of 7 hours.

One sees petrified wood everywhere in the Swell, but Chimney Canyon has a fine site.

MAP 31, CHIMNEY CANYON

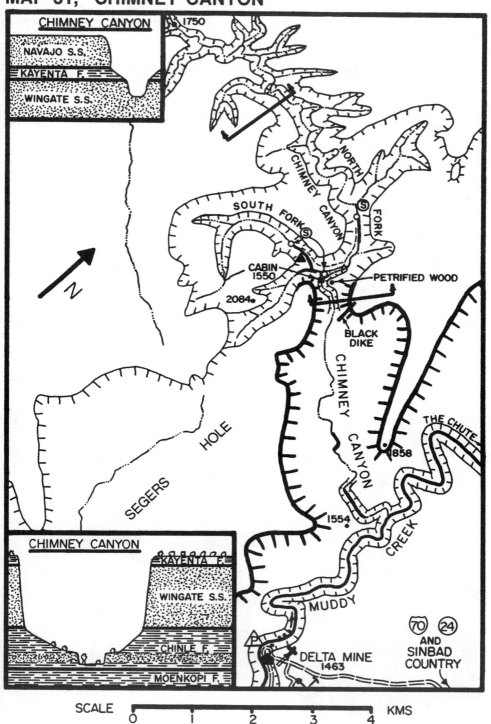

CHIMNEY CANYON

NAVAJO S.S.

KAYENTA F.

WINGATE S.S.

1750

SOUTH FORK

CHIMNEY CANYON

NORTH FORK

CABIN 1550

2084

PETRIFIED WOOD

BLACK DIKE

CHIMNEY CANYON

THE CHUTE

1858

SEGERS HOLE

1554

CREEK

CHIMNEY CANYON

KAYENTA F.

WINGATE S.S.

CHINLE F.

MOENKOPI F.

MUDDY

DELTA MINE 1463

70 24 AND SINBAD COUNTRY

N

SCALE   0   1   2   3   4   KMS

The Chute--of Muddy Creek

Location and Access The Chute of Muddy Creek is located in the extreme southern end of the San Rafael Swell. The Chute is found on the inside of the Reef and in between Tomsich Butte and the Delta(Hidden Splendor) Mine. Muddy Creek in this section cuts down into the Coconino Sandstone, thus making a very narrow and deep trench. It does the same thing here as the San Rafael River does in the north end of the Swell as it flows through the Black Boxes. These two canyons are very similar except there's a lot less water and no obstacles in Muddy Creek. To get to this canyon, exit I-70 at mile post and Exit 129 and drive south to Tomsich Butte; or leave Highway 24 at Temple Junction, which is between mile posts 136 and 137. From there drive west to the middle of the Swell and turn south towards Tomsich Butte. You could also begin the hike at the Delta Mine. However, most of the best parts of The Chute are easier to reach from Tomsich Butte.

Trail or Route Conditions If you begin at the Delta Mine, then simply get into the stream and walk up-canyon. From Tomsich Butte, turn left or south and drive as far as you can. That will be just before the stream crossing. Cross the creek and walk along the very old and faded mining road as shown on the map for about 2 kms, then it's into the water and walking down-stream. In the part labeled *Coconino Narrows,* you'll be in the water about 50% of the time, while in the area of the log jam, you'll be in water 90% of the time(in dry years there will be much less water). The water is normally less than ankle deep and there are no obstructions as one finds in the Black Boxes of the San Rafael River. Horses can walk all the way through The Chute.

Elevations The river bed at Tomsich Butte, 1554 meters; bottom end of The Chute, 1432 meters.

Hike Length and Time Needed From Tomsich Butte to the Delta Mine is about 25 kms one way. This can be done in one day, but you'd need two cars. It's perhaps best to begin and end the hike at one car-park. Plan on a full day's hike.

Water Take all the water you'll need in your car and in your pack. Treat river water first.

Maps USGS or BLM map San Rafael Desert(1:100,000), or Wild Horse (1:62,500).

Main Attractions A deep, dark and narrow canyon. Maybe the best narrows hike in the San Rafael Swell.

Ideal Time to Hike Spring through fall, but if it's too early or late in the season the water will be very cold. Summer might be best, because you're in the water so often. Winter is out of the question, unless it's the middle of a drought. In years with heavy snowfall in the mountains kayakers sometimes make a run through this canyon from sometime late in May to early June. Don't get into this gorge with a rainy weather forecast!

Hiking Boots Wading type boots or shoes.

Author's Experience The author camped at the Tomsich Butte car-park and walked down-stream on April 19, 1986. At first his feet felt like blocks of ice, then a little later they warmed up OK. He walked to within 4 kms of Chimney Canyon and returned in 8 hours.

At a log jam in the narrows of The Chute of Muddy Creek.

MAP 32, THE CHUTE--OF MUDDY CREEK

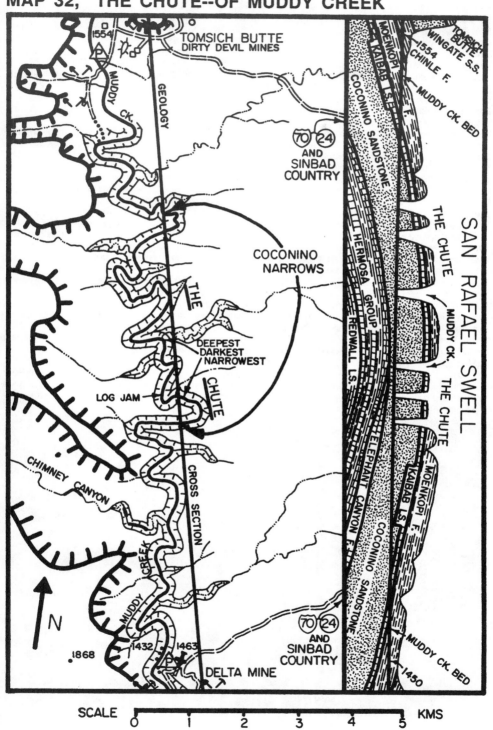

SCALE

0 1 2 3 4 5 KMS

Upper Muddy Creek and Poor Canyon

Location and Access This hike is along upper Muddy Creek as it enters the inner parts of the San Rafael Swell and where it cuts through the southwestern part of the Reef. To reach this area turn west at Temple Junction on Highway 24 between mile posts 136 and 137 and drive to the middle of the Swell, then turn south and head for Tomsich Butte. Or leave I-70 at mile post and Exit 129 and drive straight south to Tomsich Butte. Look at the map closely. Your goal is to get to the Torval Albrecht Cabin or the second car-park just west of Tomsich Butte where there's been a road washed out. This second car-park is easier to reach if you have a car. Also, the old army truck shown in the foto on page 49 has been dismantled by someone and half of it has been carted away. The roads leading into this area are very good most of the time and any car can make it to Muddy Creek unless you're there right after a heavy rain storm.

Trail or Route Conditions At one time there was a road bulldozed up along Muddy Creek on the north side, but that track is so washed out now that it can hardly be seen. However, it's easier and faster if you just get out in the small stream and wade part of the time as you walk up-canyon. Not far above the Albrecht Cabin is the mouth of Poor Canyon. It has a small stream in the lower end and is very deep. Further along, the canyon walls will be seen getting lower and lower. The first big canyon west of Poor is a good one but there's a blocking falls near the mouth. There's lots of room to explore in this canyon complex which has many side drainages and shaded campsites.

Elevations The river just west of Tomsich Butte, 1550 meters; the mesa above, 2000 meters.

Hike Length and Time Needed One can hike here for half a day, a full day, or make an overnight camp and spend a couple of days. There are many canyons to explore. Horses can be used here too.

Water Always carry water in your car and in your pack. Treat Muddy Creek water if you're staying over night. Poor Canyon water at the spring source should be good. However cattle are grazed in the area during some winter months each year.

Maps USGS or BLM maps San Rafael Desert and Salina(1:100,000), or Wild Horse(1:62,500), and Emery IV NE(1:24,000).

Main Attractions Poor Canyon is very deep and moderately narrow, plus there are many other canyons in the region that could prove interesting. There's at least one petroglyph panel as shown on the map. Much of this area is part of the Muddy Creek Wilderness Study Area.

Ideal Time to Hike Spring or fall, but if you're there too early or late in the season, you'll get cold feet. Hiking in summers can probably be fun too, as you can cool off in the creek.

Hiking Boots Wading boots or shoes.

Author's Experience The author walked along the north side of Muddy Creek to the mouth of Poor Canyon and explored half of that drainage. He didn't wade on that cold late-winter day, but on a another trip he waded further up Muddy Creek to the first drainage above Poor Canyon. That round-trip from Tomsich Butte lasted about 5 hours.

Poor Canyon, with its soaring Wingate and Navajo Walls, is one of the better hikes.

MAP 33, UPPER MUDDY CREEK & POOR CANYON

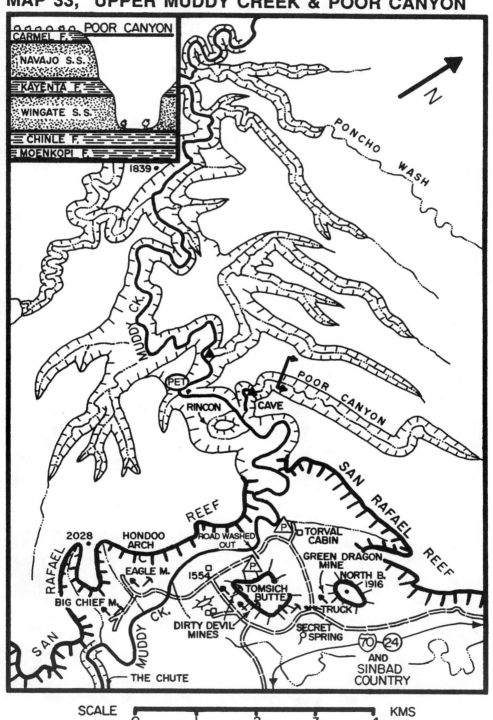

POOR CANYON

CARMEL F.
NAVAJO S.S.
KAYENTA F.
WINGATE S.S.
CHINLE F.
MOENKOPI F.

1839

N

PONCHO WASH

MUDDY CK.

POOR CANYON

PET

RINCON

CAVE

SAN RAFAEL REEF

REEF

2028

HONDOO ARCH

ROAD WASHED OUT

P

TORVAL CABIN

GREEN DRAGON MINE

EAGLE M.

1554

P

NORTH B. 1916

RAFAEL

BIG CHIEF M.

MUDDY CK.

TOMSICH BUTTE

DIRTY DEVIL MINES

TRUCK

SECRET SPRING

70 24

SAN

THE CHUTE

AND SINBAD COUNTRY

SCALE   KMS
0   1   2   3   4

Devils Canyon

Location and Access Devils Canyon is located in the west central part of the San Rafael Swell and just south of Interstate Highway 70. To get there, drive along I-70 to mile post and Exit 114 and turn south onto the Copper Globe Road. This exit is just across the highway from a rest area. Drive this good road downhill to the southeast to Justensen Flats, a camping area just south of the freeway. Continue southeast for another km then the road turns south and drops into the upper part of Devils Canyon. Higher clearance cars can go all the way to the bottom of the canyon, but some may have to be parked at the 2150 meter car-park as shown on the map. This Copper Globe Road runs on to the mine of the same name.

Trail or Route Conditions Devils Canyon is completely wild and untouched even though I-70 is less than a km away in some places. From where you park your car, either near Justensen Flat or at the bottom of the drainage, just walk down-canyon in the dry creek bed. In the upper and middle sections of the canyon, you will find some moderately good narrows and several potholes. In the lower end of the canyon is a good spring which is piped to a stock trough. Cattle use it during the winter months each year. Instead of returning the same way, strong hikers could walk cross-country south to Kimball Draw, then road-walk up Cat Canyon to the Copper Globe Mine area. From the mine you can go north along the Copper Globe Road back to the head of Devils Canyon and your vehicle. This however is too long of a hike for most people to do in one day. For most it's best to walk down into the narrows and return the same way. Better visit the Copper Globe Mine while in the area. Read about it in the history part of this book. Take a shovel if you have a car, to insure you get past one rough spot near the bottom of upper Devils Canyon. If you're lucky the BLM will have graded the road for your arrival. Horses can only go down part way through this canyon.

Elevations Justensen Flats, about 2150 meters; lower end of canyon, 1800.

Hike Length and Time Needed From Justensen Flats to the spring at 1800 meters, is about 18 kms one way, or 36 kms round-trip. A very long day-hike. If you were to make a loop-hike including Kimball and Cat Canyons, it would be walking 48 to 50 kms. Far too long, but the author did it once!

Water Always carry water in your car and in your pack. You'll find a safe drink at the spring and stock tank marked 1800 meters, but it's a dry canyon otherwise.

Maps USGS or BLM map San Rafael Desert(1:100,000), or San Rafael Knob(1:62,500).

Main Attractions Some pretty good narrows and easy access. This section is part of the Devils Canyon Wilderness Study Area. Also the Copper Globe Mine.

Ideal Time to Hike Because of the higher altitudes, spring, summer or fall.

Hiking Boots Any dry weather boots or shoes.

Author's Experience The author hiked from the Justensen Flats area all the way down Devils, then up Kimball and Cat Canyons and back to his car in 9 1/2 hours.

The San Rafael Swell has many deep, dark, narrows such as this one in Devils Canyon.

MAP 34, DEVILS CANYON

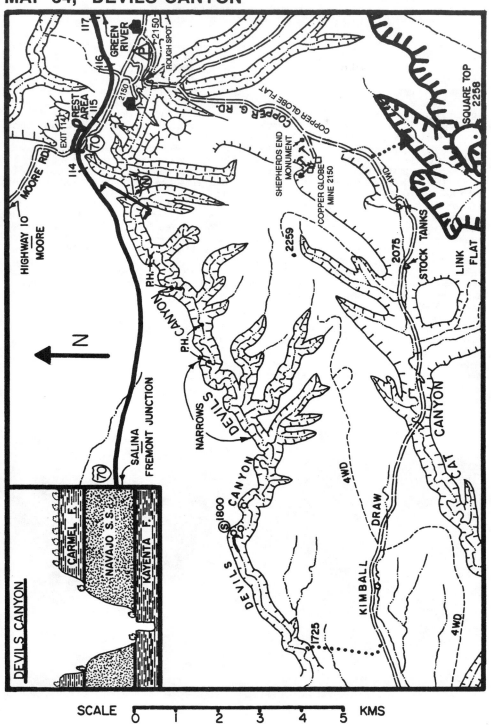

SCALE 0 1 2 3 4 5 KMS

San Rafael Knob and the Copper Globe Mine

Location and Access The highest point in the San Rafael Swell is known as the San Rafael Knob. It's located in the west central part of the Swell and at the very head of both Devils and Reds Canyons. This peak is composed of Navajo Sandstone and is the last remaining remnant of a once larger butte or mesa. The altitude of 2414 meters almost puts it in the alpine category. To reach this peak, drive along Interstate 70 to between mile posts 114 and 115 and turn south onto the Copper Globe Road. In the same area as Exit 114, is a rest stop and the beginning of the Moore Road, which is a short-cut running northwest into Castle Valley. Once on the Copper Globe Road drive southeast to Justensen Flats, a popular camping place at 2150 meters elevation. Continue southeast and to the point where the Copper Globe Road turns to the right or south and heads into upper Devils Canyon. Instead of turning right, continue straight ahead and in the direction of the Knob which will be directly in front of you. About one km beyond the road junction and at the foot of a minor butte, stop and park. With care any car can be driven to the trailhead at 2175 meters. The road continues east, but apparently doesn't get any closer to the mountain. An alternate route would be to drop down into Devils Canyon on the way to the Copper Globe Mine and use another old track as shown on the map. However, the last time the author was in the area, this road was simply not being used even by ORV's. This track apparently ends in the area of the Knob? Riders on horseback can get to the base of the Knob if the old vehicle tracks can be located and used?

Trail or Route Conditions From the car-park, leave the road and route-find southeast in the direction of the peak. You will first cross a shallow canyon with no trouble, then will parallel still another drainage which is the upper-most end of Devils Canyon. Further along and with the Knob in front of you, cross this upper drainage at a convenient place. You will likely find an old and un-used track in the area north of the Knob. This old road apparently begins in the bottom of Devils as shown on the map. The author hasn't tried to make the connection. As you near the peak, first locate and climb the northwest ridge. As you climb up the mountain you will notice a small grove of Douglas fir trees growing in the sheltered north face of the peak. At the upper end of this ridge, cut across the north face to the northeast ridge, then climb up to the southwest until you reach the summit. On top is an old USGS bench mark dated 1938.

Elevations Car-park, 2175 meters; San Rafael Knob, 2414 meters.

Hike Length and Time Needed From the car-park to the top and back should take the average person about 4 or 5 hours or half a day. However, some may want to walk an old track to the edge of the plateau for some interesting views down into Reds Canyon.

Water Always carry water in your car and in your pack, as there's none in the area.

Maps USGS or BLM map San Rafael Desert(1:100,000), or San Rafael Knob(1:62,500).

From the Copper Globe Mine(with the huge pile of wood) one can see San Rafael Knob in the distance.

MAP 35, SAN RAFAEL KNOB & COPPER GLOBE MINE

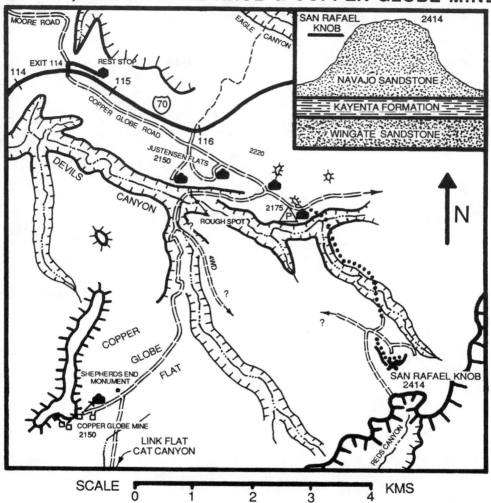

SAN RAFAEL KNOB 2414
NAVAJO SANDSTONE
KAYENTA FORMATION
WINGATE SANDSTONE

MOORE ROAD
EAGLE CANYON
EXIT 114
REST STOP
114
115
70
COPPER GLOBE ROAD
116
JUSTENSEN FLATS 2150
2220
2175
P
ROUGH SPOT
DEVILS CANYON
4WD
COPPER GLOBE FLAT
SHEPHERDS END MONUMENT
SAN RAFAEL KNOB 2414
COPPER GLOBE MINE 2150
LINK FLAT
CAT CANYON
REDS CANYON

N

SCALE 0 1 2 3 4 KMS

Main Attractions A fun hike to the highest point in the San Rafael Swell, great views from the top in all directions and a chance to visit the old Copper Globe Mine on the same trip. A man by the name of Alan S. Pike still held a valid mining claim to the mine as of August, 1989. Most of the time higher clearance cars can make it to this mine, but take a shovel anyway to help get over one rough spot near the bottom of Devils Canyon. It seems the BLM occasionally grades this road, but then heavy rains each summer make the road rough again. Read more about the mine in the history section of this book.

Ideal Time to Hike Because of the higher elevations, spring, summer or fall.

Hiking Boots Any dry weather boots or shoes.

Author's Experience The author parked at the car-park, then did the climb to the summit in 1 hour, 18 minutes. Round-trip was 2 hours, 43 minutes.

This is Slipper Arch which is about half way up the North Fork of Coal Wash.

One of the best petroglyph panels around is found at the mouth of Three Fingers C.

The Best Hikes

The Best Hikes as judged by the author. Based on scenic beauty, lots of deep and dark narrows, challenges of passage, and interesting geology. Included is the geologic formation most prominently featured. Your list of best hikes may differ.

1. **The Chute, of Muddy Creek**, Coconino Sandstone
2. **Lower Black Box (Swazys Leap)**, Coconino Sandstone
3. **Upper Black Box**, Coconino Sandstone
4. **Little Wild Horse Canyon**, Navajo Sandstone
5. **Eardley Canyon (Straight Wash)**, Coconino Sandstone
6. **Crack Canyon**, Kayenta Formation and Navajo Sandstone
7. **Lower Muddy Creek**, Wingate and Navajo Sandstone
8. **San Rafael Reef (North and South)**, Wingate and Navajo Sandstone
9. **Upper San Rafael River Gorge**, Wingate and Navajo Sandstone
10. **Black Dragon Canyon and San Rafael River**, Wingate and Navajo Sandstone
11. **Canyons of the Southern San Rafael Reef**, Kayenta Formation and Navajo Sandstone.

The Best Hikes to see Indian rock art, either petroglyphs or pictographs, and the geologic formation featured.

1. **Cottonwood Draw**, Petroglyphs, Navajo Sandstone
2. **Upper San Rafael River Gorge**, Pictographs, Wingate Sandstone and Chinle Formation
3. **Black Dragon Canyon**, Pictographs and Petroglyphs, Navajo Sandstone
4. **Wild Horse Creek**, Pictographs and Petroglyphs, Navajo Sandstone
5. **Spring Canyon**, Petroglyphs, Chinle (Moss Back Member) Formation

Indian Art with vehicle access, or with very little walking.

1. **Buckhorn Wash**, Petroglyphs and Pictographs, Wingate and Navajo Sandstone
2. **Three Fingers Canyon**, Petroglyphs, Navajo Sandstone
3. **Buckhorn Flat-Cedar Mtn. Cliffs**, Petroglyphs, Entrada or Dakota Sandstone Boulders
4. **Head of Sinbad**, Pictographs, Wingate Sandstone
5. **Dry Wash** (near Moore), Petrographs, Dakota Sandstone

Dutchman Arch, found on the north side of Head of Sinbad.

The Cleveland--Lloyd Dinosaur Quarry

If you're visiting the San Rafael Swell and have the time, and are there at the right time of year, you should plan to visit the Cleveland-Lloyd Dinosaur Quarry. This is one of the more productive dinosaur quarries in the world. To get there drive south out of Price on Highway 10. Between highway mile posts 56 and 57, or between mile posts 49 and 50, turn to the south or east and drive to either Cleveland or Elmo. From either of these towns there are signs to follow to the quarry. It's about 20 kms east of these towns on a good and well maintained dirt and gravel road.

The quarry is open on weekends from Easter to Memorial Day. In summer, from Memorial Day to Labor Day it's open Thursday through Monday, and from 10 a.m. to 5 p.m. (closed on Tuesday and Wednesday). This quarry is administered by the BLM, and the person at the site is a BLM employee. The site has a visitor center with a dinosaur skeleton, books for sale, picnic tables, toilets, water taps, and a building over the quarry itself.

Reports of fossil bones in this area reached the University of Utah in 1928 from local cowboys and sheepherders. University of Utah geologists made a preliminary investigation and began digging in 1931.

Princeton University dug here in the summers of 1939-41 to obtain an exhibit specimen. The expedition was partially financed by Malcolm Lloyd Jr., a Princeton law graduate. For this reason, and because of the quarry's proximity to Cleveland, Utah, it became known as the Cleveland--Lloyd Quarry.

There was no digging from 1941 to 1960, then the University of Utah commenced a five year project with several cooperating schools and museums. Dr. William Lee Stokes, a former Cleveland resident, was in charge of this project.

Over the years some 12,000 bones have been taken from the quarry, representing at least 70 different animals. Over 60 cast and original skeletons have been assembled from these bones and are on display across the United States and in other parts of the world.

The quarry region was not always dry and hilly. Geologists believe that about 147 million years ago this area was a shallow, fresh-water lake with a muddy bottom. The vegetation surrounding the lake was attractive to plant-eating dinosaurs, who occasionally became trapped in the mud and made easy prey for meat-eating dinosaurs. Some carnivores who ventured into the water and muck also became trapped, and as the years passed the area became a concentration of the bones of at least ten different types of dinosaurs.

The bones became scattered and the bog dried up. Both were covered with volcanic ash, and rivers and shallow seas deposited thick layers of sand and mud on top. Meanwhile, the bones became fossilized. Millions of years later, water and wind eroded the layers to produce the topography that can presently be seen.

The bones are now fairly close to the surface and can be removed from the clay with ice picks and whisk brooms. Three-quarters of the bones uncovered are from **Allosaurus**, a large carnivore. Also present are fossilized remains of plant-eating **Stegosaurus, Camarasaurus, and Camptosaurus.** In the mid-1970's James H. Madsen Jr. described two previously unknown dinosaurs from bones uncovered here. These small carnivores are known as **Stokesosaurus clevelandi** and **Marshosaurus bincentesimus.**

There have been new discoveries at the quarry in recent years. In 1987, geologists unearthed a fossil dinosaur egg believed to be that of an Allosaurus. It measured 5 x 10 cms(2 x 4 inches) and was the first egg found at this quarry. It is also the first fossil egg found from the Upper Jurassic period which lasted from 155 to 136 million years ago. Tests on the egg indicated it had an embryo inside.

Adapted from the BLM publication, **Cleveland-Lloyd Dinosaur Quarry, National Natural Landmark.**

ACCESS ROUTES TO THE CLEVELAND--LLOYD DINOSAUR QUARRY

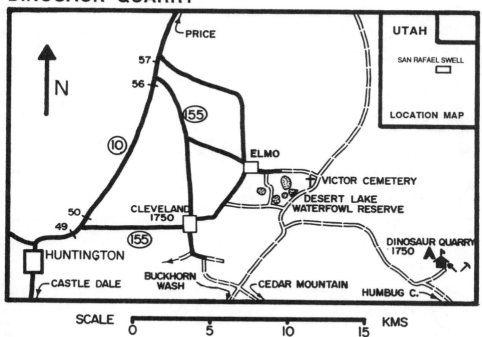

The dinosaur skeleton inside the visitor center at the Cleveland-Lloyd Dinosaur Quarry .

USGS Maps of the San Rafael Swell

The USGS maps covering the San Rafael Swell are a real hodge-podge of cartography. There are three sets of maps which will be of interest to anyone touring the region, and at three different scales. The ones the author likes best are the new metric maps, which are at 1:100,000 scale. Just two of these cover the majority of the Swell: Huntington(1980) and San Rafael Desert(1986). The Salina and Loa maps might be helpful in some cases.

The San Rafael Desert map was formerly a planimetric map with no contour lines, but it's now been updated into a normal topo map. For those who might be frightened by the word "metric", all the small squares you see on these maps are sections, and each section is one square mile. So these maps are really a combination of the metric and English systems. As far as accuracy and updating of roads are concerned, the metric 1:100,000 scale maps are the best by far. The older maps don't even have Highway 24 on them, let alone the newer constructed Interstate 70.

Besides the USGS metric maps, the BLM puts out their own version of the same map. The maps of these two agencies are the same except for different colors. The USGS maps show forests as green, whereas the BLM maps show land ownership such as private, state, federal government, national parks, etc, in different colors. With the BLM maps you'll know if you're walking on someone else's land. You can buy the BLM maps at any office in the area, whereas the USGS maps must be bought at USGS offices and some stores in Moab and Price.

The maps at scale 1:62,500 you may be using are San Rafael Knob, The Wickiup, Tidwell Bottoms, Wild Horse, and Temple Mtn. All other maps on the index chart are at scale 1:24,000. These all date from the 1950's and are often outdated. The nice thing about using the metric maps is that just two of these smaller scale maps cover the entire Swell, and at one scale. If you're in an area where two different scale maps must be used, it's very confusing.

Another very good map to have along, and one which shows all the access routes and some places which are of interest to tourists, is the Utah Travel Council Map 2, Southeastern Central Utah. This one is at 1:250,000 scale, which makes it a bit limited as to any real detail, but it does show the I-70 Highway and has contour lines. This map gives one an excellent overall view of the entire region, as well as kilomage (milage) along the main traveled routes. This map is probably sold out by now, and the old 8 map series of the state of Utah has now been replaced by newer maps. In this new series look for the maps titled Southeastern Utah and Northeastern Utah. Along with the above maps by the Utah Travel Council, a highway map of the state of Utah is necessary for some people new to the area.

BLM Offices in Southeastern Utah

Moab District Office, 82 E. Dogwood, P. O. Box 970, Moab, 84532, Tele 259-6111
Grand Resource Area, Sand Flats Road, P. O. Box M, Moab, 84532, Tele 259-8193
Price River Resource Area, 900 North 7th East, Price, 84501, Tele 637-4584
San Rafael Resource Area, 900 North 7th East, Price, 84501, Tele 637-4584
San Juan Resource Area, 435 North, Main, P. O. Box 7, Monticello, 84535, Tele 587-2141

USGS MAPS OF THE SAN RAFAEL SWELL

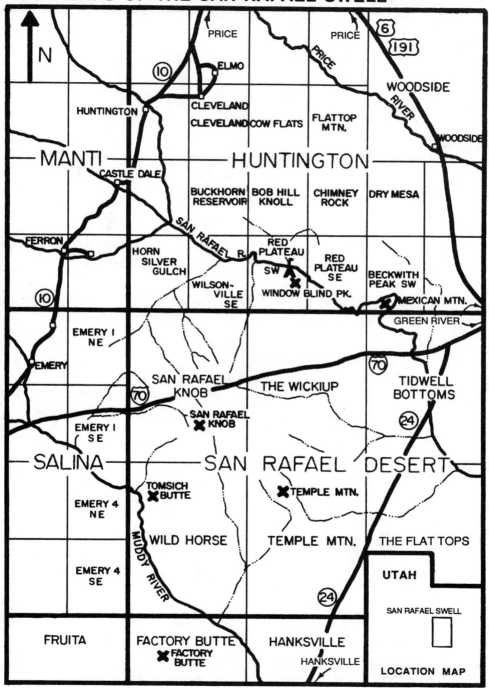

GEOLOGY OF THE SAN RAFAEL SWELL

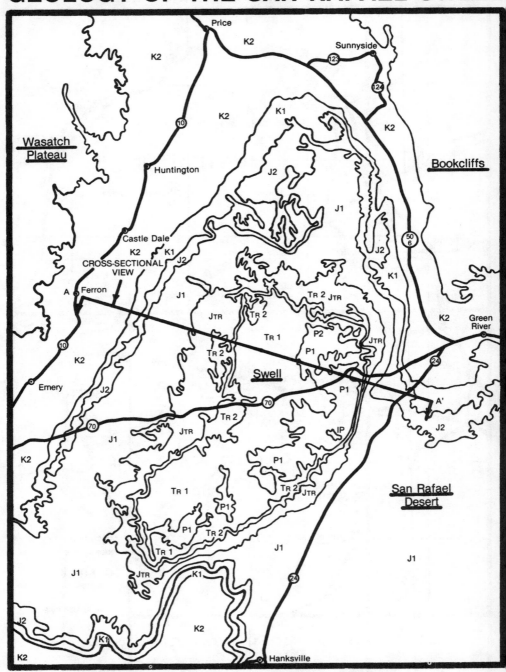

By A. Lynn Jackson   **BUREAU OF LAND MANAGEMENT**

KEY

GEOLOGIC MAP

Cretaceous	K2	Mancos Group
	K1	Dakota, Cedar Mountain and Buckhorn Conglomerate
Jurassic	J2	Morrison Formation
	J1	San Rafael Group
	JTR	Glen Canyon Group
Triassic	TR 2	Chinle and Moss Back
	TR 1	Moenkopi and Sinbad
Permian	P2	Kaibab Limestone
	P1	Coconino and Elephant Canyon
Pennsylvanian	IP	Hermosa Group

CROSS SECTION

 Shale and Mudstone

 Sandstone

 Conglomerate

 Limestone

 Dolomite

 Evaporite (Salt, anhydrite)

 Granite and Metamorphics

 Fault (showing direction of movement)

GEOLOGIC CROSS SECTION

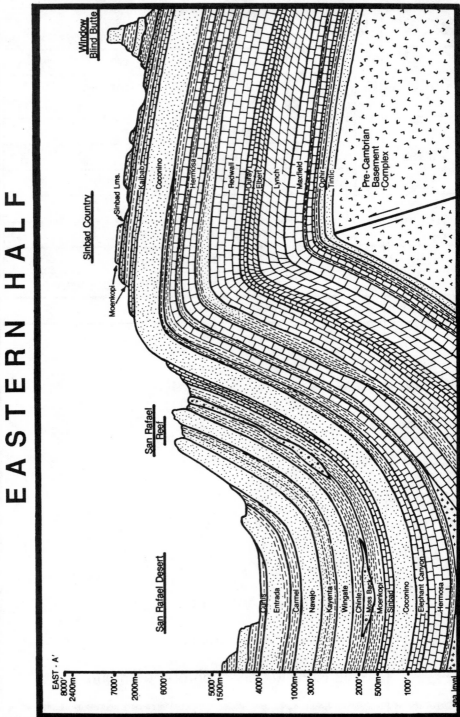

EASTERN HALF

Window Blind Butte

Sinbad Country

San Rafael Reef

San Rafael Desert

EAST - A'

8000'
2400m

7000'
2000m

6000'
5000'
1500m

4000'
1000m

3000'
2000'
500m

1000'

sea level

Moenkopi

Sinbad Lms.

Kaibab

Coconino

Hermosa

Redwall

Ouray

Elbert?

Lynch

Maxfield

Ophir

Tintic

Pre-Cambrian
Basement
Complex

Curtis

Entrada

Carmel

Navajo

Kayenta

Wingate

Chinle

Moss Back

Moenkopi

Sinbad

Coconino

Elephant Canyon

Hermosa

WESTERN HALF

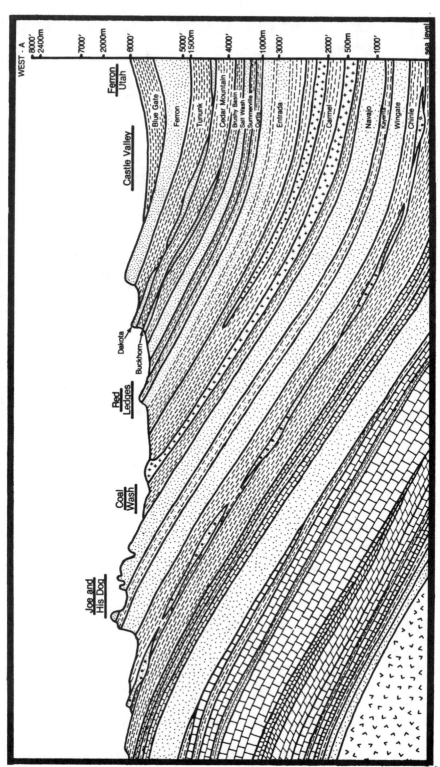

WEST - A

8000'
2400m

7000'
2000m

6000'

5000'
1500m

4000'

1000m

3000'

2000'

500m

1000'

sea level

Ferron
Utah

Castle Valley

Red
Ledges

Coal
Wash

Joe and
His Dog

Blue Gate

Ferron

Tununk

Cedar Mountain

Brushy Basin

Salt Wash

Summerville

Curtis

Entrada

Carmel

Navajo

Kayenta

Wingate

Chinle

Dakota

Buckhorn

STRATIGRAPHIC SECTION

Years Before Present	Geologic Age		FORMATIONS		Thickness (meters)	CHARACTERISTICS
	C R E T A C E O U S	M A N C O S	Blue Gate Shale		450 to 600	Shale. Drab to bluish-gray. Marine deposit. Forms broad lowlands and slopes around outside margins of Swell.
		G R O U P	Ferron Sandstone		30 to 150	Sandstone. Light brown to buff. Forms cliff. Large round concretions found in some areas. Beach deposit.
			Tununk Shale		125 to 150	Shale. Drab to bluish-gray. Marine deposit. Forms lowlands and slopes.
			Dakota Sandstone		0 to 20	Sandstone. Light to yellowish-brown. Forms cliff where present. Beach deposit. Thickness highly variable.
			Cedar Mountain Fm.		50 to 60	Mudstone, siltstone, shale. Varicolored - maroon, gray, green. Forms slopes. Alluvial (stream) deposit with volcanic ash. Buckhorn Member is composed of conglomerate, dark brown to black. Forms cliff up to 8 to 10 meters
				Buckhorn Conglom. Member		
130 million	J U R A S S I C		Morrison Formation	Brushy Basin Member	75 to 125	Mudstone, siltstone, bentonite, limestone - interlayered. Varicolored maroon, gray, green. Alluvial deposit. Forms slopes. Contains dinosaur bed at Cleveland-Lloyd Quarry.
				Salt Wash Member	60 to 100	Sandstone, mudstone, siltstone - interlayered. Varicolored. Forms broken ledges with small cliffs. Alluvial deposit.
		S A N R A F A E L G R O U P	Summerville Fm.		60 to 125	Siltstone, mudstone, gypsum - interlayered. Reddish to chocolate brown. Forms steep ribbed slopes and cliffs. Tidal flat deposit.
			Curtis Fm.		60 to 75	Sandstone, siltstone, shale - interlayered. Light gray to green. Lower section forms cliffs, upper section forms slopes. Shallow marine deposit.
			Entrada Sandstone		125 to 150	Sandstone, siltstone. Reddish-brown, earthy. Forms steep to rounded cliffs. Combination of near shore and shallow marine deposit.
			Carmel Fm.		75 to 100	Siltstone, gypsum, shale, limestone - interlayered. Red to brown. Forms broad valleys and slopes. Shallow marine deposit.
180 million - ? -	T R I A S S I C	G L E N C A N Y O N G R O U P	Navajo Sandstone		150 to 165	Sandstone. Buff to white. Massively cross-bedded. Forms cliffs and rounded domes. Contains small isolated limestone lenses. Desert eolian (wind) deposit, with small intermittent playa lakes. Some investigations have indicated a subaqueous deposition for the dunes that characterize the Navajo.
			Kayenta Fm.		50 to 60	Sandstone, siltstone - interlayered. Red to brown. Forms broken ledges. Alluvial deposit.
			Wingate Sandstone		100 to 115	Sandstone. Pale orange to red. Cross-bedded. Forms sheer vertical cliffs and pinnacles. Desert eolian deposit.
			Chinle Formation		150 to 200	Siltstone, mudstone, sandstone - interlayered. Varicolored - maroon, gray, green. Moss Back Member is light to dark brown sandstone and conglomerate which forms cliff at base of formation. Alluvial deposit with interlayered volcanic ash.
				Moss Back Member		
			Moenkopi Formation		150 to 200	Sandstone, siltstone. Buff to reddish and chocolate brown. Forms thin horizontal ledges and slopes. Sinbad Limestone member is buff to gray cliff forming unit near base of formation. Tidal flat and shallow marine deposit. Ripple marks abundant. The Sinbad Member forms the surface throughout "Sinbad Country."
225 million				Sinbad Limestone Member		
	P E R M I A N		Kaibab Limestone		0 to 25	Limestone. Gray to buff. Forms cliff where present. Marine deposit.
			Coconino Sandstone		150 to 250	Sandstone. Buff to white. Large scale cross-beds. Forms cliffs in deeper canyons of Swell. Lateral equivalent of White Rim Sandstone in Canyonlands. Eolian and shallow off-shore marine deposit.
280 million			Elephant Canyon Formation		60 to 75	Sandstone, limestone - interlayered. Buff to gray. Forms ledges and slopes in deepest canyons. Shallow, near shore marine deposit.
	P E N N S Y L	P V A N N I A N	Hermosa Group Undifferentiated		200 to 300	Limestone, sandstone, shale. Gray. Only the top 30 meters of formation exposed on Swell. Forms cliff in deepest canyons. Thickens rapidly east of the Swell. Predominantly of marine origin.

310 million	MISSISSIPPIAN	Redwall Limestone	200 to 250	Limestone. Not exposed on Swell, known only from drill holes and outcrops in other areas. Lateral equivalent of Redwall Limestone in Grand Canyon. Marine deposit.
350 million	DEVONIAN	Ouray Limestone	50 to 60	Limestone. Thin beds of green shale. No exposures on Swell. Shallow marine deposit.
		Elbert Formation	75 to 100	Sandstone, dolomite. No exposures on Swell. Shallow marine deposit with associated mudflats and beaches.
500 million	CAMBRIAN	Lynch Dolomite	125 to 200	Dolomite. No exposures on Swell. Off-shore marine deposit.
		Maxfield Limestone	125 to 200	Limestone. Thin beds of green shale. No exposure on Swell. Off-shore marine deposit.
		Ophir Formation	50 to 60	Sandstone, siltstone, shale, limestone - interbedded. No exposures on Swell. Near shore. Shallow marine deposit.
570 million		Tintic Quartzite	50 to 60	Sandstone, conglomerate. Not exposed on Swell. Sandstone which has been metamorphosed becomes quartzite. Beach deposit.
	PRECAMBRIAN	Granite	?	Basement complex of igneous and metamorphic rock. Total thickness and depth unknown.

Large potholes (or tanks) in the Navajo Sandstone (mouth of Three Fingers Canyon).

GEOLOGIC HISTORY

NOTE - REEF defined

STRUCTURE

The San Rafael Swell forms a large kidney-shaped structural upwarp, called an anticline, which is 125 kms long and 65 kms wide. The eastern border of the Swell is referred to as "the Reef", where the strata have been folded into a nearly vertical position and forms an almost inpenetrable topographic barrier. The folding of this strata resulted from movement along an ancient deep-seated vertical fault in Precambrian rocks. This caused the younger overlying rocks to drape over the fault zone as the western fault block was uplifted. Strata on the other three margins of the Swell have been folded much less severely, resulting in the formation of what geologists refer to as an "asymmetric" anticline.

PRE CAMBRIAN

At the core of the Swell are ancient rocks of Precambrian age—over a billion years old. Very little is known of the nature or origin of these ancient rocks, as they are not exposed on the Swell. Data from drill holes indicate these rocks form a highly complex system of granite and metamorphic rock types. But what mysterious mountains or vast seas these rocks may have been associated with will never be known with any certainty.

CAMBRIAN, DEVONIAN AND MISSISSIPPIAN

Beginning about 600 million years ago, when life began to inhabit the earth in many diverse and abundant forms, the San Rafael area became part of a vast continental margin and seaway that ran from Alaska to Mexico. Of course, the San Rafael Swell as we know it today did not exist at that time, as the rocks which we see today had not yet been deposited and the land surface was relatively flat, sloping westward into a deep seaway. This ancient seaway is referred to as the Cordilleran Geosyncline (a vast, deep, linear trough where thick sequences of stratified rocks were deposited over long periods of time).

For 350 million years this seaway persisted, depositing sediments of Cambrian, Devonian and

Looking south from Cedar Mtn. Overlook at Window Blind Butte and Calf Canyon.

Mississippian age. At times the shoreline would move eastward, covering the Swell area with deep quiet waters which deposited mudstones, limestones and dolomites. Gradual climatic changes and tectonic episodes (processes related to structural movements in the earth's crust) would then push the shoreline and sea back to the west, resulting in partial erosion of the previously deposited sediments, and subsequent deposition of continental siltstones and sandstones. This type of erosive period resulted in what are referred to as unconformities, represented by the wavy lines separating formations in the stratigraphic column.

PENNSYLVANIAN AND PERMIAN— THE PARADOX BASIN

The final episode of this great era which directly affected the Swell region, began and ended with deposition of this sequences of evaporites (salt and gypsum) in a large structurally isolated section of the Cordilleran Geosyncline, referred to as the Paradox Basin. The salts formed from rapid evaporation of the shallow seawater in the Basin. Seawaters became very salty due to a lack of circulation with waters of the main body of the Cordilleran sea. This lack of circulation was caused by an ancient ancestor of the San Rafael Swell known as the Emery Uplift, which formed a moderate subaqueous (below sea level) barrier between the two seas, in approximately the same location as the present day Swell. This uplift also caused Pennsylvanian aged sediments to thin rapidly over the Swell area and resulted in salt being deposited only on the southeastern flank of the uplift (see cross-section).

TRIASSIC AND JURASSIC

About 250 million years ago the character of the Swell region began to change significantly. The Cordilleran seaway and the Paradox Basin were pushed far out of the region by uplift of the Sevier orogenic belt (a linear region subjected to mountain building by deformation and folding) in western Utah and eastern Nevada, and the Uncompahgre Uplift in western Colorado. The region encompassed by the old Emery Uplift and Paradox Basin became the site of deposition of thick sequences of continental sediments deposited by streams and lakes, wind and occasional volcanic ash falls from volcanoes to the west and southwest. The colorful strata of the Navajo and Wingate sandstones which form such a prominent part of the Swell today, were formed during this time under arid Sahara-like

Assembly Hall Peak, seen just south of the San Rafael Campground.

desert conditions. Dinosaurs began to inhabit the area toward the end of this time period.

CRETACEOUS

Roughly 130 million years ago, as the mountains bordering the region (and supplying the source for the sediments) were gradually eroded away, a new sea encroached upon the region from the south. The thick marine shales of the Mancos Group were deposited in this sea. A fierce shoreline battle was waged over the Swell region for the next 60 million years, between a low coastal plain and beaches to the west, and a deep sea to the east which stretched far into Colorado and New Mexico. The Ferron and Emery Sandstones were deposited as beaches during this time along with coal deposits which formed in lagoonal swamps behind these beaches. Several other thick coal bearing formations were deposited over the region during this time. They are found today on the Wasatch Plateau to the west of the San Rafael Swell, but have long since been removed by erosion from the Swell area.

LARAMIDE OROGENY—
BIRTH OF SAN RAFAEL SWELL

The Mancos seaway was gradually pushed out of the region beginning 50 to 60 million years ago. The sea would never return to the region. An intense mountain building process began during the end of the Cretaceous period, known as the Laramide Orogeny. It was during this period of mountain building that the present day San Rafael Swell began to form along with other prominent uplifts of the Colorado Plateau. The Rocky Mountains also began to form during the Laramide Orogeny. The region became a scene of fierce erosion in the high areas, coupled with deposition of the eroded sediments in high intermountain lake basins. Thick lake deposits laid down over the San Rafael region during this period have long since been removed by erosion.

VOLCANIC ACTIVITY

The Laramide Orogeny raged on for 25-30 million years, molding and shaping the face of the San Rafael Swell area and surrounding regions. The period ended with volcanic activity underneath and around the margins of the San Rafael Swell and Colorado Plateau. This resulted in emplacement of the Henry, LaSal and Abajo Mountains in southeastern Utah, and the outflow of volcanic basalts in the

The San Rafael Reef just south of Interstate 70 and the Chinle--Moenkopi Valley(Moenkopi Formation left; Chinle Formation, center; and the Wingate Sandstone, right--the highest peaks).

southwestern portions of the San Rafael area.

EROSIVE SCULPTURING

Tectonic activity during the past 10 million years has lifted the entire Colorado Plateau region. The rivers and streams flowing through the area at the beginning of that time have silently cut deep into the Plateau's surface, removing thousands of meters of Tertiary and Cretaceous strata from the San Rafael Swell, and exposing and carving the fanciful features of the San Rafael Swell that today delight the eye and intrigue our imaginations.

One of several miners cabins near Tomsich Butte. The southwestern Reef in the background.

Tunnel entrance to the Uneva Mine in what the author calls Second Canyon along the eastern Reef.

CHINLE FORMATION IN THE SAN RAFAEL SWELL AND CAPITOL REEF NATIONAL PARK

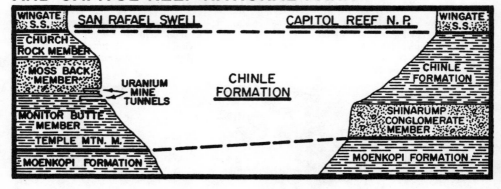

One of the most interesting and studied geology formations of the San Rafael Swell is the Chinle Formation. The following is an excerpt from the Geological Survey Bulletin #1239 (1968), Altered Rocks and Ore Deposits of the San Rafael Swell, by Hawley, Robeck and Dyer.

[The Chinle Formation of Late Triassic age crops out in a belt around the Swell and as remnants on isolated buttes and mesas in the Sinbad Country. It is represented in the Swell by four units, named in ascending order: the Temple Mountain, Monitor Butte, Moss Back, and Church Rock Members. The Moss Back Member is composed predominantly of light-colored sandstone and conglomerate and was deposited in a broad river system. The Monitor Butte, Temple Mountain and Church Rock Members, in contrast, are mainly composed of varicolored claystone, siltstone and fine-grained sandstone which were probably deposited in lakes, flood plains and smaller river systems. The formation appears to become richer in sandstone to the north and northwest, as reflected particularly by the character of the Church Rock Member and also by an increase in thickness of the Moss Back Member to the northwest.

Channel-fill sandstones and conglomerates of the Temple Mountain, Monitor Butte and Moss Back Members are the host rocks of most of the uranium deposits of the San Rafael Swell.

The thickness of the Chinle Formation ranges from about 65 meters 2 kms north of Tomsich Butte, to at least 110 meters locally. It averages about 90 meters near the Delta Mine (Hidden Splendor) in the southern part of the Swell, 110 meters near Temple Mountain in the southeastern part, and 105 meters on Mexican Mountain in the northeast corner. According to others the Chinle is 110 meters thick at Straight Wash, 105 meters in Buckhorn Wash, and about 80 meters thick near the Lucky Strike Mine.

The Moss Back Member of the Chinle Formation, composed mainly of sandstone or conglomerate more resistant to erosion than the overlying and underlying strata, forms a bench or ridge, depending on its dip, that encircles the Swell inside the San Rafael Reef. The Moss Back is the host rock of the large uranium deposits of the Temple Mountain district, as well as of smaller deposits including those of the Cistern, Lucky Strike, and Dirty Devil Mines.

Sandstone and conglomerate which crop out above the Monitor Butte and Temple Mountain Members in the Swell were formerly included in the Shinarump Conglomerate. Stewart (1957) showed, however, that the rocks generally mapped as Shinarump in southeast Utah contain three main units that can be distinguished by aerial distribution and lithology; these units were named the Shinarump, Monitor Butte, and Moss Back Members. Stratigraphic studies and mapping show that the sandstone-rich medial Chinle of the Swell correlates with the Moss Back Member, whose type section is in the eastern part of White Canyon area, San Juan County, Utah.] above

The small geology cross-section shows the Chinle as it appears in the Swell and in locations to the south, either in the Capitol Reef National Park or the Dirty Devil River area southeast of Hanksville (in generalized form). This conglomerate, whether called the Moss Back or Shinarump, is made of coarse sand and small rocks. In areas where it's exposed, you can always find pieces of petrified wood lying about. This is the same basic formation as that found in the Petrified Forest National Park in Arizona.

PROPOSED WILDERNESS STUDY AREAS(WSA'S)

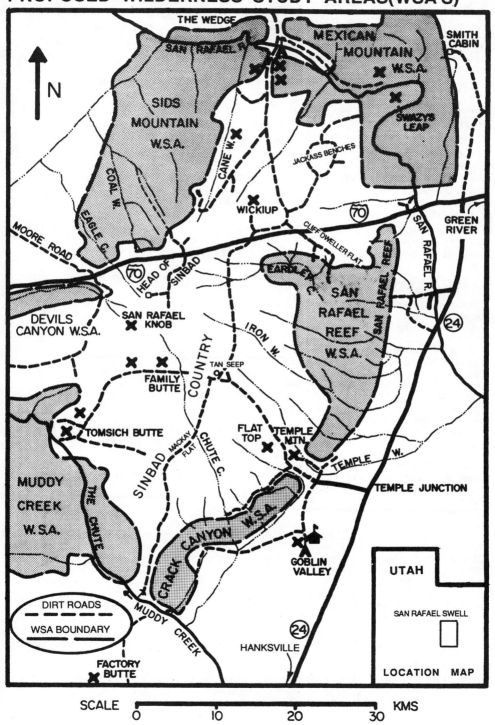

Further Reading

A Guide to Nine Mile Canyon, Chuck Zehnder (author-publisher), The Sun Advocate, Price, Utah.

Canyon Country Geology, Barnes, Canyon Country Publications, P.O. Box 963, Moab, Utah.

Canyon Country Prehistoric Indians, Barnes and Pendleton, Canyon Country Publications, P.O. Box 963, Moab, Utah.

Canyon Country Prehistoric Rock Art, Barnes, Canyon Country Publications, P.O. Box 963, Moab, Utah.

Centennial Echos from Carbon County, Daughters of the Utah Pioneers of Carbon County.

Geologic History of Utah, Hintze, Brigham Young University, Provo, Utah.

Geological Survey Bulletin, 1239, 1968, Hawley, Robeck and Dyer, US Government Printing Office.

Petroglyphs and Pictographs of Utah, Volume One--Eastern Utah, K. B. Castleton, Utah Museum of Natural History, Salt Lake City, Utah.

Stone House Lands, Joseph M. Bauman, Jr., University of Utah Press, Salt Lake City, Utah.

Utah's Scenic San Rafael, Owen McClenahan (author-publisher), Castle Dale, Utah.

Standing Up Country (The Canyonlands of Utah and Arizona), Crampton, Peregrine Smith Books, Salt Lake City, Utah.

The Archeology of Eastern Utah (emphasis on the Fremont Culture), J. Eldon Dorman, College of Eastern Utah Prehistoric Museum, Price, Utah.

The Wild Bunch at Robbers Roost, Pearl Baker, Abelard-Schumen, Green River, Utah.

Other Guide Books by the Author

Climbers and Hikers Guide to the World's Mountains(3rd Ed.), Kelsey, 800 pages, 377 maps, 380 fotos, waterproof cover, 14cm x 21cm(5 1/2" x 8" x 1 1/2"), ISBN 0-9605824-2-8. Approximately US $25.00 (Mail orders approximately US $27.00). (3rd Edition due in the spring of1990).

Utah Mountaineering Guide, and the Best Canyon Hikes(2nd Ed.), Kelsey, 192 pages, 105 fotos, ISBN 0-9605824-5-2. US $8.95 (Mail orders US $10.00).

Canyon Hiking Guide to the Colorado Plateau(2nd Printing), Kelsey, 256 pages, 117 hikes and maps, 130 fotos, ISBN 0-9605824-1-5. US $9.95 (Mail orders US $11.00).

Hiking and Exploring Utah's Henry Mountains and Robbers Roost, Kelsey, 224 pages, 38 hikes or climbs, 163 fotos, including The Life and Legend of Butch Cassidy, ISBN 0-9605824-6-0. US $8.95 (Mail orders US $10.00).

Hiking and Exploring the Paria River, Kelsey, 208 pages, 30 different hikes from Bryce Canyon to Lee's Ferry, including the Story of John D. Lee, Mountain Meadows Massacre and Lee's Ferry, 155 fotos, ISBN 0-9605824-7-9. US $8.95(Mail Orders US $10.00).

Hiking and Climbing in the Great Basin National Park--A Guide to Nevada's Wheeler Peak, Mt. Moriah, and the Snake Range, Kelsey, 192 pages, 47 hikes or climbs, 125 fotos, ISBN 0-9605824-8-7. US $8.95(Mail Orders $10.00).

Boater's Guide to Lake Powell, *featuring* Hiking, Camping, Geology, History and Archaeology, Kelsey, 288 pages, 256 fotos, ISBN 0-9605824-9-5. US$10.95(Mail Orders US$ 12.00).

Climbing and Exploring Utah's Mt. Timpanogos, Kelsey, 208 pages, 14 basic routes, Also Featurning--History of Provo & American Fork Canyons, Sundance, Heber Creeper, Timp Hike, Timp Cave, Air Plane Crashes, Hiking Deaths and Rocky Mountains Goats & Geology,170 B+W fotos, ISBN 0-944510-00-0. US $9.95(Mail Orders $11.00).

China on Your Own, and The Hiking Guide to China's Nine Sacred Mountains(3rd and Revised Ed.), Jennings/Kelsey, 240 pages, 110 maps, 16 hikes or climbs, ISBN 0-9691363-1-5. US $9.95(Mail Orders US$11.00)(Please order this book from Milestone Publications, P.O. Box 35548, Station E, Vancouver, B.C., Canada, V6M 4G8).

Primary Distributor for all of Michael R. Kelsey's guidebooks:
Wasatch Book Distributions, P.O. Box 1108, Salt Lake City, Utah, USA, 84110, Tele. 801-575-6735.